Approaching Disability

D1558385

Disability Studies is an area of study which examines social, political, cultural and economic factors that define 'disability' and establish personal and collective responses to difference. This insightful new text will introduce readers to the discipline of Disability Studies and enable them to engage in the lively debates within the field. By offering an accessible yet rigorous approach to Disability Studies, the authors provide a critical analysis of key current issues and consider ways in which the subject can be studied through national and international perspectives, policies, culture and history.

Key debates include:

- the relationship between activism and the academy;
- ways to study cultural and media representations of disability;
- the importance of disability history and how societies can change;
- national and international perspectives on children, childhood and education;
- political perspectives on disability and identity;
- the place of the body in disability theory.

This text provides real-world examples of topics that are important to debates and offers a much-needed truly international scope on the questions at hand. It is an essential read for any individual studying, practising or with an interest in Disability Studies.

Rebecca Mallett is Senior Lecturer in Education and Disability Studies, Sheffield Hallam University, UK.

Katherine Runswick–Cole is Senior Research Fellow in Disability Studies and Psychology, Manchester Metropolitan University, UK.

Approaching Disability

Critical issues and perspectives

Rebecca Mallett and
Katherine Runswick-Cole

LONDON AND NEW YORK

First published 2014
by Routledge
2 Park Square, Milton Park, Abingdon, Oxon OX14 4RN

and by Routledge
711 Third Avenue, New York, NY 10017

Routledge is an imprint of the Taylor & Francis Group, an informa business

British Library Cataloguing in Publication Data
A catalogue record for this book is available from the British Library

Library of Congress Cataloging in Publication Data
Mallett, Rebecca.
Approaching disability : critical issues and perspectives / authored by Rebecca
Mallett and Katherine Runswick-Cole.
  pages cm
  1. Disability studies. 2. People with disabilities. I. Runswick-Cole,
  Katherine. II. Title.
  HV1568.2.M35 2015
  362.4–dc23   2014001684

ISBN: 978-0-415-73589-6 (hbk)
ISBN: 978-1-408-27906-9 (pbk)
ISBN: 978-1-315-76546-4 (ebk)

Typeset in Bembo
by Wearset Ltd, Boldon, Tyne and Wear

Printed and bound in the United States of America by Publishers Graphics,
LLC on sustainably sourced paper.

To our parents
Kathleen and Ray Mallett
Maureen and Adrian Runswick

Contents

Figures

Preface

How to use this book

Our aim in this book is to offer an engaging and accessible path into the study of disability for an international audience. The book offers critical perspectives on key disability issues, directs you to further resources and encourages you to explore disability in its broadest terms.

The book is intended for undergraduate and postgraduate students, researchers and academics, as well as practitioners, disabled people, activists, allies and family members. Its discussion of disability in a global context will challenge all readers to examine their own cultural assumptions and to bring a wider dimension to their thinking.

As you will discover in Chapter 1, Disability Studies is an area of study that challenges the view of disability as an individual deficit or defect that can be cured or treated through medical intervention or rehabilitation by 'experts'. In other words, as Pfeiffer and Yoshida (1995:480) have described, it involves a shift in focus 'away from a prevention/treatment/remediation paradigm to a social/cultural/political paradigm'. Making this shift can be quite daunting as it demands that we overturn many of our long-held beliefs and attitudes towards ability as well as disability.

To help you make this paradigm shift, the book outlines key approaches, perspectives and issues that will help you examine social, political, historical and cultural factors that define and shape our collective and individual relationships with difference. We will explore how the study of disability occupies a unique position, overlapping with the humanities, natural sciences and social sciences in a myriad of exciting ways. As attitudes towards disability and disabled people are not, and have not been, the same across times and places, we will also pay particular attention to different historical and geographical contexts.

The scholarship within, and associated with, Disability Studies is far too large to fit between the covers of one book, so our intention here is to introduce you to a wide and diverse range of critical issues and perspectives which you can use to approach and explore disability.

Unlike many other introductory texts to Disability Studies, within these chapters we also focus on *how to do* Disability Studies. This includes explorations of how to analyse a cultural text for its representation of disability, the challenges of researching disability in history and the practicalities of researching with disabled children.

At every step, we offer suggestions for further thinking and reading. We encourage you to investigate further any areas that grab your interest. The study of disability can take some surprising turns and take you to some fascinating places.

Structure of the book

The book consists of nine chapters (eight main chapters plus a final chapter of concluding thoughts). It has been designed to have a dual purpose: to be coherent from start to finish but also to enable you to dip into it, depending on your interests.

Each main chapter has a concise introduction, and a conclusion that summarises what the chapter is about. The chapters also include a number of features that will guide you towards key points in the discussion and offer moments for further thinking. These are:

Action Points: these are tasks or activities for you to complete, if you want to. They encourage you to take a break from reading and to reflect on what you have read through carrying out an activity or task.

Key Issues: these alert you to some of the key areas of discussion within studies of disability. You may want to return to these as you read the book.

Key Concepts: these highlight key thinking tools or ideas that help to develop your understanding. Again, you may wish to return to the key concepts as you read further chapters.

Suggestions for Wider Reading: these include a short list of specific suggested readings at the end of each chapter. We suggest you go to these texts to learn more about the key ideas, arguments and debates in each of the chapters.

Outline of the book

Part I, 'Approaching disability', introduces you to the study of disability in the United Kingdom as well as to international approaches from different global locations.

Chapter 1 begins by introducing you to Disability Studies as an area of academic study in the United Kingdom. It explores how disability is understood not simply as a biological deficit but also as a socio–political category. The chapter traces the emergence of the discipline in the United Kingdom and the relationship between the academic community and the disabled people's movement, before introducing the social model of disability. The chapter debates nine challenges that have been made to the social model of disability and responses to them from proponents of that model. The chapter also details how these challenges have helped structure the rest of the book.

Chapter 2 continues this introduction to Disability Studies by outlining and exploring a range of international approaches. The chapter sets out a number of approaches to disability from different geographical locations, including Nordic approaches, North American approaches, and approaches to disability from countries in the global South.

Together, Chapters 1 and 2 provide the basic theoretical concepts used to approach disability. We suggest that you read these two chapters first. You may also find it useful to return to them as you read on.

Part II, 'Critical perspectives', consists of four chapters, each exploring perspectives on a particular aspect of disability: childhood, culture, history and identity politics.

Chapter 3 focuses on disabled children and their childhoods. It begins by exploring definitions of childhood before moving on to discuss the impact of literature from the sociology of childhood and from developmental psychology on the way disabled children's childhoods are constructed and understood. The chapter concludes by asking how disabled childhoods might be understood in a 'post-able' world.

Chapter 4 explores the ways in which disability, impairment and disabled people are represented in cultural texts, such as books, films and television programmes. In order to do this, the chapter reflects on the importance of culture for understanding disability, before taking the reader through a step-by-step guide to the process of deconstructing and analysing a cultural representation of disability. Within the chapter, there are numerous examples of texts that have been analysed (such as the television show *South Park*), and we offer many suggestions for further reading around this topic.

Chapter 5 examines the shifting historical conceptions of disability over time. It examines why it might be important to consider how responses to impairment and disability have changed over the decades, and explores some of the barriers to researching 'disability' from a historical perspective. Using historical examples, it argues that studying the *contexts* of events allows us to better understand *how* people with impairments have been on the receiving end of oppression, exploitation and genocide, and argues that this offers an opportunity to better understand our contemporary society.

Chapter 6 considers disability as a question of identity. It traces the relationship between disability politics and activism, reflecting on political action by disabled people. The chapter goes on to consider the intersections between disability and other political identities, particularly gender and sexuality. The focus then turns to considering the limits of identity politics and possible alternative approaches.

Part III, 'Critical issues', focuses on two critical issues within Disability Studies.

Chapter 7 focuses on the lives of disabled children in the social world. In Chapter 3 we explored perspectives on disability and childhood, and here we return to the lives of disabled children to discuss approaches to their participation in research, giving an example of a case study from research.

Chapter 8 debates the theorisation of 'bodies' in the social study of disability. We describe in Chapter 1 some of the ways in which impairment and the body have been positioned within Disability Studies and return to the body here to expand upon these arguments.

Chapters 7 and 8 include a further feature:

Debating Points: these are there to provoke your thinking and/or to encourage you to debate these issues with friends, peers or colleagues.

Part IV is entitled 'Conclusion and future directions'. Chapter 9 reflects on our journey through Disability Studies and on the approaches, issues and perspectives we have considered throughout the book. We also take this opportunity to look to the future and to consider the ways in which the study of disability might develop in the coming years.

We hope that you enjoy your journey into and through Disability Studies, and hope that this book will challenge you to think differently about ability and disability, normal and abnormal, ordinary and extraordinary.

Acknowledgements

We would like to thank Alison Foyle at Routledge Education for her enthusiasm for our book and for her support.

We are particularly grateful to the students on the BA (Hons) Education and Disability Studies degree course at Sheffield Hallam University from 2007 to 2014, who were our inspiration for writing this book and our guinea pigs for much of the material herein. In particular, our thanks go to student turned friend and colleague Jenny Slater: your continued passion for this subject acts as reassurance that we aren't the only ones to find it fascinating.

We would like to thank Heather Hollins for sharing her disability history wisdom with us and our students.

We would like to acknowledge the support of our institutions: the Research Institute for Health and Social Change at Manchester Metropolitan University and the Department for Education, Childhood and Inclusion at Sheffield Hallam University.

Huge thanks go to the many friends and colleagues we have met and conversed with through our beloved research networks, including the Disability Research Forum, Sheffield Hallam University, UK; the Theorizing Normalcy and the Mundane conference series, UK; the Critical Disability Studies Research Community @MMU, UK; the Ontario Institute for Studies in Education, University of Toronto, Canada; the Child, Youth and Family and Disability Conference Series, UK; the Critical Autism Network, UK; and the Disabled Children's Research Network, UK.

We would like to thank our friend and colleague Dan Goodley for his inspiration for our thinking and his support for our writing. Without him, we would not have met and this book would never have been written.

Katherine would like to thank Jonathan, William and Imogen for your tolerance, support and, most of all, for your love.

Rebecca would like to thank Ezekiel, Paul, Ross, Ali and (in advance) Chloe for enduring her endless analyses of all things 'disability' with grace, love and unwavering affection.

Part I

Approaching disability

Chapter 1

Approaching disability

Foundational perspectives

Introduction

The aim of this chapter is to enable you to identify, describe and explain the foundational issues and concepts within Disability Studies. In order to introduce you to the key issues in this area, the chapter begins by exploring different meanings of 'disability' using legal, individual, medical and sociological definitions. The development of Disability Studies and the role of disabled people within the discipline are also examined. Finally, the social model of disability, which is sometimes described as British Disability Studies' 'big idea' (Hasler, 1993), is introduced, explored and challenged.

Section 1: What is disability?

Action Point: What is disability? Write a sentence defining the term 'disability'. How do you understand the word? How would you explain its meaning to someone else? Keep your definition and return to it at the end of the chapter.

As you will realise from trying to answer the questions above, defining 'disability' is not a simple matter. If we look to a dictionary definition, the *Oxford English Dictionary* (2007:556) tells us that disability is:

1   **a.** Lack of ability (*to* discharge any office or function); inability, incapacity; weakness. **b.** An instance of lack of ability. Chiefly in *pl.* Now *rare.*
2   A physical or mental condition that limits a person's movements, senses, or activities; (as a mass noun) the fact or state of having such a condition.
3   Incapacity in the eye of the law, or created by the law; a restriction framed to prevent any person or class of persons from sharing in duties or privileges which would otherwise be open to them; legal disqualification.

Thus, the *OED* presents a variety of definitions of what disability is. The first definition describes 'disability' in terms of 'lack'. This reflects an understanding of disability known as the individual model of disability, which defines disability in terms of a tragic problem for isolated, unfortunate individuals (Oliver, 1990). The individual model focuses on a disability as what the individual cannot do or what is wrong with them. The second *OED* definition defines disability in terms of a 'condition'. This definition reflects what has been called a medical model of disability (ibid.). The medical model

deems disability to be a functional limitation that is biologically or physiologically determined. The medical model emphasises individual pathology, individual (personal)
deficit and individual medical treatment. The third definition in the OED frames disability in terms of a legal definition. Clearly, legal definitions of disability vary from
nation-state to nation-state, but in the United Kingdom a disabled person is defined in
the Equality Act 2010 as having a disability for the purposes of the Act if he or she has a
'physical or mental impairment' and 'the impairment has a substantial and long-term
adverse effect on [his or her] ability to carry out normal day-to-day activities'.

Internationally, the United Nations Convention on the Rights of Persons with Disabilities (UNCRPD), which 'aims to promote, protect and ensure the full and equal
enjoyment of all human rights and fundamental freedoms by all persons with disabilities,
and to promote respect for their inherent dignity' (United Nations, 2007: Article 1),
defines a 'person with disabilities' in the following terms: 'Persons with disabilities
include those who have long-term physical, mental, intellectual or sensory impairments
which in interaction with various barriers may hinder their full and effective participation in society on an equal basis with others.'

All of the definitions above – individual, medical and legal – define disability as
something that an individual person *has*. In contrast to this, Disabled People International's (DPI) definition of disability does something different. DPI (1982 cited in
Goodley, 2011:6) offers a distinction between impairment and disability:

- IMPAIRMENT: is the functional limitation within the individual caused by physical, mental or sensory impairment.
- DISABILITY: is the loss or limitation of opportunities to take part in the normal
  life of the community on an equal level with others due to physical and social
  barriers.

The DPI definition describes disability in social terms, and as the consequence of social
barriers. Impairment and disability are seen as distinct. Impairment is produced by functional limitations of the body, but disability is the result of physical and social barriers.
As we shall discuss in Section 2 and throughout this chapter, a model of disability that
defines disability as a form of social oppression is what usually distinguishes the study of
disability within Disability Studies from approaches within other disciplines, such as
psychology or medicine.

Key Issue: 'Person with a disability' or 'disabled person'?
There has been a great deal of debate about the 'correct' language to use when talking
about people and disability. This is because it is through 'language' that our ideas and
assumptions are shaped, and these, in turn, directly affect the ways people are treated and
valued (Mallett and Slater, 2014). As Titchkosky (2001) has explored, our choice of language has a material impact upon the lives we all lead.

Many people use 'people with disabilities'; this is referred to as 'people first' language
and is preferred because it is thought to stress the person (or 'personhood') before disability. However, in Britain the preferred term used by the disabled people's movement is
'disabled person' (Barnes, 1992; Carson, 2009). This term stresses the view that disability is
something done to a person, not something a person individually has. Shakespeare
(2006:33) has criticised others for 'quibbling' over the use of 'person with a disability' or

'disabled person', claiming that both terms can be supportive of disability rights and social inclusion, but, as Aubrecht (2012), drawing on Titchkosky (2001), argues, language choices are very significant and are worth in-depth consideration.

In a discussion on language preferences, Aubrecht (2012:34), states: 'my description of myself as a disabled person reflects an interest in reclaiming the living significance of disability in how I understand what it means to be recognized as a person within ablest social and cultural environments.' In other words, by shifting the language you can also shift the focus from understanding disability as abnormal difference *in* an individual and towards understanding disability as being done *to* an individual by society. This chapter focuses on this shift in understanding and examines its implications.

Section 2: The emergence of disability studies and its relationships with the disabled people's movement

In the United Kingdom, Disability Studies has been described as a 'ragbag' of ideas covering a diverse range of issues (Oliver and Barton, 2000:1). These issues include 'oppression, emancipation, representation, struggle, inclusion, independence, discrimination, rights, genocide and so on' (ibid.:1). What unites most approaches within contemporary Disability Studies is the rejection of any model of disability that locates (the *problem* of) disability *within the person* (Albrecht *et al.*, 2001). Disability is instead seen as a social issue: (the *problem* of) disability is firmly positioned in terms of *barriers* in the social world, not '*problems*' within the individual. The idea that disability should be understood as a sociological concept, rather than as a biological difficulty for tragic, isolated individuals, is key to understanding the discipline of Disability Studies in the United Kingdom.

Action Point: Accurately locating the 'problem' is an important idea within Disability Studies. What would your answers be to the following questions:

- What does it mean to talk about the 'problem' of disability?
- Who has the 'problem'?
- Does the 'problem' need to be solved?
- If so, who takes, or should take, responsibility for solving the problem?

A further distinguishing feature of Disability Studies is that it is an interdisciplinary study, which means that it cuts across traditional disciplinary divides. As a result, a range of people from different disciplines have made significant contributions to Disability Studies, including people writing from psychology (Finkelstein, 1980; Goodley, 2011), sociology (Oliver, 1990); medical sociology (Bury, 1997), literary theory and cultural studies (Mallett, 2009; Snyder and Mitchell, 2006) and education (Barton, 1997; Slee, 1997). Currently, in UK colleges and universities Disability Studies is taught as part of a range of academic and professional courses including social work, education, nursing, health care, cultural studies, sociology and psychology, and as a discipline in its own right at undergraduate and postgraduate levels.

Despite its popularity, Disability Studies is a relatively new discipline. Before the 1990s, discussion of disability within academia usually took place within the fields of medicine and psychology (Barnes, 2008). This meant that the experiences of disabled people were largely seen in terms of individual biological and psychological processes, rather than as social issues. In the 1940s, the medical sociologist Talcott Parsons argued that the 'normal' state of being for humans was good health. Parsons saw 'normal' people as able to contribute to the economy and family life, and as playing a crucial role in holding society together (Thomas, 2007). Anyone who deviated from that 'norm', including 'the sick' and 'the disabled', was viewed as deviant and as a threat to the maintenance of a 'healthy' society (ibid.). Managing health and illness became a key concern for Parsons. In his book *The Social System* (1951), Parsons identified the 'sick role'. He argued that 'the sick' and 'the disabled' were not to be held responsible for their condition and could be excused from work or contributing to family life, but only if they adopted his understanding of 'the sick role', which required people to follow doctor's orders and to try to 'get better'. Failure to comply with medical treatments and/or to seek rehabilitation was seen as a threat by the 'deviant' individual to the health of society.

Key Concept: The 'sick role' (Parsons, 1951)

In 1951, Parsons identified 'four aspects of the institutionalized expectation system relative to the sick role' (1951:436). Briefly, for the person who occupies the 'sick role', these four aspects are as follows:

1   The 'sick' person is not to be held responsible for his or her incapacity, as it is beyond his or her control.
2   The 'sick' person is released from social role obligations (such as work and contributing to maintaining family life).

Only on condition that:

3   the person tries to get well;
4   the person seeks appropriate help (i.e. from a physician) and follows advice given.

However, early as 1960s there were challenges to traditional approaches to disability. Goffman (1963) began to examine the stigma associated with disability, and the idea of stigma was taken up by Paul Hunt (1966), a disabled person himself, in his book *Stigma: The Experience of Disability*. Indeed, many academics in the field of Disability Studies are themselves disabled activists (Oliver, 1990). The close links Disability Studies has with disabled people have had the welcome effect of blurring the distinction between the researcher and the researched (Goodley and Lawthom, 2006).

A key example of the contribution to Disability Studies made by disabled people is the work of the Union of the Physically Impaired Against Segregation (UPIAS), a group of people with physical and sensory impairments. In the 1970s, UPIAS was extremely influential in developing thinking about disability. The group's origins stemmed from a letter that Paul Hunt, who was resident in a Cheshire Home, sent to *The Guardian* in 1972, which called for a consumer group to represent people living in institutions (the letter is reproduced in Figure 1.1). Working alongside Hunt, Vic Finklestein was another key player in UPIAS. Finklestein was banned from South Africa in 1968 for his anti-apartheid activism. He made the connection between the struggle of Black South Africans for emancipation and disabled people's struggles for equality (Shakespeare, 2006).

Sir, – Ann Shearer's account of the CMH conference *of* and not *on* the so-called mentally handicapped, challenges our patronising assumptions about such people. It also has important implications for anyone who genuinely wants to help other disadvantaged groups. For instance, practically every sentence in her article could apply with equal force to the severely physically handicapped, many of whom also find themselves in isolated and unsuitable institutions, where their views are ignored and they are subject to authoritarian and often cruel regimes. I am proposing the formation of a consumer group to put forward nationally the views of actual and potential residents of these successors to the workhouse. We hope in particular to formulate and publicise plans for alternative kinds of care. I should be glad to hear from anyone who is interested to join or support this project. – Yours faithfully,

Paul Hunt
61 Chettle Court,
Ridge Road,
London N8

Figure 1.1 Letter to *The Guardian* (London), 20 September 1972, p. 5 (Hunt, 1972).

Initially, UPIAS members concentrated on discussion and debate, but in 1976 UPIAS published *Fundamental Principles of Disability*, in which it stated that its members' struggle was developed from *a social theory of disability*. Crucially, the document was a socio-political reinterpretation of disability (Barnes, 2008). In the UPIAS document, a fundamental distinction was drawn between the biological and the social; this was the origin of the DPI definition of disability given above. UPIAS (1976 cited in Oliver 1996:25) defined disability as opposed to impairment as follows:

> we define impairment as lacking part of or all or of a limb, organ or having a defective limb, organ or mechanism of the body; and disability as the disadvantage or restriction of activity caused by a contemporary social organisation which takes no or little account of people who have physical impairments and thus excludes them from the mainstream of social activities. Physical disability is therefore a particular form of oppression.

Before UPIAS, 'disability' was defined as a biological flaw within an individual. UPIAS redefined disability as social disadvantage imposed on top of people's 'impairments'. UPIAS's aim was to replace segregated facilities with opportunities for people with impairments to play a full part in mainstream society (Shakespeare, 2006).

At the same time as UPIAS published its *Fundamental Principles*, Disability Studies was developing as an academic subject. In 1975, the Open University introduced a course entitled 'The Handicapped Person in the Community'. This was the first undergraduate course in Disability Studies in the United Kingdom. In 1979, the first postgraduate programme emerged at the University of Kent (Oliver and Barton, 2000). However, it was not until the creation of the international journal *Disability, Handicap and Society* in 1986 (renamed *Disability and Society* in 1993) that academic interest in the subject of disability really began to take off (Barnes, 2008). In 1990, Mike Oliver published *The Politics of Disablement*, which has been described as the first comprehensive account of the socio-political interpretation of disability (Barnes, 2008). In 1991, Colin Barnes published *Disabled People in Britain and Discrimination: A Case for Anti-discrimination Legislation*, which provided extensive evidence of the institutional discrimination faced in education, employment, benefits, health and social care, the built environment, leisure, the media and in politics. The study was carried out with and by disabled people (Barnes, 2008).

Disability Studies is now firmly embedded as an academic subject in British universities and colleges (Barnes, 2008). This is demonstrated by the number of established research centres and the research activity being carried out. For example, the Centre for Disability Studies was established at the University of Leeds in 1992 (www.leeds.ac.uk/disability-studies); in 2005, the Disability Research Forum was established at the University of Sheffield (now based at Sheffield Hallam University) (www.disabilityresearchforum.wordpress.com); the Centre for Disability Research at the University of Lancaster was established in 2008 (www.lancs.ac.uk/cedr/about.htm); the Centre for Cultural Disability Studies at Liverpool Hope University was set up in 2010 (www.ccds.hope.ac.uk/index.htm); and Critical Disability Studies at Manchester Metropolitan University was also established in 2010 (www.cdsmmu.wordpress.com).

Barnes (2008:2) describes the relationship between the disabled people's movement and academic institutions as continuing to be 'generally productive'. 'Nothing about us without us' (Charlton, 2000) is a famous slogan adopted by the disabled people's movement, and the involvement of people with personal experience of disability has continued to be important within the discipline. Just as Mike Oliver (1994:2) wrote about the importance of personal experience and identified himself as a 'disabled sociologist and political activist', many of the key contemporary figures in the discipline of Disability Studies have identified themselves as disabled people, including Colin Barnes, Tom Shakespeare and Donna Reeve. Others have identified themselves as close allies of disabled people, including Dan Goodley, who has worked alongside people with the label of learning difficulties; Sara Ryan, a mother of a disabled child; and Linzi Carlin, who has a disabled sibling. In the United Kingdom, the link between disabled people and the academy has been seen as crucial but also as a source of ongoing tension between the academy and disabled people (Oliver and Barton, 2000). Moreover, the place of non-disabled people in research on disability has been hotly debated (Branfield, 1998, 1999; Drake, 1998; Duckett, 1998).

Oliver and Barton (2000:7) claim that it 'is an inescapable fact that the relationship between disability studies and disabled people is essentially a parasitic one and there are real concerns about abuse, exploitation and colonisation'. Academic researchers, including disabled and non-disabled people, in their 'ivory towers' stand accused of exploiting relationships with disabled people in order to advance their own careers: writing papers, going to conferences and, indeed, publishing books. Barnes (2008) cautioned against the severing of links between disabled people and the academy warning, that it would be the end of the discipline.

Section 3: Disability studies (in the United Kingdom): the 'big idea'

In 1981, Mike Oliver first used the phrase 'the social model of disability'. He used it in the context of a training course for social workers and disability equality training with other 'disability' professionals (Barnes, 2008; Oliver, 2004). A model is what social scientists call a 'heuristic device' that is intended to aid understanding, in this case in the area of disability (Barnes, 2008). Oliver (2004:7) explains that by using the social model he was trying to give his students 'a way of using the idea that it was society and not us [people with impairments] that should be the target for professional interventions and their professional practice'.

Key Issue: Disability Equality Training (DET)
Disability Equality Training, often shortened to DET, focuses on the barriers and attitudes that disable people with impairments. DET highlights the role of organisations in the removal of those barriers and in the changing of attitudes (Walker, 2004).

Language is a key issue for DET because while language is often thought to be merely descriptive of people, objects and events, it is in fact more than just communication. When people talk to each other, they are framing and changing the things they are talking about.

A number of organisations publish lists of what is 'unacceptable' language to use with and about disabled people. Manchester City Council's version of the list is as follows:

1   Afflicted with – This conveys a tragic or negative view about disability
2   Suffering from – This confuses disability with illness and also implies that a disability may be a personal burden. Increasingly, disabled people view their disability as a positive rather than negative experience
3   The blind – Lumping everyone together in this way is felt by many to take away their individuality. The most appropriate term to use here is 'people with visual impairments', or 'blind people'
4   Victim of – This again plays to a sense that disability is somehow a tragedy
5   Cripple or crippled by – Use the term 'the person has…'
6   Wheelchair bound – Disabled people are not tied into their wheelchairs. People are wheelchair users or someone who uses a wheelchair. A wheelchair offers the freedom to move around and is a valuable tool
7   Deaf and dumb – This phrase is demeaning and inaccurate. Many deaf people use sign language to communicate and dumb implies that someone is stupid. Use 'a person with a hearing impairment', or 'a deaf person', or 'sign language user'
8   The disabled – There is no such thing as the disabled. Use the term 'disabled people'
9   People with disabilities – The term 'disabled people' is the preferred term within the social model of disability. 'People with disabilities' suggests that the disability 'belongs' to the disabled person, rather than 'disabled person', which accurately implies that society disables the individual, thus adopting the social model of disability
10 Handicapped – This term is inappropriate, with images of begging and disabled people being cap in hand
11 Invalid – The term literally means not valid
12 Able-bodied – The preferred term is 'non-disabled'. 'Able-bodied' suggests that all disabilities are physical and ignores unseen disabilities, and that disabled people are not able
Source: Manchester City Council (no date)

Action Point: Reread the list above and consider the following questions: Do you agree with the list and the explanations above? Do they reflect any of the approaches to disability we have discussed? Are there any contradictions in the list above?

In contrast to medical, individual and, indeed, many legalistic understandings of disability, the social model of disability seeks to move the focus away from the limitations of impaired bodies and to look instead at the difficulties caused for disabled people by disabling environments, barriers, attitudes and cultures. The aim then is to expose and remove barriers to disabled people's participation in all areas of life, including education, work environments, the benefits system, health and social services, housing, transport, and the devaluing of disabled people in the media (including newspapers, films, television and the web) (Barnes, 2008).

Social model thinkers, including Finkelstein (1980), Oliver (1990) and Gleeson (1999), have drawn heavily on the work of Marx. They offer a materialist account of disability in which disability is linked to the spread of capitalist society – a society that is organised on the founding principle of the need for cooperative production of commodities for sale (Ransome, 2010). Marxist materialists argue that the spread of capitalist commodity production and exchange resulted in the 'repression of certain forms of social embodiment' (Gleeson, 1999 cited in Thomas, 2007:54). In other words, the shift towards a capitalist society in the nineteenth and twentieth centuries created a situation in which people with impairments were excluded from capitalist society because they were deemed unable to contribute to the production of commodities for sale and thus became 'disabled' people. While capitalist societies have usually identified the 'deserving poor' in order to determine who is eligible for state aid, Oliver (1990) points out that who is and who is not 'deserving' usually depends on the judgements of professionals. Indeed, the rise of capitalism coincided with what Oliver (ibid.) describes as the rise of the professional class (including doctors, teachers, psychologists and social workers), who have created and sustained a situation in which systems of knowledge define disability as individual pathology. As Marxist materialists argue that people with impairments have come to face exclusion as a direct result of the capitalist system, Finkelstein (1980) and Oliver (1990) suggest that social inclusion can only be achieved once the capitalist system is replaced by a more equitable social system (Tregaskis, 2002).

The social model has been crucial to the disability movement in the United Kingdom. Shakespeare (2006:30) identifies three key contributions of the social model and their impact on British disability activism and academia:

1   The social model identifies the need for barrier removal. This gave disabled people a political strategy based on a civil rights model around which they were able to organise and protest. The need for barrier removal has underpinned the drive for anti-discrimination legislation and practice.
2   The social model has had an impact on how disabled people see themselves. The model enables disabled people to reject individual deficit, tragedy models of disability and to assert their rights to equality, focusing on the need for society, not disabled individuals, to change.
3   The social model shifted the discussion about disability within academia away from medical sociology, which focused on 'sick' and 'disabled' individuals, and towards a study of disability that explored social and cultural processes.

Key Concept: The social model
With each thinker comes a slightly different version of the 'social model of disability', but all versions have a number of elements in common. Depending on the thinker, different elements will be emphasised at different times. A 'social model' approach to disability is concerned with:

- the rejection of a medical model approach to disability;
- a challenge to individualised approaches to disability;
- valuing the direct experience and understanding of disability by disabled people themselves;
- addressing issues of marginalisation, oppression and discrimination;
- identifying and removing disabling barriers produced by social and cultural institutions.

The social model of disability has undoubtedly been a powerful tool to challenge the discrimination of disabled people in Britain and yet it is also a highly contested idea, generating lively and sometimes passionate debate within Disability Studies in Britain.

Action Point: Before we move on to the next section, are there any issues or problems with a 'social model' approach to disability?

Section 4: Criticisms of the social model

The social model of disability has generated much discussion and debate within the field of Disability Studies, and the criticisms and counter-arguments concerning the social model are numerous and complex. In this section, we explore some of the key areas of debate, although this list of nine challenges is by no means exhaustive.

Challenge 1: The social model has not gone far enough

While the strengths and weaknesses of the social model have been hotly contested, it is, perhaps, worth noting that this debate has not been universally welcomed. Indeed, the person who coined the term 'the social model of disability', Mike Oliver (2004:18), claims that 'in the last twenty years we have spent too much time talking about the social model and its usefulness and indeed its limitations and not devoted enough attention to actually implementing or attempting to implement it in practice'. Oliver's frustration is driven by the fact that disabled people continue to be an oppressed group within society who do not have equal access to jobs, education, transport and public housing, buildings and amenities (Oliver, 2004). Oliver is not alone in expressing his frustration that the social model has not gone far enough in terms of implementation, and others have expressed similar concerns about the nature of the academic debate while the oppression of disabled people continues (Barnes, 1991; Oliver and Barton, 2000).

However, it has also been argued that, rather than not going far enough, in some senses the social model has gone too far. Despite acknowledging the contribution the social model has made to disabled people's lives, Shakespeare (2006) regrets the dominance of the social model in British Disability Studies. He observes that the social model has become the litmus test by which activists and academics assess interventions and initiatives. He argues that social model orthodoxy has stifled debate and that, as a result, failure to follow the social model is seen as 'inappropriate, misguided or even oppressive' (ibid.:32). Shakespeare goes so far as to describe the social model as an 'obstacle to the further development of the disability movement and disability studies' (ibid.:33).

While Shakespeare rightly points out the dominance of the social model in British Disability Studies, a flurry of new theories and approaches from other disciplines (queer theory, critical race theory, feminism, postcolonial theory) and from other countries (including the Nordic countries, North America and the global South) have started to enter Disability Studies. We will explore these in Chapter 2.

Challenge 2: The social model devalues and is hostile to medicine

As the social model defines disability as being produced by social arrangements that exclude disabled people, Shakespeare (2006:31) has also questioned how the social model can accommodate the role of medicine in the lives of disabled people, because if 'disability is about social arrangements, not physical or mental impairments, then attempts to mitigate or cure medical problems may be regarded with intense suspicion'.

Yet Oliver (2004:21) argues that 'endorsement of the social model does not mean that individually based interventions in the lives of disabled people, whether they be medically, rehabilitative, educational or employment based, are of no use or always counter-productive'. In addition, Barnes (2008) argues that *individual* medical, re/habilitative, educational or employment-based interventions may be useful to disabled people but that they are limited in terms of developing an inclusive society, particularly when these interventions are constructed by 'non-disabled people' for 'disabled people'.

It is possible to accept the value of medicine in the lives of disabled people and to adhere to the principles of the social model of disability, but only, perhaps, with a sense of scepticism about the 'power' of medicine in the lives of disabled people and its limitations in terms of achieving equality for disabled people.

Challenge 3: Barrier removal is not enough to end discrimination against disabled people

At the heart of social model thinking is the emphasis on removing the physical and social barriers to disabled people's participation. However, it has been argued that barrier removal alone cannot end discrimination against disabled people. There are two lines of argument to support this view. The first is that barrier removal will not challenge the (often historical) cultural values in society which position disabled people as 'other' (Oliver, 2004). Indeed, it has been argued that solely economically based materialist accounts of disability devalue the impact of culture and prejudice in explaining the exclusion of disabled people (Tregaskis, 2002). Oliver (2004) acknowledges the role that culture plays in creating a disabling society, and this was already a theme taken up by Barnes (1992) in his key text *Disabling Imagery and the Media: An Exploration of the Principles for Media Representations of Disabled People*. Social model accounts can acknowledge the role culture plays in the creation of disability, and we will be exploring the valuable contributions cultural and historical perspectives can make to Disability Studies in Chapters 4 and 5. However, for Oliver (1990, 1996) it remains the case that it is the situation of material deprivation which disabled people find themselves in that should be the primary focus of attention.

The second limitation of barrier removal is linked to the place of the body and impairment in Disability Studies. As we have seen, social model pioneers such as Finkelstein, Oliver and Barnes were keen to focus on the material aspects of disability, rather than on bodies and the effects of impairments. However, Sally French, herself a disabled person, declared: 'I believe that some of the most profound problems experienced by people with certain impairments are difficult, if not impossible to solve by social manipulation' (1993:17). French's (1993) assertion that social manipulation, or barrier removal, could not solve all the issues disabled people face is a key challenge for social model thinkers. Again, Oliver (2004) counters the claim that a focus on barrier removal has meant that the body has been left out of Disability Studies by arguing that the body and impairment have in fact been the focus of social model writers (Oliver *et al.*, 1988; Zarb and Oliver, 1993 cited in Oliver, 2004). Yet many do not agree, and the place of impairment in the social model remains a highly contested issue.

Challenge 4: What about the body?

The role of the body in understanding disability has been widely debated. Social model thinkers stand accused of writing the body out of Disability Studies. Oliver (2004:85) counters this attack with the assertion that 'the social model is not about the personal experience of impairment but the collective experience of disablement'. And yet the problems of what to do with, and say about, the body remain.

Disabled feminist accounts have continued to question analyses that avoid a discussion of disabled people's subjective experience, including how they experience their bodies. Morris (1996:13) articulates this feeling as follows:

> [t]here was a concern among some disabled women that the way our experience was being politicised didn't leave much room for acknowledging our experiences of our bodies; that too often there wasn't room for talking about the experience of impairment, that a lot of us feel pressurised into just focusing on disability, just focusing on social barriers.

The focus on the body has led to calls for a social theory of impairment (Hughes and Paterson, 1997). The aim of a social theory of impairment is to take the discussion of the body back from medicine and to talk about the disabled body more positively (Tregaskis, 2002). In traditional medical discourses, disabled bodies are seen as grotesque and lacking, but social theory perspectives on impairment create spaces to challenge the idea of that 'perfect' or 'imperfect' bodies exist independently of the language used to describe, or label, them (Butler, 1993). We will be discussing these particular issues, and their implications for the study of disability, in more detail in Chapter 8.

One of the reasons the sociology of the body is problematic for the social model is that it challenges one of the central concepts that underpin the social model: the impairment/disability divide. A social theory of impairment demands that disability and impairment are experienced together, not separately: '[d]isability is experienced in, on and through the body, just as impairment is experienced in terms of the personal and cultural narratives that help to constitute its meaning' (Hughes and Paterson, 1997:334–335).

Building on the notion of the interaction between bodies and culture, Thomas (2007:135) talks of impaired bodies as being *biosocial*. Doing so allows her to talk about bodies being simultaneously 'biological, material and social'. Closely linked to the notion of the sociology of the body is what Thomas (2007) calls 'impairment effects'. She explains the concept of an impairment effect with an example (ibid.). She describes a woman with a 'missing hand' carrying out an everyday activity: boiling a kettle. Thomas describes how the person with the missing hand does this differently from a two-handed person; this is as an impairment effect. If a person is then restricted in some additional way because they boil a kettle differently – for example, they are denied the opportunity to become a parent, or get a job – then this is disablism. This example, Thomas (ibid.) argues, illustrates the interaction of the 'biological' with the 'social'.

Thomas (1999) and Reeve (2002, 2006) have also explored what they term the psycho-emotional aspects of disablism. Thomas (2007:72) describes psycho-emotional disablism as follows: 'social barriers "out there" certainly place limits on what disabled people *can do*, but psycho-emotional disablism places limits on who they *can be*.' For Thomas (2007), psycho-emotional disablism describes how a disabled person's sense of 'self' can be affected by the experience of being treated less favourably than non-disabled people, and by the hurtful words and unkind actions of others in personal encounters. Feminists such as Thomas and Reeve have been criticised for focusing on the 'internal' aspects of disablism and for focusing on personal experience rather than material oppression.

Challenge 5: The social model fails to take into account multiple or simultaneous oppression

The social model has also been challenged for failing to take into account issues of multiple or simultaneous oppression. Disabled people may also experience disadvantage on the grounds of gender, age, race and sexuality. For example, this has led Thomas (1999:124) to argue that it is important to acknowledge the gendered nature of disability. Feminists such as Thomas (1999) and Morris (1992, 1993) have also sought to challenge the view that Disability Studies should maintain a distinction between 'public issues' and 'private troubles'. However, Oliver (2004) answers the question of multiple oppression by arguing that just because the social model has been slow to integrate the divisions of race, gender, sexuality and age, this does not mean that it is not possible for these issues to be incorporated. Yet the issue of 'private' troubles becoming 'public' issues remains a source of tension between feminist and social model materialist accounts of disability.

Such tensions also exist between other marginalised groups (particularly those based on race and sexuality), and we will discuss the implications of these tensions for the lives of disabled people and for the disabled people's movement as a whole in Chapter 6.

Challenge 6: The social model does not include all people with impairments

A further criticism of the social model is that it has failed to include all people with impairments. It has been noted that the social model was pioneered by a group of physically disabled white, middle-class men, and that this may explain tensions between social model approaches and some feminist approaches (Morris, 1996). Barnes (2008) accepts that the UPIAS statement was originally drafted to include only people with physical impairments, but he argues that it was adopted by the disabled people's movement in order to include people with physical, sensory and cognitive impairments. However, there have continued to be calls for the social model to be inclusive of all people with impairments, not least to include people with the label of learning difficulties (Chappell et al., 2001) and mental health service users (Beresford et al., 2010), a point we shall return to in Chapter 6. Indeed, another complication, as Watson (2002) shows, is that not all impaired people consider themselves to be disabled, so it may also be the case that not all people with impairments would include themselves in the social model approach to their own lives.

Challenge 7: The social model has little to say about disabled children

Stalker and Connors (2001:19) have commented that the 'social model of disability has paid little attention to disabled children'. It can be argued that disabled children constitute another group of people with impairments that has been neglected by the social model of disability, in so far as the original proponents of the social model of disability had little to say about disabled children's lives. However, the social model has had a big impact on the lived experiences of disabled children, not least in the areas of inclusive education and play and leisure (as we shall explore in Chapter 7), and disabled children have been the focus of research that has been underpinned by social oppression models of disability (see, for example, Shakespeare et al., 1999; McLaughlin et al., 2008; Goodley and Runswick-Cole, 2010b, 2011a, b). As we will see in Chapter 3, disability perspectives and the experiences of disabled children also have an important part to play in challenging and reshaping orthodox understandings of childhood.

Challenge 8: The social model: a Western model of disability?

As we have seen, the social model of disability is very much associated with the development of British Disability Studies. This has led to criticisms of the social model as a Western ideology that has been imposed on the developing world (also known as the majority world and/or the global South) contexts. Ghai (2002) has questioned the relevance of theories developed in the industrialised Western world for the majority world. Furthermore, Grech (2009) argues that majority-world issues remain excluded from, or included in piecemeal fashion in, Western Disability Studies literature, noting, as feminists have done before him, that the social model is the product of white, middle-class, educated, Western disabled academics (Grech, 2009). Grech (ibid.) goes on to argue that impairment *does* matter (see also Chapter 2). While Oliver (1990) argues that it is the experience of disablement, rather than impairment, that is the source of disabled people's oppression and exclusion, Grech (2009) argues that it is difficult to sustain this approach in majority-world contexts in which 'hard labour' is the only way to survive and impairment issues can mean the difference between survival and failure to survive.

Barnes (2009:3) acknowledges that 'applying western ideas about impairment and disability to non-western cultures is fraught with difficulty'. However, he maintains that 'the disabling tendencies associated with western influenced economic and cultural development: industrialisation, urbanisation, self reliance and "able bodied" normality, are replicated across the globe' (ibid.:10). Despite Ghai's (2002) concern that by attempting to export the social model to majority-world contexts, academics are following in the traditions of others who have tried to colonise the majority world with ideas and practices, Barnes (2009) maintains that it is possible to use the social model to challenge global disability issues.

Challenge 9: The emergence of Critical Disability Studies

Finally, as Davis (1997 cited in Meekosha and Shuttleworth, 2009:49) tells us, '[a]s with any new discourse, disability studies must claim space in a contested area, trace its continuities and discontinuities, argue for its existence, and justify its assertions'. Disability Studies is constantly changing, and new debates will, inevitably, be incorporated into and move on from the challenges we identify above. The field of *Critical* Disability Studies (Meekosha and Shuttleworth, 2009; Goodley, 2013) is already emerging. Critical Disability Studies seeks to change the study of disability in a number of ways:

1   to challenge the dominance of the concerns of the global North within Disability Studies writing;
2   to 'move away from the preoccupation with binary understandings – social versus medical model, British versus American disability studies, disability versus impairment' (Meekosha and Shuttleworth, 2009:50);
3   to welcome ideas from cultural studies and humanities writing about disability, as well as engaging with psychological and psychoanalytic approaches to disability (Goodley, 2011), which would previously have been firmly positioned within individual and deficit models of disability;
4   to see the social model of disability as *but one* of a number of tools of analysis.

As Goodley (2013:632) tells us, 'Critical disability studies start with disability but never end with it: disability is *the* space from which to think through a host of political, theoretical and practical issues that are relevant to all.'

Crucially, Critical Disability Studies approaches do not seek to abandon the social model of disability but to theorise disability and disablement by drawing on a range of resources (from feminist, postcolonial and queer thinkers, among others) and in this way to move *on*, *with* and *through* the social model of disability to expose and challenge the oppression of disabled people. We shall return to the intersections between disability and other identity positions in Chapter 6.

Action Point: Write a paragraph summarising the arguments for and against the social model of disability by considering a question posed by Shakespeare and Watson (2001): is the social model of disability 'an outdated ideology'?

Conclusion

Despite these various challenges that the social model of disability faces from within the discipline of Disability Studies and from outside it, the social model has, as Shakespeare

(2006) reminds us, served an important role within the disabled people's movement and contributed to some key policy and practice changes, not least in terms of disability discrimination and equality legislation in the United Kingdom (the Disability Discrimination Act 1995, the Special Educational Needs and Disability Act 2001 and the Equality Act 2010). It remains the case that the social model of disability can be used as a powerful tool with which to expose the disabling tendencies of modern Western society (Barnes, 2008). The social model has been, and we suspect it will remain, central in the discipline of Disability Studies both in the United Kingdom and elsewhere.

Action Point: Look back at your definition of disability. Where does it stand in relation to the medical, individual, legal and social approaches to disability we have explored? Has your view of disability developed while reading this chapter? If so, in what ways?

In the next chapter, we continue exploring approaches to the study of disability and move away from a British-centric conception of disability and Disability Studies by considering international approaches. We will examine Nordic, North American and global South perspectives.

Suggestions for Wider Reading

Goodley, D. (2011) *Disability Studies: An Interdisciplinary Introduction*, London: Sage.
Oliver, M. (1990) *The Politics of Disablement*, Basingstoke: Macmillan.
Oliver, M. (1996) *Understanding Disability: From Theory to Practice*, Basingstoke: Macmillan.

Chapter 2

Approaching disability

Global perspectives

Introduction

> In the UK, the hallmark of belonging to Disability Studies is some kind of adherence to the social model of disability (even as a prelude to heavily critiquing it).
>
> (Thomas, 1999:8)

As Thomas suggests, in Britain 'Disability studies is centrally the study of the disabling society' (Swain *et al.*, 2003:1). Accordingly, social oppression models of disability dominate; indeed, British Disability Studies often seems to demand an unquestioning adherence to the social model of disability. This chapter seeks to broaden the debates beyond British perspectives and to consider critical approaches to Disability Studies and key issues that have been emerged from outside the United Kingdom. Following Chataika (2012:252), the chapter adopts the terms 'global North' and 'global South' to refer to 'the broad division of countries in relation to resources and power. Global North nations are usually known as 'developed, high income, thriving, or first world countries' (Stubbs, 1999 cited in Chataika, 2012:252). Global South nations are located in Africa, Central and Latin America, and most of Asia and the Middle East (see Figure 2.1), and are usually referred to as 'developing, low-income, failing, majority world, or third world countries' (ibid.:252).

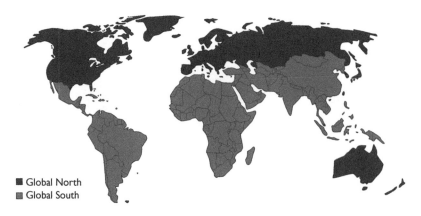

■ Global North
■ Global South

Figure 2.1 Map showing the 'global North' and the 'global South'.

First, this chapter explores critical perspectives on disability and Disability Studies from the global North, focusing on Nordic, North American and Australian perspectives. The focus then moves to the global South and the critiques made by, among others, Meekosha (2004), Ghai (2001, 2002) and Grech (2009, 2010) that challenge the dominance of ideas from the global North within Disability Studies. Here, the chapter considers ideas from global South contexts and discusses the influence of postcolonial theory in Disability Studies.

While we identify a range of critical perspectives in this chapter that have developed from outside the United Kingdom, we are not suggesting that these approaches are the *only* approaches used within that region or that they are not used elsewhere. Just as the social model of disability has been 'exported' from the United Kingdom to other countries, Disability Studies approaches from across the globe have influenced the United Kingdom and each other. You might find it useful to refer back to this chapter as you encounter these, and other, international perspectives in later chapters in the book.

Section 1: Nordic approaches

The Nordic countries are made up of Denmark, Finland, Iceland, Norway and Sweden (see Figure 2.2). Nordic perspectives on disability have challenged the dominance of British-centric approaches in the global North. While there are, of course, individual differences between the Nordic countries in their approaches to disability and Disability Studies, this chapter focuses on what are generally termed 'Nordic' approaches to disability.

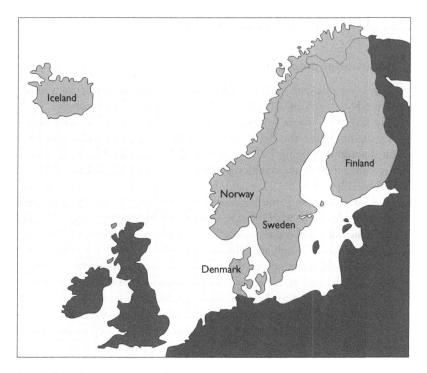

Figure 2.2 Map showing the Nordic countries.

Not surprisingly, the development of Disability Studies in the Nordic countries differs from that in the United Kingdom. Traustadóttir (2004) sketches out a history of Disability Studies in the Nordic countries since the 1960s. She describes how the development of Disability Studies and the disabled people's movement in those countries has been heavily influenced by the existence of extensive welfare state services. The provision of welfare is underpinned by the belief that human rights should be extended to all, including disabled people (ibid.). As early as 1967, a Norwegian White Paper argued that there was a need to shift the focus in disability policy. Instead of putting the sole emphasis on considering how to change disabled people so that they could 'cope better' in the environment, the emphasis was put on also changing the environment to fit the needs of people with impairments (Tøssebro, 2004). In the 1960s and 1970s, critiques continued to emerge from the Nordic countries of the dominance of medical understandings of disability, a phenomenon linked to increasing criticisms of the practice of disabled people living in institutions, which was common in the 1960s and 1970s. This criticism of the institutionalisation of disabled people stemmed from a shift in thinking about the nature of 'disability' and the turn away from seeing the individual as the sole source of the 'problem of disability' towards a more relational model in which the role of the environment was also considered to play a part in the creation of disability (Traustadóttir, 2004).

In the 1990s, Disability Studies continued to develop in the Nordic countries. In 1992, *FUN: Forskning om utveklingshemming i Norden*, the Nordic Intellectual Disability Research Organisation, was set up followed by the Nordic Network on Disability Research in 1997, which aims to advance research and development in the field of disability, and in 1999 the *Scandinavian Journal of Disability Research* was launched (Traustadóttir, 2004). The creation of the research network and the journal were key developments in the discipline of Disability Studies.

The Nordic relational model of disability

Nordic approaches contrast with British approaches to Disability Studies in a number of ways. First, as we have seen in Chapter 1, the development of Disability Studies in Britain is closely linked to the development of the disabled people's movement, with activists pushing the discipline and debates forward. However, in Nordic countries such a link has been described as being less significant, and leadership has often been found in the academy, rather than in the disabled people's movement (Goodley, 2011).

Second, and crucially, while social model thinking has all but dominated British Disability Studies since the 1980s, this has not been the case in the Nordic countries (Traustadóttir, 2004). As Tøssebro (2004:3) explains, in Nordic countries disability has been defined as '*a mismatch between the person's capabilities and the functional demands of the environment*' (emphasis in the original). This suggests that there is a gap between individual functioning and the demands of the society or environment. In this sense, disability is 'a relationship, and it is relative to the environment' (ibid.:3), hence this approach is known as the Nordic relational model of disability (Goodley, 2011). Tøssebro (2004:3) illustrates the relational nature of disability with an example: '[a] blind person is not disabled when speaking on the telephone and is exceptionally able when the lights have gone out.'

By defining disability as the result of a relationship *between* the person *and* the environment, the Nordic relational model differs from the British social model, which firmly locates disability within the environment, not the person with an impairment (Shakespeare, 2006). In Nordic countries, disabled people and academics are familiar with the British social model but see it only as one possible approach to understanding disability (Tøssebro, 2004). Like Disability Studies in Britain, Nordic Disability Studies has certainly taken an 'environmental turn', but this draws on a 'family of ideas', not one uniform approach (ibid.:3). The differences between British and Nordic approaches to disability are also due in part to the difficulties involved in translating the language of the British social model into the Nordic languages. Traustadóttir (2004) explains that the distinction between 'disability' and 'impairment' does not easily translate into Nordic languages, and this linguistic difference has played its part in explaining why a relational model of disability has driven and been driven by empirical research in the Nordic countries (Goodley, 2011).

A further difference between Britain and the Nordic countries is the basis for service provision. In Britain, the campaign for services has usually been driven by a rights-based discourse – borrowing from other minority-group models, including those relating to gender, race and class (see the minority-group model in the next section). However, services in the Nordic countries have been built on the principle of 'normalisation': the principle that disabled people should be able to lead 'normal' lives. In the Nordic countries, normalisation principles informed the early beginnings of the self-advocacy movement, and self-advocacy continues to be an important element of Nordic disability activism (Traustadóttir, 2004). Normalisation principles suggest that through the 'empowerment' of disabled people it is possible to make patterns of everyday living for disabled people that are as close as possible to the regular circumstances of life in the wider society (ibid.).

Key Concept: Normalisation principles

Normalisation principles are a strong component of current Nordic Disability Studies (Goodley, 2011), and, although they are often associated with the Nordic countries, discussion and application of the principles have taken place beyond those countries. In the United States, for example, Wolfensberger (1980) is strongly associated with the development of the principles of normalisation as follows (adapted from Wolfensberger, 1980 cited in Chappell, 1992:36):

- the use of culturally valued means to enable people to lead culturally valued lives;
- the use of culturally normative means to provide conditions that are at least as good as those of the average citizen;
- the enhancement of the behaviour, appearance, experience and status of the culturally devalued person;
- the use of cultural means to support the behaviour, appearance, experience and status which are themselves culturally normative.

Normalisation has been used as a principle to improve services in the Nordic countries, Britain and the United States (Chappell, 1992). However, Chappell (ibid.) outlines a number of limitations of normalisation theory:

- It maintains, rather than challenges, the power of professionals in the lives of disabled people.

- It works with existing structures and tries to change them; it does not challenge the underlying assumptions of service provision.
- It offers a theory of services and not provision; it does not locate disability in a political context,
- It assumes that there is consensus between service users and service providers in terms of sharing the same goals and ideas about how to achieve them. This approach ignores the possibility of tensions and conflict of interests between service users and service providers in how services should be delivered.
- Normalisation is a functionalist theory (see Parsons' 'sick role' in Chapter 1): professionals play a key part in 'restoring' disabled people to their social roles.
- Normalisation theory fails to recognise the power imbalance between service users and professionals. Service users need professionals and are reliant on them for the provision of services.
- Normalisation theory risks presenting disabled people as 'deviant'.

British social model	Nordic relational model
• Approaches to disability have been driven by the close links between the disabled people's movement and academics.	• Academics have often taken the lead in Nordic countries to develop approaches to disability.
• Disability Studies in Britain has been dominated by social model orthodoxy.	• Nordic academics are familiar with the social model but they see it as only one approach to understanding disability.
• Campaigns for welfare are based on a rights-based model.	• Welfare provision is based on the principles of normalisation.
• The language of the social model makes a clear distinction between 'disability' and 'impairment'.	• In Nordic languages, the difference between 'disability' and 'impairment' cannot easily be translated.

Figure 2.3 Summary of the similarities and differences between the British social model of disability and Nordic relational model.

Action Point: Consider what these two approaches have in common. Write a paragraph comparing and contrasting them.

This chapter explores a range of critical approaches that enrich the study of disability and we now turn to our next international perspective: North American approaches.

Section 2: North American perspectives

The history of disability activism in the United States can trace its development to the traditions of radical feminism, the Black American civil rights movement and the gay, lesbian, bi- and transsexual (LGBT) movement. Just as these movements sought to develop a positive 'minority' identity in order to challenge oppression, disabled people have also sought to challenge the oppression of disabled people by non-disabled people by developing a positive minority identity. This approach is known as the 'minority-group model'. For Hahn (1997:174), the 'minority-group' model

> asserts that disabled men and women have been subjected to the same forms of prejudice, discrimination, and segregation imposed upon other oppressed groups which are differentiated from the remainder of the population on the basis of characteristics such as race or ethnicity, gender, and aging.

The minority-group model shares many of the principles of the British social model of disability, including an emphasis on society, and not the individual, as the locus of the 'problem' of disability, and a focus on prejudice and discrimination in society (Mallett, 2007). The minority-group model emphasises the social construction of disability and minoritisation of disabled people. Activism is, therefore, driven by what is seen as the collective experience of marginalisation. The focus on the empowerment of a minority group means that, unlike in the United Kingdom, the 'people first' language of 'people with disabilities' is the preferred terminology; the aim is to recognise humanity before the label. In the United Kingdom, by contrast, the term 'disabled people' is used to emphasise the social construction of disability and the disablement of people with impairments.

Disability Studies in the United Kingdom and in the Nordic countries is most often understood as a 'social scientific' endeavour. However, this is not the case universally (Thomas, 1999). Indeed, the 'disciplinary landscape' (Mallett, 2007:55), as we shall see, varies, and in North America in particular, Disability Studies has become more widely 'woven into the critical matrix' (Snyder *et al.*, 2002:3), and has increasingly been used to understand culture, language and literature. Despite the growth of interest in Disability Studies in the United States, Davis (1995) points out that although many Americans, both inside and outside of academia, are sensitive to issues of race and gender, disability is regularly left out of theory development and analysis, and often remains the missing 'third dimension' in US cultural studies (LaCom, 2002). Nevertheless, cultural and literary analyses from the United States have yielded useful critical approaches for understanding disability.

Cultural and literary approaches to disability

Cultural and literary analyses of disability take as their starting point the view that disability is socially constructed. Such approaches take the view that bodies are not objectively 'good' or 'bad' or 'normal' or 'impaired'; rather, views about bodies are the product of complicated cultural processes and practices that shape thinking about bodies within a particular historical moment and context (Mallett, 2007). As a result, novels, films and performance become key sites for analysing the 'creation' of disability (Davis, 1995, 1997, 2002a; Mitchell and Snyder, 1997, 2001a; Snyder and Mitchell, 2006).

For Davis (1995), cultural texts are significant sites not only for the creation of disability but also for the construction of the normal world. His influential book *Enforcing Normalcy: Disability, Deafness and the Body* (ibid.:23) argues that '[t]o understand the disabled body, one must return to the concept of the norm, the normal body'.

Davis contends that in order to understand 'disability', we must begin by examining the idea of 'normal'. Indeed, he draws our attention to what he describes as the hegemony, or domination, of the 'world of norms' (1995:23). The world of norms is one in

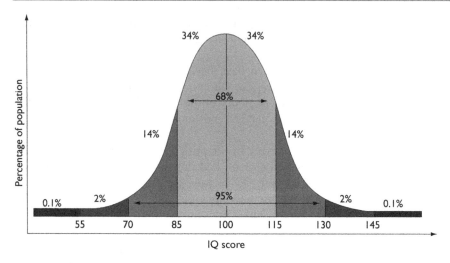

Figure 2.4 The bell curve.

Note
The diagram above shows the 'normal' range or distribution for intelligence based on the Intelligence Quotient (IQ) scores. People who score between 70 and 130 are considered to fall within the 'normal range' for intelligence. Those who score above 130 are above average and those who score below 70 are below average and consequently often labelled with a learning disability.

which intelligence, height, weight and many other aspects of the body are measured in comparison to the 'normal'. In some disciplines, such as psychology and medicine, the 'normal' range is often depicted on a bell-shaped graph that offers a visual representation and statistical description of the limits of normal.

As Rod Michalko (2002:91), who writes from Canada, tells us, 'normal' is 'understood within the paradigm of "nature"'; to be 'normal' is natural, and differences that fall outside of the bell curve are considered to be 'abnormal' and 'unnatural'. Often implicit in the identification of those who are 'abnormal' or 'unnatural' is the need to find a 'cause' for their differences and to offer rehabilitation and/or cure. Bell-curve understandings are taken as a given, as a statistical truth, and underpin much of contemporary thinking in the global North about a/typicality, dis/ability and ab/normality. These understandings lead to the assumption that the disabled person is in some sense 'damaged', while the observer or assessor of the disabled person's function or appearance remains 'undamaged' (Davis, 1995:14). 'An able body', Davis argues, 'is the body of a citizen; deformed, deafened, amputated, obese, female, perverse, crippled, maimed and blinded bodies do not make up the body politic' (ibid.:71–72). And yet, despite the power of the 'norm' and the current acceptance of the idea that deviance from the norm is 'unnatural', in *Enforcing Normalcy* Davis (ibid.:24) has sought to disrupt the contemporary power of the 'norm' by noting 'the rather remarkable fact' that

the constellation of words describing this concept – 'normal', 'normalcy', 'normality', 'norm', 'average', 'abnormal' – all entered the European languages rather late in human history. The word 'normal' as 'constituting, conforming to, not deviating or different from, the common type or standard, regular, usual' only enters the English language around 1840. (Previously, the word had meant 'perpendicular'; the carpenter's square, called a 'norm', provided the root meaning.) Likewise, the word 'norm', in the modern sense, has only been in use since around 1855, and 'normality' and 'normalcy' appeared in 1849 and 1857, respectively.

In describing the surprisingly recent origin and history of the word 'normal', Davis (ibid.:24) aims to question 'assumptions of universality of the concept'. He troubles the presupposition of 'the problem' of disability as an abnormal condition and reveals the idea of a 'norm' to be a feature of a certain kind of society (ibid.:24), rather than an 'objective' fact.

> **Action Point:** Aimee Mullins: The opportunity of adversity
> Link: www.ted.com/talks/aimee_mullins_the_opportunity_of_adversity.html
>   Aimee Mullins is a Paralympian and disability activist. Visit the link above to listen to her discussion of the definition of the word 'disability'. What does this tell you about how the meaning of the word 'disability' changes over time and the importance of paying attention to language?

Davis's work has important implications for the lives of disabled people, but he singles out the impact of 'norms' on children, in particular, as they are 'ranked in school and tested to determine where they fit into a normal curve of learning, of intelligence' (1995:23). We shall return to normalcy in the discussion of the lives of disabled children in Chapter 5.

In the United States, the study of disability has diversified into history, culture, literature, discourse and meaning, while much work in Nordic countries and the United Kingdom is located in the social sciences. So far, we have focused on ideas from the global North. In Section 4, we will turn our attention to the perspectives from the global South, but first we make a brief stop in Australia.

British social model	North American approaches
• Implicitly influenced by wider 'class' politics	• Explicitly influenced by, and positioned in relation to, wider 'minority' politics
• Located in social sciences	• Located in the humanities
• 'Disability' is the result of social structures	• 'Disability' is a social and cultural construction
• Focuses on identifying barriers and removing those barriers in order to end discrimination	• Focuses on revealing the roles of 'norms' and 'normal' in creating exclusion and prejudice
• Focus on resisting discriminatory attitudes and changing social policy	• Focus on resisting demeaning cultural ideas of disability and fostering a sense of pride

Figure 2.5 Summary of the similarities and differences between the British social model of disability and North American literary and cultural approaches.

Section 3: Disability down under: Australian perspectives

It is fitting that our section on Australian perspectives sits between our sections on the global North and the global South. Australia is one of a few countries to occupy a rather precarious position. While Australia has a global North economy and living standards, geographically it lies in the southern hemisphere. As Meekosha (2011:669) has neatly summarised, the complexities do not stop there:

> Not all populations in the South are poor: the global periphery includes countries with rich classes (e.g. Brazil and Mexico) and relatively rich countries (e.g. Australia). Even Australia, however, is regarded by global capital as a source of raw materials (timber, coal, uranium, iron ore) and holds a peripheral position in global society, culture and economics.

Moreover, like many other countries of the global South, Australia also has a history of colonialism which has left a continuing legacy of poverty and dependence among sections of its population.

Key Concept: Colonialism
The term 'colonialism' refers to the process of establishing and maintaining 'colonies' in a territory by people from another territory. One of the most famous periods of colonialism was the period of 'European colonialism', which spanned over 300 years between the sixteenth and the mid-twentieth centuries. During this time, several European powers (most notably Portugal, Spain, Britain, France and the Netherlands) established colonies (sometimes also called 'empires') in Africa, Asia and the Americas. Many colonies have experienced complicated histories, with the 'colonised' populations fighting and/or negotiating with their 'colonisers' for the right to rule themselves (independence). In this sense, colonialism is often talked of as a set of unequal relationships between the 'colonisers' and the indigenous population. Such histories have had many consequences way beyond the period of colonial rule, and *postcolonialism* (see p. 29) is a concept that attempts to make sense of those legacies.

Meekosha (2011:670) discusses the experiences of Australia's indigenous communities and suggests that in a context where survival is the goal, 'concepts of disability and impairment seem inadequate and the concept of social suffering may be more appropriate'. She describes how in

> [m]any remote indigenous communities in [the] Australian outback each house may contain over 20 people, sanitation and water is sporadic, there is no fresh food available, there is little employment, while alcoholism, rheumatic heart disease and chronic otitis media are rife.

(Ibid.:670)

She does this not to position these experiences as 'personal tragedies' or to blame indigenous communities for their situation, but to highlight the need to historically and culturally locate these experiences as the result of 'the dispossessing actions of the global North' (ibid.:671). The idea of 'social suffering' allows her to talk about group 'burdens' and collective 'wounds'.

An important theoretical concept that has come from Australia is 'ableism'. Fiona Kumari Campbell was not the first to use the word but was the first to offer a sustained examination of what its associated ideas could offer Disability Studies. She distinguishes 'ableism' from 'disablism' in the following way:

> *disablism* focuses on the negative treatment towards disabled people and social policy. I argue that while this approach is commendable, it still distorts research and policy responses. Why? *Disablism* is concerned with disabled people as Other (those people) – Other than 'us'.
>
> (2012:213; emphasis in the original)

Instead, she seeks to flip the focus onto able-bodied perspectives and position ableism as

> a network of beliefs, processes and practices that produces a particular kind of self and body (the corporeal standard) that is projected as the perfect, species-typical and therefore essential and fully human. Disability is then cast as a diminished state of being human.
>
> (Campbell, 2009:5)

To liken it to an area you may be familiar with, *disablism* is similar to sexism, while *ableism* is similar to the idea of patriarchy. Ableism is concerned with the structures, practices and processes that assume, and work in favour of, those whom it deems 'able', and, in doing so, seeks to 'erase' disability. Campbell (2012:213) provides a good summary of the sorts of work ableism does: '[a]bleism denotes the meaning of a healthy body, a normal mind, how quickly we should think and the kinds of emotions that are acceptable to express.'

Ableism is a far-reaching concept with much to offer the study of disability. We shall return to it in Chapter 3, where we imagine a 'post-able' world for children who are, currently, 'disabled'.

We move now to other parts of the southern hemisphere and consider perspectives on disability, and Disability Studies, from the global South.

Section 4: Disability in the global South

Disability Studies has been widely criticised for failing to include perspectives from the global South and, in particular, what have been termed 'postcolonial perspectives'. Ghai (2001) and Grech (2009) have argued that disability issues affecting the global South are excluded from mainstream Disability Studies or are, at best, included in piecemeal fashion. Several writers, such as Anita Ghai (2001), Helen Meekosha (2004) and Shaun Grech (2009), have argued that the dominance of the British social model in global Disability Studies analyses is unhelpful, as the social model is the product of white, middle-class, Western, disabled, educated academics and can, therefore, offer only a limited analysis of the experience of disability in the global South. As Priestley (2001:3) notes, 'the academic literature of disability studies consistently privileges minority world accounts (especially, those from Western Europe and North America). The result is that disability (in both medical and social model senses) has been framed within a minority worldview.' While the British social model focuses on the impairment/disability binary and the social production of disability, Grech (2009) sees impairment as the *key* issue for disabled people in environments where survival often relies on 'hard labour'. For Grech (ibid.), the political rhetoric of the social model risks rendering invisible the basic survival needs of disabled people in the global South.

Key Issue: Troubling 'progress'

A key issue in this area of Disability Studies centres around making assumptions about what it means for a country to be 'developing' or to be in the process of 'modernising'. From a Western or Eurocentric position, it may seem common sense to assume that countries are all heading towards the same destination, with some further ahead than others. However, this view is highly problematic. McRuer (2007:8) has highlighted how the term 'development', 'especially since World War II, has come to connote seemingly-natural "stages of development" in a capitalist progress narrative, with "developed," "underdeveloped," and "developing" societies positioned at various points along a world market spectrum'. He explores how organisations such as the World Bank and the United Nations have played a part in 'securing these meanings for development and in making them seem self-evident' (ibid.:8). It is the 'natural' and 'self-evident' nature of these ideas that we wish to query here.

In Chapter 5, we will discuss the need to *historically contextualise* all studies of disability. In this chapter, we are arguing not only for the need to *geographically contextualise* studies of disability, but also that those contexts are not to be judged against standards which are based on the view that ideas and values in the global North are inherently more advanced. This includes, but is not limited to, the assumption that the (British) social model is the best model for understanding disability.

Another problem when doing Disability Studies in global South contexts centres on the idea of 'rights'. Disability Studies in the global North is often based on the notion of human rights. As we have seen, the British and North American approaches draw heavily on individual-rights-based models to advocate for disabled people. However, as Grech (2009:91) has noted, rights are a 'Western invention, founded on Western values'. The discourse of individual rights sits uncomfortably within cultures where family and community are key to survival. Indeed, in some cultures individual rights are subsumed within obligation to the community (Grech, 2010). In this context, rights-based legislation, including the United Nations Convention on the Rights of Persons with Disabilities (United Nations, 2007), represents a *Western* utopian ideal.

There is, then, a need for a different approach that avoids universalism: 'The basic approach is to start where people live, with their concerns and resources and the particular political ecology in which they are interacting. What is disabling for them there?' (Whyte and Ingstad, 2007:3). Local cultural contexts and sensitivities must play their part in the field of Disability Studies. As Meekosha (2008:18) writes, '[t]he time is ripe for developing southern/Majority World perspectives on disability. [...] We need to develop southern theory of disability that challenges the implicit values and concepts of contemporary disability studies and includes the lasting impact of colonialism.'

Key Concept: Postcolonialism
For our purposes, *postcolonialism* is an area of study that attempts to account for, and make sense of, the contemporary legacies of colonial rule. Postcolonial theory, in particular, looks at literature and society in two ways: (1) how the writer, artist, cultural worker, and his or her context reflects a colonial past; and (2) how that person survives and discovers new ways of creating and understanding the world (Chataika, 2012). It may also deal with literature written by people living in formerly colonial nations who take those colonies as their subject matter. The theory is based upon the concepts of otherness and resistance (ibid.).

Postcolonial theory challenges the dominant views about both disabled and colonised people emanating from the global North. Disability Studies theorists have drawn on postcolonial perspectives to compare the experience of disability to that of colonialism and imperialism (Shakespeare, 2000). This is not surprising, perhaps, as both disabled and colonised people have been depicted as 'an irrational, unreasonable, propertyless, uncivilized class of people' (Goodley, 2011:38). Sherry (2007) points to the overlaps between postcolonial and disability theory and describes how both disabled people and colonised people are represented as victims of the colonisers. For example, Frank (1997 cited in Sherry, 2007) describes the doctor–patient relationship as 'medical colonization', while the reluctance to recognise American Sign Language as a distinct culture has been represented as a form of 'colonialism' (Lane, 1993 cited in Sherry, 2007).

Sherry (2007:10) acknowledges disability and postcolonialism as "two important, and inter-related, discourses in the social construction of the nation and of those bodies deemed worthy of citizenship rights' and comments that 'rhetorical connections [...] are commonly made between elements of postcolonialism (exile, diaspora, apartheid, slavery, and so on) and experiences of disability (deafness, psychiatric illness, blindness, etc.)'. However, despite these overlaps, Sherry (2007) cautions against using the term 'colonialism' simply as a metaphor for disability, or 'disability' as a metaphor for colonialism, which he characterises as a naïve approach.

When rejecting this naïve use of metaphor in the study of disability and postcolonialism, Sherry (2007:17) calls instead for 'a culturally specific examination of disability and impairment'. Disability is certainly a global issue (there are 400 million disabled people in the global South, which is equivalent to 66–75 per cent of all disabled people; Goodley, 2011). However, the challenge is to approach disability in the global South in culturally sensitive ways.

There is now a wide range of literature that focuses on studying and researching disability and disabled people in the global South in ways which acknowledge the cultural, social, political and economic particulars of the country or region being explored. As we could not possibly include the whole world in this chapter, we have had to be selective. In the final part of this chapter, we are going to explore approaches to, and critical perspectives on, disability from two places (the country of India and the continent of Africa). However, to enable you to travel further afield, should you wish to do so, Figure 2.6 provides some suggested academic sources that offer more detail on some countries in Africa, Asia, Central and South America and the Middle East.

Africa	Moswela and Mukhopadhyay (2011) on Botswana
	Kiani (2009) on Cameroon
	Baffoe (2013) and Kassah et al. (2012) on Ghana
	Cobley (2012) and Opini (2010, 2012) on Kenya
	Eleweke (2013) on Nigeria
	Berghs (2010) on Sierra Leone
	Loeb et al. (2008) and Maart et al. (2007) on South Africa
	Nuwagaba et al. (2012) on Uganda
	Munsaka and Charnley (2013) on Zimbabwe
Asia	Gartrell (2010) on Cambodia
	Dauncey (2012), Deng and Holdsworth (2007) and Guo et al. (2005) on China
	Kalyanpur (1996) and Staples (2011) on India
	Jayasooria (1999) on Malaysia
	Kim (2010) on Korea
	Lamichhane (2012) and Maya Dhungana (2006) on Nepal
	Brolan et al. (2013) on the Philippines
Central and South America	Moraes (2012), Dos Santos (1997) and Souza et al. (2013) on Brazil
	Grech (2008) on Guatemala
	D. J. Campbell et al. (2012) on Haiti
Middle East	Miles (2013) on Iraq
	Burton et al. (2013) on occupied Palestine and Crabtree (2007) on the United Arab Emirates

Figure 2.6 Disability Studies and the global South: suggested academic sources.

Action Point: Choose a country in the global South, it might be one you live in or have been to, or one you'd like to visit, and do a literature search. What can you find out about disability issues, disability legislation and the experiences of disabled people in that country?

You could start by visiting the UB Enable website to find out whether your chosen country has signed and ratified the UN Convention on the Rights of Persons with Disabilities.

Postcolonial disability studies: India

Anita Ghai is a disabled feminist academic who writes from an Indian context (2001, 2002). Ghai (2001) acknowledges that disability has been portrayed as a global issue with universal meanings and nuances but, like Sherry (2007) and others (Meekosha, 2004; Grech, 2009) concerned with postcolonialism and disability, Ghai (2001) questions the assumption of universality of the experience of 'disability' across the globe. Ghai (2002) describes India as an 'emerging superpower' with a population of one billion people, 70 million of whom, she says, are disabled – and yet she points to the absence of disability in social theorising in India. Ghai (2001) questions the contemporary and seemingly universal 'fight for rights' for disabled people, which fails to question whose agenda and ethos are being privileged within the rights discourse. Like Grech (2009), Ghai (2001) sees the individual rights agenda as a construct belonging to the global North that is difficult to translate into an Indian context.

Ghai (2002) allies herself with postcolonialism and urges disability scholars to attend to the specific social and cultural context in which disabled people in India live (Ghai, 2001). Indian culture is one in which the meaning of 'disability' is embedded in 'multiple cultural discourses' (ibid.:27), and 'labels such as "disability", "handicapped", "crippled", "deaf" and "blind" are used synonymously' (Ghai, 2002:90). Moreover, in India the apparent binary of 'disability/ability' seems culturally inappropriate, as disability is usually simply represented as 'horror and tragedy' (ibid.:89). In India, disabled people are characterised as 'eternal children' in need of charity or pity (ibid.:27), and labels such as '"*Bechara*" (poor thing)' reinforce the status of victim (ibid.:90).

The role of faith, of belief in God or gods, is a central tenet of Indian culture. However, as Grech (2009) points out, the British Marxist materialist social model of disability has ignored faith within its discussions of disability and impairment. 'Eurocentric secularism' (Grech, 2010:91) has led to a lack of engagement with the role of religious beliefs in communities. Yet in India, responses to disability embedded within faith-based stories and cultures have a direct impact on the day-to-day experience of disability. Ghai (2001:27) tells us that disability is seen as 'lack' or a 'flaw' and is often associated with 'deceit, mischief and evil', and that these images of disability are linked to the view that the cause of disability and impairment is the 'wrath of God' (karma) for past sins or misdemeanours committed by the disabled person or his or her parents, from which there is no acquittal (Ghai, 2002). There is a danger of presenting India or other countries in the global South as somehow 'less developed' in their attitudes to disability without recognising that many of these attitudes, based on pity and lack or flaw, persist in the 'developed' global North. Moreover, India has not been immune to the ideas of the colonisers, and Western medical explanations of disability have been thrown into the cultural mix, leading to a focus on medical intervention without any attention being paid to the social nature of disability (Ghai, 2001).

In the Indian context, as elsewhere, poverty and disability go hand in hand. However, in a context where day-to-day survival is a struggle, the birth of a disabled child, and the associated implications for the impact on family income, is considered to be 'a fate worse than death' (Ghai, 2001:29). In India, nearly half of all children are out of school, and nearly two-thirds of those children are girls. In this context, the chances of disabled children receiving education are virtually non-existent (Ghai, 2001). Indeed, the interconnections of poverty, gender and disability are made very visible in India, where the tradition of arranged marriages and the requirement to pay a dowry to the husband's family mean that 'disabled people are severely hampered in their efforts to get married' (ibid.:34). India continues to be a culture where female infanticide is widespread, and so the killing of a disabled child may not be regarded by some as a crime (Ghai, 2002).

Despite the harsh realities of life in India for disabled people and the lack of cultural sensitivity demonstrated by many disability academics in the global North, Ghai (2002) does not reject out of hand the sociological explanations of disability coming from the global North. She suggests instead that social oppression theories of disability may offer worthwhile '*strands*' in the Indian disability discourse and suggests that postcolonialism can be used to destabilise 'totalizing', or dominant, discourses from the global North (ibid.). For Ghai (ibid.:96), postcolonialism offers the opportunity to 'question the claims of a universalistic disability identity and a universal disability culture'.

Action Point: Read an interview with Anita Ghai, disability activist and academic
Visit: www.bbc.co.uk/ouch/interviews/13_questions_anita_ghai.shtml

Disability, development and postcolonialism: Africa

Writing from South Africa, Chataika (2012:253) also seeks to 'explore the themes frequently bypassed, ignored or rejected by the dominant Global North disability studies'.
In doing so, she brings together Disability Studies, postcolonial theory and development
studies, noting that there has so far been little work done to ensure that the disciplines
complement one another. Indeed, Grech (2010:88) notes 'the virtual abandonment of
disability issues by development studies'. For Chataika (2012:254), development is concerned with 'empowerment whereby local people take control of their own lives,
expressing their own demands and seeking their own solutions to their problems', and
within this definition she includes disability issues.

Chataika (2012:255) notes that disability and development across Africa has 'largely
been spearheaded by the Global North development agencies and researchers', who
work with local people but with the latter as junior (and relatively powerless) partners
in the relationship Indeed, the Southern African Federation of the Disabled (SAFOD)
argues that disability research in Africa 'has to be socialised and claimed back by the
people concerned' (ibid.:255), and yet the social hierarchies that exist between global
North and global South, which position the global South as lacking, remain largely
intact. Chataika (2012) calls for a Global Critical Disability Studies in which there is
meaningful dialogue between Disability Studies in the global North and global South.
In building a Critical Disability Postcolonial Studies, Chataika (ibid.:264) seeks to challenge common assumptions about the location of knowledge and to acknowledge the
colonial legacy of 'them and us', which leads to exclusion and oppression in the global
South.

A common assumption that it is important to avoid here is of talking about Africa as
if it were one place. 'Africa' is a large continent and, like Asia, Central and South
America, and the Middle East, should not be considered a homogeneous entity. Across
the continent there are many differences to be noted. In terms of legislation, for
instance, Kenya passed national legislation (the Persons with Disability Act) in 2003,
signed the UN Convention on the Rights of Persons with Disabilities in 2007, and has
active disabled people's organisations (Opini, 2010; Cobley, 2012). However, Botswana
has yet to ratify the convention (Moswela and Mukhopadhyay, 2011), and although it
has some national policies, it does not have national legislation relating to discrimination against disabled people. Interestingly, at the time of writing, Cameroon, like the
United States, has signed but not ratified the convention. We make this point to reinforce the need never to assume that the global North is ahead of the game.

Within many African countries there are also differences in wealth, employment
opportunities, sanitation, access to housing and health care, availability of support and
acceptance in the community. Cobley (2012:373) recounts a Kenyan study conducted
by the African Union of the Blind (AFUB) in which

> 95 interviewees were asked to talk about their experiences of discriminatory atti-
> tudes in various contexts. Almost 75% of participants had faced discriminatory

attitudes within their own communities, while 30% had faced discriminatory attitudes in the workplace. [...] According to the study report, much of this discrimination arose from 'deep, entrenched stereotypes prevailing in Kenyan society that portray people with disabilities as burdens, useless, good for nothing, and curses'.(AFUB 2007:11)

Other studies have shown that such attitudes may not be universal. Maart *et al.* cite a 1995 study by Asindua which found a significant difference in support available to urban and rural dwellers: '[a] community-based rehabilitation (CBR) programme in Kenya found that rural dwellers experienced better support than urban dwellers. Villages were home to one specific ethnic group with a chain of extended families making community participation and voluntary work much easier' (2007:265–266).

As is hinted at here, it has been suggested that one way to challenge the 'them' and 'us' divide which Chataika (2012) highlighted is to practise *ubuntu*. Mji *et al.* (2011) report on the formation and first meetings of AfriNEAD (the African Network on Evidence-to-Action on Disability), in which *ubuntu* was highlighted as crucial in nurturing relationships and collaborations in work carried out to improve the lives of disabled people. *Ubuntu* is described as follows:

> [t]he cultural principle of *ubuntu* (as used in South Africa, or other linguistic variations used throughout Africa) refers to a social system of interrelatedness whereby people's humanity is determined not by their personal qualities, but in terms of how they relate to all in their community (Boon 1996). The idea that 'a person is a person through other persons' encapsulates the essence of the *ubuntu* philosophy, contrasting sharply with more individualized Western views.

We quote Mji *et al.* (ibid.:365) at length here because the principle of *ubuntu* is key to understanding how Disability Studies could be done differently and how perspectives from the global South have global resonance and relevance. Mji *et al.* go on to note that under the principle of *ubuntu*, urging disabled people to fight for 'independence' in their work and home life, for instance, is positioned as a particularly Western preoccupation. Instead, *ubuntu* 'is a more interconnected way of being that locates people not as independent individuals striving for self-actualisation but as interdependent beings who are part of a collective' (ibid.:366). If disability support programmes and Disability Studies were to take *ubuntu* as their guiding principle, perhaps efforts could be refocused on ensuring rights to 'interconnectedness' and 'relationships'.

Action Point: If 'interconnectedness' and the nurturing of 'relationships' were placed at the centre of approaches to disability, what changes would be made?

Conclusion

The aim of this chapter has been to broaden the approaches to Disability Studies and to move away from purely British-centric debates. Nordic, American and Australian approaches enrich Disability Studies by introducing the ideas of relational models of disability, normalisation, minority-group perspectives, normalcy and ableism. The chapter has also attended to voices from the global South challenging the dominance of the 'minority world' in Disability Studies. Disability Studies must pay attention to local cultural contexts of disability, and while, as Ghai (2002) suggests, this does not mean that social oppression models of disability should be abandoned, Disability Studies must reflect on its colonising tendencies in order to build meaningful dialogues between Disability Studies in the global North and the global South.

Action Point: After reading this chapter, do you think the social model of disability has relevance in the global South? Write a paragraph outlining your thoughts.

Suggestions for Wider Reading

Chataika, T. (2012) 'Disability, development and postcolonialism', in Goodley, D., Hughes, B. and Davis, L. J. (eds) *Disability and Social Theory: New Developments and Directions*, Basingstoke: Palgrave Macmillan, pp. 252–269.

Davis, L. J. (2006) [1995] 'Constructing normalcy: The bell curve, the novel, and the invention of the disabled body in the nineteenth century', in Davis, L. J. (ed.) *The Disability Studies Reader*, 2nd edn, New York: Routledge, pp. 1–15.

Ghai, A. (2001) 'Marginalisation and disability: Experiences from the Third World', in Priestley, M. (ed.) *Disability and the Life Course: Global Perspectives*, Cambridge: Cambridge University Press, pp. 26–37.

Part II

Critical perspectives

Chapter 3

Critical perspectives on disability and childhood

Introduction

This chapter focuses on how the concepts of 'children' and 'childhoods' are understood and how they affect the lives of 'disabled' children. We begin by looking at definitions of 'child' and consider what it means to say that 'child' and 'childhood' are social constructions; we do so by paying attention to the historical and global contexts in which 'child' and 'childhood' are constructed. The chapter then moves to consider the roles that the disciplines of the 'sociology of childhood' and 'developmental psychology' have played in framing the ab/normal, dis/abled child. Finally, the chapter offers a view of disabled childhoods that shifts the discourse away from notions of 'deviance from the norm' that have so often characterised approaches to disabled children. Instead, we draw on the concept of 'ableism' (Campbell, 2009) and argue for the recognition of the potential of *all* children, whether or not they are dis/abled.

Section 1: What is a child?

Action Point: What is a child? Write a sentence explaining the term 'child'. How do you understand the word? Keep your definition and return to it at the end of the chapter.

As we saw in Chapter 1, definitions of concepts such as disability are often more complex and multifaceted than they may first appear. This is particularly the case for the concept of 'child'. Even in legal terms, the definition of 'child' is not straightforward. The United Nations Convention on the Rights of the Child defines a 'child' as 'a person below the age of 18'; this certainly seems straightforward. However, the Convention adds the caveat that this is the case 'unless the relevant laws recognise an earlier age of majority' (UNICEF, 1989:Article 1). This means that although under the Convention a child is usually considered to be a person under the age of 18, signatories of the Convention (of which there are currently 192 states) are able to pass national laws that vary the age at which a child is able to make decisions for him- or herself. So, for example, the United Kingdom is a signatory of the United Nations Convention on the Rights of the Child, and childhood in the United Kingdom is generally considered to end at 18. However, in the United Kingdom the age at which a young person can give consent for sex is 16, not 18. On the other hand, some groups of children in the United Kingdom, especially those considered to be 'vulnerable', can have their entitlements to services associated with being a child extended beyond the age of 18. For example, the

Children (Leaving Care) Act 2000 states that local authorities in England and Wales must keep in touch with care leavers until they are at least 21, and they should provide assistance with education, employment and training. Furthermore, recent proposals regarding changes to services for disabled children and young people have introduced education, health and care plans that will set out the needs of the young person from birth until they are 25 (DfE, 2011). This move is controversial, as although the change in the way services are delivered is intended to smooth disabled children and young people's transition to adulthood, the existence of a plan from birth to 25 for disabled people could also been seen to obscure a disabled person's adult status at the age of 18. Sadly, disabled adults have often been treated like children and have been considered unable to make choices or to have opinions. In relation to sexuality, Shakespeare *et al.* (1996) have exposed the extent to which disabled adults are not expected or permitted to do things that non-disabled people do, as a consequence of this infantilisation of disabled people.

The impact of the Convention on the Rights of the Child goes beyond the role it plays in constructing the 'child'. The Convention is an international treaty that has played a significant role in promoting the human rights of children. It establishes the principle, in international law, that states must ensure that *all* children (including disabled children) must

> benefit from special protection measures and assistance; have access to services such as education and health care; can develop their personalities, abilities and talents to the fullest potential; grow up in an environment of happiness, love and understanding; and are informed about and participate in, achieving their rights in an accessible and active manner.
>
> (UNICEF, 1989:n.p.)

Article 23 of the Convention is specifically concerned with disabled children in recognition of the segregation and discrimination they face across the globe.

Section 2: The 'new' sociology of childhood

The UN Convention on the Rights of the Child not only describes the rights and protections to be offered to children under international law, but also reflects a relatively new vision of 'the child'. The Convention is underpinned by the view that children are subjects in their own right; they are to be seen neither as the property of their parents nor simply as the objects of charity. The Convention sees the child as a member of a family and a community, but, crucially, as an individual with rights and responsibilities (UNICEF, 1989).

This shift towards seeing the child as an individual with rights and responsibilities represents an important change in the way that children and childhood are described. These alterations are related to significant changes in sociological approaches to childhood. Writing from the United Kingdom, James and Prout (2001), among others, have been at the forefront of a reappraisal of childhood. This revisionist approach has been termed 'the new sociology of childhood'. James and Prout have disrupted traditional images of children as 'the property of parents' and as 'passive' and 'vulnerable'. In contrast, they, as new sociologists of childhood, have pointed to evidence that suggests that children are, rather, *active agents* in their social worlds (ibid.). 'The new sociology of childhoood' has led to a change in attitudes in so far as children's social relationships and cultures are considered to be important and valuable *in their own right*, and not simply important as a time of preparation for adulthood.

The shift in approaches to understanding the nature of children and childhood is underpinned by social constructionist understandings of childhood. In other words, 'childhood' should be seen as a social construction, rather than simply a developmental or a natural phenomenon.

Key Concept: Social constructionism

The phrase 'social construction' is one of the most disputed in sociology (Hacking, 1999). However, put simply, to say that the 'child' is socially constructed is to suggest that knowledge of the 'child' is a matter of social interpretation, rather than a neutral description of a natural phenomenon (Ransome, 2010). Social constructionist approaches have been applied to a range of sociological phenomenon, including intellectual disability (Rapley, 2004), whiteness (Frankenberg, 1993) and gender (Lorber and Farrell, 1990). We shall return to social constructionism in Chapter 6 in relation to identity politics and in Chapter 8 in relation to the discussion of faeces and pain.

Historical and global contexts

For James and Prout (2001), childhood is a social construction that can never be separated from other variables such as class, gender or ethnicity. The notion of 'child' as a social construction is supported by the view that understandings of 'child' in twenty-first-century England are different from understandings of 'child' in different historical periods. Ariès (1962) published a hugely influential text, *Centuries of Childhood*, in which he argued that although 'childhood' is often presented as a straightforward, natural phenomenon, 'childhood' is actually a very new concept; indeed, he suggests that in the medieval period childhood simply did not exist; infancy and adulthood were distinguished without an intervening period of childhood being acknowledged. While some of Ariès' interpretations of history have been contested, changes in understandings of 'childhood' over time are evident. For example, it was not until the 1950s that the notion of 'the teenager' emerged as a stage distinct from childhood and adulthood (West, 2007). The focus on children as active social agents with their own rights and responsibilities represents a further change in how 'child' is being constructed.

As we saw in Chapter 2, ideas from the global North have dominated Disability Studies. Just as the British social model is the product of white, middle-class, Western, disabled, educated academics, offering only a limited analysis of the experience of disability in the global South, so too the 'new sociology of childhood' is the product of white, middle-class Western academics. Boydon (1990) has coined the term 'globalization of childhood' to argue that 'Western' or 'global North' concepts of childhood are being inappropriately imposed on countries in the global South (Mills, 2013). As we have already seen in relation to the UN Convention on the Rights of Persons with Disabilities in Chapter 2, 'the notion of individual rights is a global North idea or construct founded on Western values' (Grech, 2010:91), and the discourse of individual rights sits uncomfortably in cultures where individual rights are subsumed within obligation to the community (Grech, 2010). Burman (2008) picks up this theme in her discussion of child labour, in which she argues that practices in the global North ignore the extent to which families in the global South are dependent on the incomes their children generate for their survival. She suggests that 'globalised models of childhood' fail to address 'the varying cultural value and position of children' (ibid.:194).

Action Point: Reflect on the following questions, perhaps on your own or with someone you know: how do you view child labour? Is Burman right to pay attention to the context in which it takes place, or is child labour always 'wrong'?

As we saw in Chapter 2, it is often the case that disability is the missing dimension in socio-cultural analyses. The sociology of childhood has also been criticised for paying attention to variables such as class, gender and ethnicity and yet failing to attend to issues of dis/ability (Goodley and Runswick-Cole, 2012a); you may already have noticed that 'disability' is absent from James and Prout's (2001) list of 'variables'.

When disability is considered in childhood studies analysis, it seems that all too often the presence of an impairment 'works to exclude disabled children from the category of "child" to the extent that their childhood is invalidated by the impairment' (Davis and Watson, 2002:159). An unquestioning acceptance of the distinction between the disabled and the non-disabled child (Davis and Watson, 2002) has served to marginalise disabled children in services, policy, practice and research. There is a sense in which 'disabled childhoods' do not count as 'proper' childhoods worthy of study within mainstream sociology of childhood. We shall take up these points again in Chapter 7 in relation to disabled children's lives in the social world.

When disabled children have been identified as a minority group, for instance in the UN Convention on the Rights of the Child, a further danger can emerge. This is that the category 'disabled children' is treated as a homogeneous group and the differences *between* disabled children are not attended to (Davis and Watson, 2002). The challenge within the sociology of childhood is, then, is to pay attention to children with impairments in theorising childhood while at the same time attending to the differences within groups of children who are often assumed to be similar. There is a need to explore the 'variety of childhoods' that dis/abled children experience (Levin, 1994 cited in Davis, 1998).

Section 3: The psychologisation of childhood

As we have seen, the new sociology of childhood rests on the principle that the 'child' is a social construction, a matter of social interpretation rather than simply a natural phenomenon. Despite the principle of the social construction of childhood underpinning approaches to the new sociology of childhood, it remains the case that one set of 'truths' about children remains largely unquestioned and undisturbed within childhood studies. These truths are rooted in the knowledge claims of the discipline of psychology. The troubled relationship between Disability Studies and psychology has been well documented; psychology and psychologists have been seen to be overly preoccupied with the identification of and eradication of difference (Oliver, 1996). However, as Goodley and Lawthom (2006:5) suggest, '[t]o situate psychology as a bounded discipline engaged with enforcing normalcy does a disservice to the dynamic nature of knowledge disciplines.'

Developmental child psychology in the global North is underpinned by the view that the developing child follows a staged universal, regular and predictable pattern (Burman, 2008). Within developmental psychology, it is often the identification and surveillance of children considered to differ from the 'norm' that have informed understandings of the 'normal child' (ibid.). Indeed, it is impossible for developmental psychology to name the 'normal' child without reference to 'abnormality'. (Return to Chapter 2 for a discussion of the role of 'normalcy' in disabled children's lives.) The 'hunt for disability' (Baker, 2002:663) is inextricably linked to the project of naming 'normal' children and childhood. The work of two developmental psychologists, Jean Piaget (1896–1980) and Lev Vygotsky (1896–1934), still underpins much of the contemporary policy and practice for children in the global North. The rise of developmental psychology has led to a fascination with the developing child as a subject and object of study (Burman, 2008).

Key Concept: Discourse analysis

Discourse analysis pays attention to what language, or discourse, *does*. Discourse analysts argue that language cannot merely describe what is there; it also constructs it. For example, it is not possible to describe 'the child' without at the same time creating a notion of what the child is. For discourse analysts, the meanings of language are also seen as multiple and shifting, rather than being unitary and fixed (Burman and Parker, 1993). Ariès' (1962) discussion of the changing use of the word 'childhood' over time illustrates this point. Discourse theorists are ambivalent about realism in its ontological form; in other words, they are unsure that there is a possibility of a reality existing independent of human activity and experience. However, discourse analysts reject realism in its epistemological form; in other words, they share the view that knowledge can never be knowledge of an extra-human dimension, such as the world of science or objective facts. The purpose of discourse analysis is to unravel the processes through which discourses are constructed and to explore the consequences of these constructions. For examples, see Nunkoosing and Haydon-Laurelut (2011) and Luna (2009).

Discourse analysis is often talked about in relation to the work of the French philosopher Michel Foucault (1967, 1970, 1973, 1977, 1980). Foucault focused on how *objects* (e.g. madness, gender and sexuality) are constructed in discourses, as well as how *subjects* are constructed (how we experience ourselves when we speak and hear others speak about us). A Foucauldian perspective on discourse problematises norms and challenges the status of 'truth' claims. We shall return to Foucauldian notions of 'power' in Chapter 5 and 'truth' in Chapter 8.

The developing child

While the concepts of 'norms', 'milestones' and 'development' are presented as unproblematic in much of the literature in childhood studies, critical developmental psychologists have challenged the developmental model (Goodley and Runswick-Cole, 2010a). Critical psychologists believe that a focus on norms denies people in general, and oppressed groups in particular, access to social justice (Goodley and Lawthom, 2006). Drawing on a critical psychology approach, Burman (2008) has confronted the claims of developmental psychology by exploring the historical and cultural origins of its assertions. Burman (ibid.:22) argues that all discourses of childhood, including developmental psychology, are cultural narratives rich in political and social meanings and she argues that '[t]he normal child, the ideal type distilled from the comparative scores of age-graded populations, is therefore a fiction or a myth'. The model of the 'developing child' presented within mainstream psychology appears to be a description of a 'real' and 'natural' entity, but it is another example of a social interpretation of childhood, albeit a very dominant one in global North contexts, that has been shaped by a particular cultural and temporal context (Walkerdine, 1993). In the global North, developmental psychology not only shapes *who* is considered to be able to speak with authority, but also influences *what* it is possible to say about children (ibid.). The cultural 'production' of childhood is shown through its historical contexts by Harriet Cooper (2013) in a fascinating chapter on the changing notion of the 'normal' child. She uses the British documentary series *Born to be Different*, scientific literature on child development and a range of childcare manuals to 'denaturalise' ideas of 'childhood' in order to reveal the oppressive power of normalcy in the lives of disabled children. Once the impacts of such notions are apparent, it is often hard to know how best to respond. Burman (2001) urges us to move away from the image of the child as developmental subject and to talk instead of diversity in childhood and to be mindful of the colonial and globalising modes of production of the 'child'.

Research from within Disability Studies often focuses on the impact of disablism on both the child and their family (Beresford, 1994; Read, 2000; McLaughlin *et al.*, 2008). The child and the family are described as being subject to disabling attitudes and practices. However, a review of the history of child development also suggests some more troubling explanations as to why disabled children and parents or carers are often researched together. While the surveillance of 'deviancy' began in earnest in the nineteenth century as populations were divided into categories of 'criminal', 'mad', 'poor' and 'feeble-minded', it was only in the early nineteenth century that child experts – paediatricians, child psychologists and psychiatrists – began to disseminate knowledge about 'normal stages' of child development and to implicate mothers within these models (Nadesan, 2005). In the twentieth century, developmental psychology considered the role of the primary carer (usually the mother) to be of crucial importance for typical child development; the work of Melanie Klein and Anna Freud introduced the idea that parenting, or more particularly mothering, is vital to a child's development. By the 1940s, mothers who failed to produce typically developing children were increasingly required to put themselves in the hands of experts in order to promote their children's normal development (ibid.). In the 1940s and 1950s, development scales provided milestones with which to track child development and at the same time to track mothers' parenting skills. Failure on the part of the child (and his or her mother) to reach the milestone within the appropriate time frame became the catalyst for immediate attention and intervention by professional experts (Nadesan, 2005). In 1967, Bettleheim published *The Empty Fortress: Infantile Autism and the Birth of the Self*, which is perhaps best known for proposing that 'refrigerator' mothers, in failing to meet the emotional needs of their infants, were responsible for the onset of childhood autism. Although now widely discredited, Bettleheim's work suggested that poor mothering produced autism in children.

'Grief' and 'loss'

Given the dominance of psychological models of child-rearing, it is not surprising that research focusing on parenting disabled children has traditionally focused on the burden and stress of having a disabled child. Bruce and Schulz (2002:9) have proposed that parents of disabled children experience 'non-finite loss', which they define as 'the on-going sense of grief experienced by parents of children with severe disabilities'. They suggest that 'non-finite loss' is a 'unique form of grieving' because, unlike other forms of grief, it never goes away; rather, 'as time passes, there are often incessant triggers in the environment which accentuate or reactivate the discrepancies and fears' (ibid.:10). According to this type of model, parents of disabled children who appear not to be grieving are in fact delusional and in denial about their child's level of difficulties (Taylor *et al.*, 1995).

Increasingly, characterisations of parents' experiences of parenting disabled children as either 'delusional' or 'grief-stricken' have been challenged by research that explores the more positive aspects of parenting a disabled child (Beresford, 1994; Darling, 2003; Green, 2001, 2002, 2003; Landsman, 1998, 2003; Read 2000; Ryan and Runswick-Cole, 2008). Influenced by a social model analysis of disability, much research has found that parents or carers of disabled children report the positive aspects of parenting a dis-abled child and locate the source of 'burden and stress' of care not in their child's impairment but in their encounters with hostile strangers, practitioners and services (Runswick-Cole, 2007). Regrettably this approach still remains under-represented within research, the media and public consciousness (Ryan and Runswick-Cole, 2008).

Children and 'norms'

As we saw in Chapter 2, the notion of 'norms' has important implications for the lives of disabled people, and, as Davis (1995) noted, the impact of 'norms' on disabled chil-dren is particularly evident in the ways in which they are ranked and tested to deter-mine where they fit on the bell curve. Writing from Iceland, Rannveig Traustadóttir (1995) has also challenged what she describes as the tyranny of 'normal' child development by asking why understandings of childhood and child development emphasise such narrow notions and levels of 'normal' attainment.

The impact of developmental psychology on children who are judged as failing to meet developmental stages and goals is that they are considered to be 'other', and, as Walkerdine (1993:456) suggests, otherness within this context can only be understood as something 'at a lower developmental level'. Goodley (2011) has pointed to the increasingly narrow definitions of 'normal' child and the accompanying rise in the number of labels for children who differ from the 'norm', including attention deficit hyperactivity disorder (ADHD), oppositional defiance disorder (ODD) and deficits in attention, motor control and perception (DAMP), among many others. More and more children, especially boys, are being labelled (Timimi *et al.*, 2011). As Baker (2002:677) points out:

> [t]he proliferation of the acronyms is a phenomenon in itself; one could choose almost any letter of the alphabet, add a 'D' to it and find a category defining school aged child as a problem or as having a particular problem that is to be recorded in the school files.

In school contexts, as we shall see in Chapter 7, difference is automatically considered to cause trouble (Allan, 2012), and the hunt for difference becomes all the more urgent as a result.

Key Issue: Questioning diagnostic labels

The critical psychiatry movement has questioned the practice of labelling children with psychiatric diagnoses such as attention deficit hyperactivity disorder (ADHD), oppositional defiance disorder and (ODD) deficits in attention, motor control and perception (DAMP).

Schizophrenia

Bipolar

ADHD

Depression

Personality disorder

Autism

Anxiety disorder

OCD

Visit: www.causes.com/causes/615071-no-more-psychiatric-labels/about

The impact of developmental psychology's preoccupation with the hunt for disability goes beyond the realms of academic accomplishment. The identification of 'deviance' is not limited to attainment but also ventures into the realms of 'emotional intelligence' and 'character traits', where normative and non-normative development is also named. In recent years, Parker (2008:20) suggests, '[t]he measurement of intelligence is then matched, or even surpassed, by a focus on what has come to be called "emotional intelligence" (Goleman, 1996)'. Emotional intelligence is defined as the ability to recognise, handle, understand and express emotions 'appropriately' (Burman, 2010). Attempts to rank children's emotional literacy (Goleman, 2009) pay scant attention to gender, race, class or dis/ability. 'Emotional intelligence' represents yet another domain in which children are marked out as 'ab/normal'. Discussion of the development of character traits often takes place within the context of developmental psychology and normative development.

For example, Masten (2001:228) states, in her discussion of resilience, that '[i]ndividuals are not considered resilient if there has never been a significant threat to their development; there must be current or past hazards judged to have the potential to derail normative development'. Resilience research has often focused on children and young people who have experienced 'at risk' factors associated with poor outcomes (examples usually cited include family breakdown, drug or alcohol abuse, or 'mental illness' of a family member). Those children who are considered to thrive as 'normally' as other children in less 'at risk' contexts are described as 'resilient' (Runswick-Cole and Goodley, 2012).

And yet, as disabled children are often described in terms of their impairments and are considered not to develop *normally*, they are excluded from the category of 'resilient' child. This exclusion is important because children who are considered to lack resilience are considered to be vulnerable and in need of protection and support from specialist services and provision. The consequence of such protection and support often results in segregation and exclusion, as we shall see in Chapter 7.

> **Action Point:** Go online and search for an Emotional Quotient (EQ) test. Have a look at the questions. To what extent do you think they are shaped by cultural variables, including gender, ethnicity, class and dis/ability?

Section 3: Rethinking disabled childhoods in a 'post-able' world?

We have seen that approaches to disability evident in the sociology of childhood and developmental psychology often devalue disabled childhoods. They are underpinned by what Fiona Kumari Campbell (2001) terms ableism. As we explored in Chapter 2, ableism refers to

> a network of beliefs, processes and practices that produces a particular kind of self and body (the corporeal standard) that is projected as the perfect, species-typical and therefore essential and fully human. Disability then, is cast as a diminished state of being human.
>
> (Ibid.:44)

Campbell (2008) argues that there has been a fascination with the production of the perfect body, so much so that bodies which are judged to fall away from the 'ideal type' are automatically considered to be lacking or lesser. Indeed, Campbell (ibid.) suggests that the preoccupation with the able body means that impairment is always and only characterised as an inherently *bad thing*, which should be 'ameliorated, cured or indeed eliminated' (Campbell, 2009:6). This view resonates with Michalko's (2002) work, which, as we also saw in Chapter 2, suggests that while 'normal' is characterised as natural, difference is characterised as 'abnormal' and 'unnatural'. Campbell seeks to offer an alternative approach that re-positions disability and exposes and challenges the assumptions of ableism. She asks us to imagine a 'post-able' world, a world in which disabled children are no longer seen as being lesser or in lack, but one in which different and diverse bodies and minds are welcomed and seen not as a bad thing but as full of potential (Runswick-Cole and Goodley, 2011).

> **Action Point:** Write a paragraph describing what a 'post-able' world would look like for disabled children. How would moving away from notions of deficit and lack to seeing disabled children as full of potential shape policy and practice for disabled children? Think about health, social care, education and leisure services. How might these be different?

Conclusion

The aim of this chapter has been to explore the ways in which disabled childhoods are constructed. We have seen how the sociology of childhood has often paid scant attention to disabled children. Developmental psychology has, on the other hand, focused its attention on disabled children but with the purpose of identifying children who are considered to deviate from the norm in terms of both development and character. We have argued for an alternative approach to disability in the lives of disabled children and asked you to imagine what a 'post-able' world, where disabled children are seen as full of potential, might look like.

Action Point: Look back at your definition of 'child'. How, if at all, would you change your definition in the light of this chapter?

As we shall see in Chapter 7, the ways in which disabled childhoods are understood have significant impact on opportunities and outcomes for disabled children's lives and for their families. This analysis is offered alongside a consideration of the research practices.

Suggestions for Wider Reading

Burman, E. (2008) *Deconstructing Developmental Psychology*, Hove: Routledge.
Curran, T. and Runswick-Cole, K. (eds) (2013) *Disabled Children's Childhood Studies: Critical Approaches in a Global Context*, Basingstoke: Palgrave Macmillan.
McLaughlin, J., Goodley, D., Clavering, E. and Fisher, P. (2008) *Families Raising Disabled Children: Values of Enabling Care and Social Justice*, Basingstoke: Palgrave Macmillan.

Chapter 4

Critical perspectives on disability and culture

Introduction

The aim of this chapter is to explore the representation of impairment, disability and disabled people in cultural texts, and to provide a variety of ways such texts can be analysed using Disability Studies perspectives. When we say *analyse*, we are referring to the examination of cultural products, such as films or television programmes, in terms of how they portray impairment or disability and for what impact they might have on the lives and experiences of disabled people.

The chapter begins by examining what we mean by the terms 'culture', 'representation' and 'texts' and asks why it might be important to consider these in relation to the study of disability. The next section will enable you to explore how impairment, disability and disabled people are portrayed, by breaking down the text (e.g. book, film, magazine article) into its component parts. We shall then explore five main approaches to analysing texts.

Section 1: Culture and its importance for understanding disability

Action Point: How would you define 'culture'? Write a sentence defining the term.

If you found this question difficult, you are not alone: 'culture' is widely considered one of the most difficult words to define (Jackson, 1989). It can refer to *a* culture, or a way of life, where a group of people (e.g. a nation or an organisation) share a set of 'beliefs, rituals, customs, and values, as well as work patterns, leisure activities and material goods' (Barnes and Mercer, 2001b:515). Using this definition, a discussion of culture is more likely to fall under *historical perspectives* on disability (as discussed in Chapter 5). However, the term 'culture' also refers to more specific activities where beliefs, attitudes and values are *communicated* in artistic, creative and/or entertaining ways. These 'cultural products', which range from opera and ballet to television programmes and advertisements, are often collectively referred to as 'cultural texts', and there is a long tradition of people analysing such texts in order to examine how a particular culture views and thinks about certain topics. This chapter draws on the discipline of Cultural Studies to explore the meanings made of impairment and disability within cultural texts.

> **Key Concept:** Re-presenting shared meanings
> 'The notion of the framing of disability issues and disabled people by news media lends credence to media scholar Doris Graber's view that journalists select the content and frame of the news, thereby constructing reality for those who read, watch, or listen to their stories' (Haller, 2010:27)
>
> A key idea in the study of culture is that texts allow us to explore the 'meanings' made of certain topics or issues. In other words, as a consumer of a cultural text we do not have access to pure, neutral, untainted 'fact', and therefore texts should not be thought of as presenting 'the truth'. Even a newspaper article is written by a certain person, for a certain newspaper, at a certain time, in a certain place, for certain reasons, and all these will have an impact on how the story is framed. This is why the term 'representation' is often used to highlight how topics and issues are re-presented and mediated through dominant collective beliefs, attitudes and values. It is because cultural texts re-present reality within a shared context that they are so useful for understanding how disability is thought about in wider society.

Texts are often said to have a two-way relationship with the cultures that produce and consume them. First, they are said to re-present the society in which they are produced. As McQuail (1989:178) comments, such research assumes that 'both changes and regularities in media content reliably reflect or report some feature of the social reality of the moment'. Cultural Disability Studies scholars have, therefore, been able to examine texts for how they reflect and represent discriminatory attitudes towards disabled people. Many have argued, as Haller (2010:iii) does, that the content of cultural and media texts 'is shaped by dominant able-bodied culture, which defines and classifies disability'. This idea of a dominant ableist culture is important, as it helps to explain why some versions of the 'truth' are paid more attention to, or dominate more, than others. (For a discussion of ableism, return to Chapter 2.)

Cultural theorist Raymond Williams (1981) has suggested that all dominant cultures have the potential to be challenged by minority cultures, and when this happens, wider change is possible. As was discussed in Chapter 1, the disability rights movement is a good example of a minority culture attempting to tell a different version of the 'truth'. In relation to cultural texts, they are said to influence the society in which they are consumed. Therefore, Cultural Disability Studies scholars' second interest is in how alternative representations might influence and encourage more inclusive attitudes towards disabled people.

Cultural Disability Studies research is predominately Euro-American, and this chapter reflects that focus. However, there is increasing interest in exploring how colonialism and postcolonialism interact with the cultural representation of disability (e.g. Barker, 2010), as well as the analysis of non-Western cultural and media texts, such as Valentine's (2001) examination of deafness in Japanese television and film, and Patrick's (1998) analysis of a film's portrayal of physical impairment in colonial Zimbabwe.

Considering the wealth of information we can glean from cultural texts, as well as the potential for meaningful cultural change, the analysis of cultural and media representations of impairment and disability is one of the most exciting areas of Disability Studies. If it is true, as Haller (2010) argues, that most non-disabled people learn about disability issues through culture and the media, rather than through personal interactions with disabled people, then it could be argued that this area should be at the forefront of activism and disability rights campaigning.

In the following sections, you will be guided through how to pull apart (deconstruct) a text and identify some of its components. Following this, five critical approaches will be outlined which will help you analyse a cultural text using Disability Studies perspectives. This aim of this analysis is to explore how disability is being portrayed and, therefore, what sorts of messages about impairment, disability and/or disabled people are being produced and consumed.

Section 2: Pulling apart: components *of* and *in* a text

Being asked to analyse a representation of disability can be daunting, but with a few tricks up your sleeve it becomes a fascinating exercise. All texts are made up of various component parts, so to understand the text we start by pulling it apart. In this section, we will explore some common components. Not all these components appear in, or are significant for, *every* representation, but it is worth knowing about them nonetheless. We will begin with components *of* the text before moving on to components *in* the text. It is important to note that many of these components overlap; indeed, analysis is more fascinating when you start to explore the overlaps and the intersections.

> **Action Point:** Take five minutes to write a list of characters with an impairment you have encountered in a film or television programme. From this list, choose one example and reflect on it as you work through the rest of this section.

Components *of the text*

Some components *of* the text are quite basic (such as when it was made), some are more complicated and require informed guesswork (such as who the intended audiences are), but all of them have an impact on how impairment, disability and disabled people are represented. Figure 4.1 provides an easy guide to identifying the components *of* the text you are analysing. What follows are some thoughts on the impact made by each of these components and, utilising the increasing and insightful Cultural Disability Studies literature, some suggestions for further reading.

Medium

Rather like the word 'culture', the definition of 'medium' is hotly debated (Ryan, 2003), but at its simplest, cultural texts are communicated in a variety of formats, or media, and what is important is recognising that *how* texts are experienced matters.

Depending on the type of medium, texts have a range of possibilities and restrictions concerning how they can represent. For example, a television programme has the possibility of sound as well as visual images, whereas radio only has sound. This is important, because, as cultural theorist Marshall McLuhan (1964) demonstrated, each medium is connected with a different pattern or arrangement among the senses and results in a different experience. Even if the factual messages in a radio report are identical to those on television, the event will be perceived differently and take on different meanings for the two audiences. This idea has been summed up in the phrase 'the medium is the message' (ibid.). It is the job of the analyst to consider how the possibilities and restrictions of the particular medium allow and/or limit the representation of disability. For example,

1 Question to ask about the text	2 Identify the component	3 Examples	4 Then ask...
What format is the text?	*Medium*	Print (newspapers, magazines, novels), television, film, art, photography	What difference does this make to how impairment and disability are represented?
What sort of text?	*Genre*	Comedy, horror, romance, tragedy, science fiction, satire, gothic *or* romantic comedy, gothic horror	
When was the text made?	*Age*	–	
Who/what made this text?	*Producer*	Author, organisation	
Who is this text made for?	*Intended audience*	Age group, gender, geographical location	

Figure 4.1 Identifying components of the text.

Medium	Suggested readings
Contemporary art	• Kuppers (2003, 2007) and Sandahl and Auslander (2009) on performance art • Siebers (2000, 2005) on aesthetics and art
Literature	• Barker (2010) and Uprety (1997) on postcolonial literature • Davidson *et al.* (1994), Keith (2001) and Yenika-Agbaw (2011) on classic children's literature • Cheyne (2013a) and Stemp (2004) on science fiction
Online (social media)	• Haller (2010) on Facebook and YouTube • Thoreau (2006) on the BBC's 'Ouch!' blog
Photography	• Hevey (1992, 1997) on charity advertising • Thomson (2001) on 'popular' photography
Pop music	• McKay on Ian Dury (2009) and on others (2013) • Church (2006) and Waltz and James (2009) on Ian Curtis and Joy Division

Figure 4.2 Exploring media: suggested academic sources.

Thomson's (2001) work on print advertising explores how photography enables audiences to 'stare' at impairment in ways other media do not permit.

There are many media in which disability is represented, and we cannot cover them all here. For the most part, this chapter will focus on film, television and newspapers. If you are interested in other formats, see Figure 4.2 for some suggestions for further reading.

Genre

Regardless of the medium, most texts work within a particular genre. A genre is like a flavour and, again, this brings with it certain possibilities and restrictions regarding how impairment and disability are represented.

Studies of cultural representation of disability are beginning to recognise the importance of this component and have focused on the difference genre can make. For instance, Mallett (2009) and White (2005) suggest that the satirical and ironic nature of television programmes like *South Park* should be taken into account when the representation of disability is analysed.

By now, you are probably realising that impairment and disability are represented in texts that you had not previously thought were 'about' disability. Bérubé (2005) makes a similar point in an article on disability and narrative. He adds that he considers it 'plausible that the genre of science fiction is as obsessed with disability as it is with space travel and alien contact' (ibid.:568). There is still much work to be done on the importance of impairment and disability to genres such as sci-fi, romance and crime fiction. Figure 4.3 offers suggestions for further reading.

Age

The age of a text should be easy to identify, and in many cases it will be. Clearly, the older a text, the more an analysis has to consider whether values and beliefs about disability and impairment have changed in the intervening years. We shall discuss the importance of *contextualising* analysis in Chapter 5, when we explore historical perspectives on disability.

However, we should also remember that some texts are based *on* older texts and others are based *in* older times, so 'age' is not as simple as it first appears. For example, *The Hunchback of Notre-Dame* is an 1831 novel by Victor Hugo, a 1923 'horror' film directed by Wallace Worsley and a 1996 musical-animated film by Walt Disney. While the 1996 film may display some awareness of disability rights, it still has to stick to the 1831 story, and this is an example of a restriction upon the representation which should always be taken into account.

Producer

A key issue is whether the person responsible for a text is disabled or non-disabled, and this will be explored further in Section 3. However, before it even becomes an issue, an analyst has to identify *who* the producer is. For some texts, identifying the author is straightforward: the author of a novel is named on the front cover of the book. For others, it is more complicated, but *all* texts have a producer of some sort. For instance, a charity can be said to have *produced* an advertisement.

To make things even more complicated, some texts have both an author and a producer. Even when you know the name of the author, you might think that the

Genre	Suggested readings
Comedy	• Mallett (2010) on television shows *Little Britain* and *The Office* and Fink (2013) on *The Simpsons*
Gothic	• Miller (2012) on gothic fiction
Melodrama	• Jarman (2012) on the novels of Jodi Picoult
Romance	• Cheyne (2013b) on romance novels
Science fiction	• Cheu (2004) on 'replicants' and aliens in film
Sentimentality	• Thomson (1996a) on nineteenth-century American fiction
Soap opera	• Wilde (2004a, b, 2010) on *Eastenders* and *Coronation Street*

Figure 4.3 Exploring genre: suggested academic sources.

producer is more important. For instance, the author of a magazine article might be named, but you might think that it is more significant that it is produced by a certain magazine (e.g. *Hello*) that runs stories within a certain genre (e.g. celebrity culture); here the components of producer and genre overlap. This can be important in magazine advertising, for instance, where the presence (or absence) of impairment and disability can tell us much about the dominant ableist culture. In a quantitative content analysis (see Section 3) of magazines within the fields of sport, fitness and fashion, Parashar and Devanathan (2006) reported that out of 3,947 advertisements, only 0.73 per cent 'contained textual and/or visual depiction of disability', with none (0 per cent) being found in the fashion magazine *Cosmopolitan*. There are a number of ways this could be further investigated; one would be to look at the inherent values around physical perfection held, and promoted, by the *producers* of the advertisements.

Action Point: Thinking about the example you selected earlier, can you identify its medium, genre, age and producer? What difference do these characteristics make to how impairment or disability is being represented?

Intended audience

When creating any cultural text, producers will have some idea of the sort of audience they are targeting. For example, producers will aim at a certain age group (e.g. children under the age of five) or a certain gender (e.g. women). Often the target will be even more specific: for instance, the target audience for *Cosmopolitan* is considered to be working women between the ages of 18 and 30. This does not mean that other sorts of people do not read that magazine, but it does mean that they were not the *intended* audience.

As was mentioned earlier, identifying the intended audience may require some educated guesswork, but the important step is to ask how this influences *how* impairment and disability are represented. A key issue in this area is whether the author or producer assumes a 'non-disabled' audience. As we saw in the case of *Cosmopolitan*, assuming a non-disabled audience often involves assuming an *able* audience, which often means that impairment and disability are *not* represented at all.

Key Issue: Assuming a non-disabled audience

It has been argued by some Cultural Disability Studies scholars that assuming a non-disabled audience makes little business sense. Recent estimates suggest that one billion people in the world are impaired. This equates to 15 per cent of the global population (World Health Organization, 2011). As Davis (1995 cited in Goodley, 2011:2) comments, this 'makes disabled people the largest minority grouping in an already crowded theatre of multiculturalism'. If you are producing a cultural text and intend to make a profit (e.g. a Hollywood film), or making profits for other people is the purpose of your cultural text (e.g. advertisements), then if you know that the annual spending power of disabled adults in the United Kingdom in 2006 was thought to be around £80 billion (Employers Forum on Disability, 2006 cited in Papworth Trust, 2012), you might start taking notice. Haller (2010) has argued that some advertisers have woken up to this spending power and have responded by including disabled people in their texts.

Components in the text

Some components are *in* the text, and many are what Norden (1994) calls 'basic tools of the trade'. We shall outline just a few, but there are many more and their presence often depends on the particular medium you are analysing. Again, some are quite basic, others are more complicated and require informed guesswork, but all of them have some impact on how disability is being represented. As we did in the previous section, in Figure 4.4 we provide an easy guide to identifying the components *in* the text you are analysing, and then offer some thoughts on their potential impact before making suggestions for further reading.

Colour and lighting

The use of colour can give clues as to the intended meaning of a text, including the emotional response the makers intend the audience to have. Paying attention to the date of a text is important here, as in the past makers had limited choices, but *The Elephant Man* (1980) is a good example of a film where the makers decided to film in black and white instead of colour. Here, the use of black and white gives weight to the sense of melodrama and the feelings of Victorian sentimentality and pity. (For an extended discussion of this film, see Darke, 1994.)

The lighting of a visual image is also significant. Discussing paintings by Rembrandt, Rose (2001) discusses how there are different types of light (such as daylight or candlelight) and how light can also be used to *highlight* certain elements. The use of lighting, like the use of colour, can be important in creating an emotional mood (for example, soft lighting can encourage a feeling of romance or, more often in terms of disability,

1 Question(s) to ask about the text	2 Identify the component	3 Useful for these Mediums	4 Then ask...
What colour or lighting is being used? How are they being used at particular points?	Colour and lighting	Television, film, art, photography	What difference does this make to how impairment and disability are represented?
How are images framed or packaged?	Framing	Television, film, literature, print (newspapers and magazines)	
What sound/music is being used? Is it being used at particular points?	Sound and music	Television, film, art	
What is the story? What path does it follow?	Narrative arc	Television, film, literature, print (newspapers and magazines)	

Figure 4.4 Summary of components *in* the text.

sadness, sentimentality and pity). The use of *highlighting* (together with the framing of the image) can have a large impact on how audiences respond to a certain character. In the Disney animation *Beauty and the Beast* (1991), light and the absence of light (darkness) are used to make the beast seem scary. As Belle gets to know him, the lighting of the beast changes to reflect the changing relationship.

Framing

How the image (still or moving) is framed can be important. Drawing on Rose's (2001) discussion of *mise-en-scène* (the spatial organisation of an image – that is, how it looks), we can say that framing can include:

- *Distance*: is it a long shot, a full shot? A head and shoulders shot? A close-up?
- *Focus*: is a certain part of the image in focus? Is the focus soft (maybe suggesting romance)? Or sharp and clear?
- *Angle*: is it overhead (looking down on the scene)? Is it eye-level? Low-level and looking up? This helps to establish what the audience should feel about a certain character. (For example, if the angle is always looking down on someone, then perhaps we are being encouraged to feel superior to that character.)
- *Point of view*: is the camera adopting a character's point of view rather than just presenting a scene?

Together with the angle of the shot, the 'point of view' can have a large effect on how audiences feel about particular characters. It can be interesting to notice which characters are, or are not, afforded a point of view. Rose (2001:49) explains that the *reverse-angle shot* is 'often used to show a conversation between two people: one is seen talking or listening from approximately the other's viewpoint as the other listens or talks'. Sometimes, in conversations between a disabled and a non-disabled person, only the non-disabled person is afforded a 'point of view'.

Sound and music

Gallez (1970:40) reminds us that 'silence as well as sound is deliberate', and it is the deliberate intentions regarding the presence, absence and type of sound that an analyst is interested in. Rose (2001) uses the work of Monaco (2000) to discuss three types of sound which you might find in a text: *environmental* sounds (noise effects that may be recorded *in situ* or dubbed on afterwards), *speech* and *music*.

As Lerner (2010:i) has stated in relation to horror films, '[f]rightening images and ideas can be made even more intense when accompanied with frightening musical sounds, and music in horror film frequently makes its audience feel threatened and uncomfortable through its sudden stinger chords and other shock effects.' In the next section, we explore the links often made between impairment, criminality and monstrosity, but the use of sound and music in encouraging the fear of impairment is, at present, an under-researched area.

Narrative arc

Davis (1995) has discussed how almost all novels have a narrative (a story) which starts with a sense of normality. Something then happens to disrupt that normality, but by the end, normality is successfully restored (that is, the story rises to a crisis and falls back to 'normal' in an arc shape). He says this usually involves impairment, illness or injury in some way and that normality is often restored with the treatment, cure or the death of the impaired person.

Although Davis (1995) is writing about novels, we would add that most films and many television programmes can also be understood by thinking about the narrative arc of the story. The importance of this is that such narrative arcs send a message to the audience that impairment causes trouble and life is easier and happier without it.

> **Action Point:** Choose a novel or a film you have read or watched recently. Does Davis's (1995) argument that narratives usually involve the loss and then the restoration of a normal body or normal mind hold true for your example? If so, how? Write a paragraph to explain this.

A particular issue within Cultural Disability Studies is the inability of scholarship to keep pace with the output of new cultural texts. If you are particularly interested in analysing a text that has not yet been written about, a good approach is to look for existing analysis of a similar medium or genre and use that to inform your own work. For instance, work by

Wilde (2004a, 2004b, 2010) on soaps would be very useful for an analysis of continuing teen-dramas such as the United Kingdom's *Hollyoaks* (1995 to the present), or Kidd's (2004) work on the 'unreal' in older children's fiction could be useful to analyse the presentations of bodily difference in the *Twilight* books (Meyer, 2005, 2006, 2007, 2008).

In the next section, we build on these ideas and offer five disability-related approaches to analysing representations.

Section 3: Analysing texts: five critical approaches

After identifying components *of* and *in* a text, the next stage is to build on these observations by applying an analytical framework. Doing this is just like looking at an image through a particular lens; depending on the lens you choose, the image will look different.

The content of texts can be analysed from a variety of perspectives, and as we are interested in the ways in which impairment, disability and disabled people are represented, this section discusses five disability-related approaches you can use to interrogate a text. The section draws on the ideas of Mitchell and Snyder (2001b) in their seminal overview of this area, on the research of Mallett (2007, 2009, 2010) in her examinations of the analysis of disability in cultural texts, and on the work of US scholar Haller (2010) on media portrayals of disability.

As will become clear, these approaches use many ideas from Disability Studies with which you will be familiar. Figure 4.5 provides a summary of the approaches and what they are particularly useful for. We present them as separate frameworks, but often researchers will combine approaches, depending on the aims of their analysis.

Critical approach		
	interested in analysing...	by using ideas from...
1 Negative imagery	meanings made of 'impairment'	medical model of disability (e.g. isolation, tragedy, individual)
2 Social realism	meanings made of 'disability'	social model of disability (e.g. oppression, control, collective)
3 Transgressive resignification	playing with established meanings	minority model of disability (e.g. transgression, reclaiming, belonging)
	interested in...	by using methods such as...
4 Quantitative content analysis	content	statistical analysis
5 Qualitative audience research	effect and impact	focus groups, interviews

Figure 4.5 Summary of critical approaches to representations of disability.

I Negative imagery: identifying demeaning images

This approach seeks to highlight and analyse the meanings made of 'impairment', and to do so uses ideas from the medical model of disability.

When scholars first investigated how impairment and disability were being represented in culture, this is the perspective they used (Mallett, 2007). It has since been developed, and in more recent work you will often find the ideas combined with other approaches. It had been assumed that disability was a marginalised issue and of interest to only a few people, but this earlier work proved it was *everywhere*. This enabled scholars to argue that Disability Studies should take culture seriously and start analysing it. Analysis done using this approach considers texts to be reliable sources 'for documenting demeaning attitudes toward people with disabilities' (Mitchell and Snyder, 2001b:197) and contends that analyses should reveal those negative and disabling attitudes. One of the tools used to do this is called 'stereotypes'.

Key Concept: Stereotypes of disability

As Hall (1997:258) states, stereotypes 'get hold of the few "simple, vivid, memorable, easily grasped and widely recognized" characteristics about a person, *reduce* everything about the person to those traits, exaggerate and *simplify* them, and *fix* them' (emphasis in the original).

It has been argued that stereotypes of people with impairments often correspond to individual and medical model ideas of disability. An example of this would be in how they 'negatively' associate having an impairment with leading a restricted and unfulfilling life. In relation to this, ideas of charity, pity and tragedy are often invoked.

Longmore (1987) identified three stereotypes of disability, Kriegel (1987) identified four, but it is Barnes' (1992) identification of 11 commonly recurring media stereotypes of disabled people that provides us with the most comprehensive tool for analysis:

1 Pitiable and Pathetic
2 Object of Violence
3 Sinister and Evil
4 Atmosphere or Curio
5 Super-Cripple
6 Object of Ridicule
7 Their Own Worst and Only Enemy
8 Burden
9 Sexually Abnormal
10 Incapable of Participating Fully in Community Life
11 Normal

They are more fully described in Barnes' (1992) report *Disabling Imagery and the Media: An Exploration of the Principles for Media Representations of Disabled People*, which was co-authored with the British Council of Disabled People (BCODP). In the second section of the report, each stereotype is described and examples are given.

The presence of stereotypes is often linked to tales of wrongdoing. As Swain *et al.* (2003:20) state:

> [c]ulture is an activity that reflects attempts by human beings to impose certain frameworks upon the ways in which we relate to each other, to established boundaries between right and wrong, acceptable and unacceptable, proper and improper, normal and abnormal.

A good example of this is the link frequently made between disability and criminality. Madriaga and Mallett (2010) consider this link in their discussion of how stereotypes of disability often involve malevolence, monstrosity, violence and/or death. They explore themes such as impairment being the result of previous 'evil' wrongdoings (e.g. in films such as *The Da Vinci Code*, 2006); impairment being the symptom or side effect of 'bad' events (e.g. in D. H. Lawrence's 1928 novel *Lady Chatterley's Lover*); people with impairments being depicted as dangerous and unpredictable (e.g. in the films *Psycho*, 1960, and *Slingblade*, 1996); and how the (often violent) death of such characters is presented as inevitable and justified. On the final point, it is worth noting that

> research has shown that on television, when fictional dramas include a disabled character they are more than three times as likely to be dead at the end of the show than their non-disabled counterparts (Cumberbach and Negrine 1992). Of these deaths over half were violent and a fifth of those were suicides, all committed by 'mentally ill' characters, supporting the belief that disabled people are also in need of protection from themselves.
>
> (Madriaga and Mallett, 2010:600)

However, all is not lost, as Madriaga and Mallett (2010) end their discussion echoing Zola's (1987) surprise at the coexistent history of disabled people being portrayed as the hero or protagonist. Examples of this can be seen on television and in literature with characters such as the OCD-labelled *Monk* (2002–2009) and Jonathan Letham's Lionel Essrog, a private detective labelled with Tourette syndrome, in his 1999 novel *Motherless Brooklyn*. The danger, though, is that such portrayals merely fall into the 'super-cripple' and/or 'atmosphere or curio' stereotypes.

There is, then, a very tight line to be followed if a producer wishes to avoid stereotyping, and one area that 'plays' with this problem is the tradition within comic novels (and now films) of having superheroes with bodily anomalies. Chemers (2004), in a review of the film *X-2* (2003), celebrates affirmative representations of difference. Using a phrase borrowed from Thomson (1997:17), he argues that the film creates 'a counter-narrative of peculiarity as eminence' alongside an exploration of wider societal fears of abnormality and difference. We shall return to this idea of 'playing' in Section 3 when we discuss an approach called *transgressive resignification*, which is better suited to analysing these sorts of 'playful' texts.

2 Social realism: acceptable or unacceptable?

This approach seeks to analyse the meanings made of 'disability' and uses the social model of disability to evaluate whether texts mislead their audiences. The general viewpoint of this approach is summed up by Pointon (1997:111) when she states: '[h]istorically, literature, film, television and other media have propagated misleading or distorted pictures of disability in our culture.' The main difference between this and the previous approach is that scholars using the approach are interested not only in identifying bad (unacceptable) representations of impairment and disability, but also in identifying and suggesting good (acceptable) representations.

Drawing on Mallett's (2007) discussion of how writings in this area use an unwritten set of criteria based on the *content* of the text and the *producer* of the text, we will outline and explore each of these in turn. These criteria are used to decide whether a text, or an element of a text (e.g. a particular character), is an acceptable or an unacceptable representation of disability.

Criterion 1: Content of the text

- If an impaired person or a disability issue or theme is depicted in terms of 'an *impaired body*' (e.g. in relation to the medical model: isolation; medicine; tragedy; suffering), then that person or theme is depicted in ways that edit out the social aspect of 'disability' and is **unacceptable**. An example of this would be a magazine interview with a cerebral palsy 'sufferer' focusing on her 'condition' and how it affected her life.
- If an impaired person or a disability issue or theme is depicted in terms of the social struggle between people with impairments and a disabling society, then that person or theme is portrayed accurately and is **acceptable**. An example of this would be a magazine interview with a person who had been diagnosed with cerebral palsy that focused on her life and how it was affected by discriminatory attitudes and practices.

You will notice the influence of the social model on these ideas, and the rejection of medical model perspectives.

Criterion 2: Producer of the text

- If the author or producer is non-disabled, he or she cannot represent 'disability' adequately and the text is therefore **unacceptable**. An example of this would be a medical professional being interviewed on a television news programme about a specific impairment or particular disabled person.
- If the author or producer is disabled, he or she can represent 'disability' adequately and therefore the text is **acceptable**. An example might be a disabled person being interviewed on a television news programme about his or her experiences.

The distinction between impaired and disabled becomes important here, because, as Watson (2002) has shown, not all impaired people consider themselves to be disabled. However, this has been and continues to be a significant area of debate within Cultural Disability Studies. We explore this by examining what could be argued to be the two ends of the 'producer' spectrum: disability charities (widely considered as consisting of non-disabled producers: see below) and disability culture (disabled authors and producers: see 'Transgressive resignification', p. 61).

Case study: critique of disability charities

In the early 1990s, as the disability rights movement grew and criticism of cultural texts started to focus on disability, heated debate centred on the advertisements of disability-related charities. As part of research into the cultural criticism of disability in cultural texts, Mallett (2007) summarises the main points made within these debates. She outlines how, through negative images used in t advertisements, disability charities were said to perpetuate the 'dominant' belief that impairments are 'undesirable; constitute a personal misfortune; give rise to special needs; and place a moral obligation to help upon the public at large' (Drake, 1996:156). Charities' management structures were criticised for being exclusively made up of non-disabled people. As Campbell (1990:n.p.) stated, '[o]ur image has been created by non-disabled people who "know" how to help those who cannot help themselves. Naturally, they got it all wrong.' The idea here was that because 'non-disabled' people cannot 'understand' what being 'disabled' is like, disability charities cannot represent 'disability' correctly (you will recognise this argument from the criteria for acceptability outlined above).

This criticism was supported by the idea that disability charities were run as 'big businesses' caught up in making the most 'profit', with Hevey (1992:21) commenting that 'if charity is big business, impairment charity is the biggest'. Such criticism led activists to campaign against high-profile disability-charity fund-raising. For instance, in the United Kingdom a 1992 demonstration against ITV's annual Telethon (a televised fundraising event) attracted 2,000 disabled people (Barnes and Mercer, 2001b), and in the United States the fight to cancel the Jerry Lewis Muscular Dystrophy Association Telethon was ongoing until 2011, when it was finally cancelled. The year before, Haller (2010) discussed its inevitable demise and in doing so gives a useful insight into the role of pity in charitable representations.

During this time, it seemed that disability charities were listening as they started to make changes. For example, Scope changed its name from the Spastics Society, and Leonard Cheshire dropped the word 'Foundation' from its name. Both organisations also radically changed their advertising, using brighter colours and more 'positive' messages which attempted to convey the barriers disabled people faced. However, disability activists remain sceptical and it can be argued that Campbell's (1990:n.p.) question 'Is the change only POSTER DEEP?' remains relevant today.

Action Point: What would your answer be to Campbell's question? Do you think that the changes disability charities have made are only poster deep? Would you agree or disagree that charities' attempts to 'repackage' themselves involved a borrowing of language from the disabled people's movement but *not* a borrowing of ethos and ideas?

These concerns about non-disabled people producing texts wrongly representing 'disability' led to a more focused argument about the under-representation of disabled people in the cultural, artistic and broadcasting industries. According to figures given by Bewick (2005:30), '[w]hile disabled people represent 13% of the UK workforce, only 1.1% of people working in broadcasting are disabled.' This is a wide gap and the key issue here is *who* has control over the message, and therefore when, how and where disabled people have an opportunity to contribute to that message. If disability charities are considered to be at one end of the producer spectrum, then at the other end is disability culture, where disabled people have rather more control. We will explore this when we discuss our third critical approach, *transgressive resignification*.

The disadvantage of the *social realism* approach is that it too easily categorises texts into 'good' or 'bad'. Most texts are far more complicated than this, and, as we have discussed in relation to charity advertising, they do not exist in a vacuum: producers are aware of past criticism and may seek to respond to it in their future work. Components such as genre likewise are rarely taken into account. One area of criticism that seeks to pay attention to the complexity of texts is *transgressive resignification*.

3 Transgressive resignification: accounting for trouble

Transgressive resignification is interested in the trouble representations can cause; it seeks to analyse the alternative meanings made of impairment or disability and uses the minority model of disability to do so.

Often associated with North American literary and cultural approaches to disability (as outlined in Chapter 2), this perspective borrows ideas from feminism, critical race studies and queer theory – areas of the humanities and social science that are interested in theorising difference and non-normativity (Mallett, 2007). It differs from the two previous approaches in that instead of calling for the removal and the prohibiting of unacceptable images, it seeks to understand them and, in some cases, embrace them. By embracing such negativity, it is responding to the idea that non-disabled people have had control over representations of disability, and its intention, when *reclaiming* potentially harmful and hurtful depictions, is to re-author them in ways that are empowering. In this sense, this approach can also be seen as influencing the production, as well as the analysis, of cultural texts, and here we explore the other end of the 'producer' spectrum: disability culture.

Case study: disability culture

During our discussion of *social realism* as a critical approach, we outlined the key issue of authorship by offering the example of disability charities. Here, we explore the other end of the spectrum and consider the arena of disability culture. It is often referred to as an alternative culture that 'celebrates a positive disabled identity and consciousness' (Barnes and Mercer, 2001b:515). The difference between impaired and disabled is significant here, too, as disability culture refers to *politically* identified 'disabled' people voicing and sharing their collective identity. (For more on 'disabled' as a *political identity*, refer to Chapter 6.) Indeed, Finkelstein (1987:1–2) has stated that disability culture

> must arise out of the spontaneous desire of disabled people to share our feelings, experiences and desires, our loves and hates, our pleasures as well as our sufferings, amongst ourselves. In other words, we have to make the choice that we want to identify ourselves as disabled people. We have to be willing to express our separate identity. There can be no disability culture without this freely made choice.

Figure 4.6 is an example of a text that was written and published within this field and demonstrates the difference in tone; it is defiant, blunt and mocking of the ignorant 'non-disabled' character. Mitchell and Snyder (2001b:208–209) state that the 'power of transgression always originates at the moment when the derided object uncharacteristically embraces its deviance as a value'. Characteristic of much work

Action Point: Read the extract of the poem below. What messages about disability are being expressed here? Are they messages that you have heard elsewhere? If not, why not?

'Now let me help unpack your load – the least that I can do –
'Because, but for the grace of God, I could be just like you!
'Does anybody help you? Or do you live alone?
'Oh, do you buy this in a tin? I always bake my own.
'You haven't got a husband? Well, build a social life –
'Perhaps you'll meet a crippled man who wants a crippled wife!'
I found this quite offensive, and told her so at length.
She said, 'My dear, I understand – you've lost your health and strength.
'I know you're being very brave, but that was rather rude –
'Next time someone helps you, try to show some gratitude.
'Of course you think life isn't fair, but when you're feeling blue –
'*Big smile!* And then remember, there's someone worse than you!'

Figure 4.6 Extract from the poem 'Do unto Others' by Janice Pink (1996:179–180) published in *What Happened to You: An Anthology of Writing by Disabled Women.*

within disability culture is this acceptance, embracing and celebratory reworking of ideas around the abnormal, deviance and deficit.

Understanding the impulse to transgress (overstep established, often ableist, boundaries) and to resignify (rewrite meanings) makes it much easier to understand texts produced within disability culture. However, it is not just texts from disability culture that benefit from this analytical approach.

Transgressive analysis: rereading texts

As an approach to texts, transgressive resignification offers a lens through which complexity, intricacy and ambiguity can be more readily appreciated. As this approach does not seek to identify good/acceptable or bad/unacceptable representations, it is better able to engage with areas of culture where anarchy, indecorum and transgression are almost expected. One area is comedy, and as analyses of shows such as the US animated show *South Park* and the British comedies *The Office* and *Little Britain* has demonstrated, the approach helps us to question whether the presence of stereotypes is *always* a bad thing (Mallett, 2009; White, 2005). This work also points to the potential for texts to parody the 'performance' of political correctness and thereby raise questions about the success of tolerance as a means for inclusion (Mallett, 2010).

This approach's ability to engage with otherwise problematic subject areas has also been used to reread the idea of the 'freak' and the 'grotesque'. Work in this area (e.g. Thomson, 1996b) has helped to interrogate and re-imagine the role of the 'freak' in culture, and has been taken up, for instance, by those interested in the emergence of medical documentaries (e.g. Van Dijck, 2002) and in the pop star Michael Jackson (e.g. Yuan, 1996). (Also see Figure 5.1 in Chapter 5, p. 80, for further examples.)

So far, all the approaches have adopted a particular understanding (model) of disability. The final two approaches focus on how to gather data about texts, their production and their consumption.

4 Quantitative content analysis: counting instances

Quantitative content analysis uses statistical methods to examine cultural texts. The approach demands a high level of technical rigour and involves selecting a specific sample of content (e.g. daily national newspapers published in March of a certain year in a certain country) and coding its contents using a set framework of questions or prompts. Its advantage, as a critical approach to texts, is that using numerical data, such as percentages, is a more objective, scientific way to analyse. As quantitative content analysis counts and summarises rather than subjectively evaluates a text, it is much easier to compare across studies and across time periods so that any changes in the representation of a topic are more easily detected. In other words, this approach can 'reveal significant trends and allow us to understand "media" behaviour towards disability topics' (Haller, 2010:33).

We do not have the space to guide you through the details of how to carry out a quantitative content analysis of a cultural text, but for a good introduction to the method you can refer to McQuail's (1989) book on media research. There have also been some important studies in this area which have looked at the representation of disability. These include Cumberbach and Negrine's (1992) examination of British television output for six weeks during 1988, highlighting the frequency of a 'personal tragedy approach' to impairment and disability involving both the medical treatment or cure of impairments and the special achievements of disabled people. Auslander and Gold's work (Auslander and Gold, 1999; Gold and Auslander, 1999) compares three Canadian and three Israeli newspapers over a three-month period, in part concentrating on the impact of gender differences between those featured in, and also those authoring, the articles. More recently, Briant *et al.* (2011) produced *Bad News for Disabled People*, a report that analysed 2,276 print articles in a variety of tabloid and broadsheet newspapers as well as also analysing findings from focus groups.

To give an idea of the sorts of results such an approach can deliver, we explore Beth Haller's research on newspapers.

Case study: read all about it – analysing the papers

Haller (2010) reports on a study that analysed 256 stories selected from 11 newspapers and news magazines published in 1998 using a 294-question code sheet. The terms used to select the stories were 'disabled', 'disability', 'disabilities' and 'handicapped'. The code sheet prompted the analyst to look for, among other things, the placement of the stories, the kinds of impairments mentioned, the kinds of sources drawn on and the language used. Some of the results were as follows:

- Placement of stories: 'slightly more than 60 percent of the stories were located in the local Metro section or the neighborhood/suburban section. Only 14 percent of the stories were in the front national news section' (Haller, 2010:30). The prominence of news stories is important because, as Biklen (1987:81) suggests, the 'media's influence may be less effective in determining a particular decision or action as it is in shaping what we consider worthy of attention'.

- Interestingly, the study also found that most of the stories were news (48 per cent) rather than feature stories (37.5 per cent), which, Haller (2010) argues, means that disability issues are being considered newsworthy, rather than merely entertainment or of general interest.
- On types of impairment, Haller (2010:32) found that 'due to the search terms used, people with disabilities in general accounted for the largest category at 54 percent'. This is a good reminder that how you select the texts for analysis sometimes skews your results. However, Haller (2010) also found that the highest mention of specific impairment was 'cognitive impairment', which is interesting given the often-assumed marginalisation of those labelled with learning impairments. Of course, being reported about in the media is not necessarily proof that you are no longer marginalised.
- On sources, only 36 per cent of stories had 'no person with a disability as a source' (Haller, 2010:33), and disabled people were much more likely to be used as examples than as sources. When they were used as a source, it was much more likely to be in feature stories (48 per cent) than news stories (17 per cent), which, as Haller (2010:33) notes, 'means they may not be used as sources on more hard-hitting issues' and 'has implications for the message that may be getting across to the public', such as the impression that disabled people cannot speak for themselves.
- On language used, Haller (2010:32) reports that the news media 'seemed to understand that the term "handicapped" is no longer an acceptable term' and that 'people with disabilities' was the term most often used.
- Haller (2010) states that the most unexpected finding of the study, and one that deserves more research, was a link between disability issues, education and children in major new stories. She later went on to analyse four years' worth of media coverage on the case of *Hartmann* v. *Loudoun County Board of Education* in an attempt to reveal more about the narratives being used in these stories.

To read more about these studies, refer to chapter 2, 'Researching media images of disability', and chapter 5, 'Autism and inclusive education in the news media', in Haller's 2010 book entitled *Representing Disability in an Ableist World*.

The disadvantage of this approach, like many of the others we have discussed, is that it does not, and cannot, 'make claims about the effect of news stories on audiences' (Haller, 2010:28). To do this, analysts have to involve the audience in their research.

5 Qualitative audience research: meanings being made

Alison Wilde (2004a:67) has observed that 'disability studies on representation have focused primarily on the content of various media rather than on its "effects"'. So far in this chapter we have mirrored this, although we have considered the *contexts* of production (e.g. who the author is) and have briefly considered the influence of the 'intended' audience on the production process. In this section, using the work of Wilde, we explore how analysis can pay attention to the 'actual' audience's response to texts.

Audience Studies, particularly in relation to television, is now an established part of Cultural and Media Studies (Rose, 2001), as is the idea that audiences receive and respond to texts in very different ways (Fiske, 1987). Within Disability Studies, there have been only a few such pieces of research, but even fewer have taken a *qualitative* approach. Qualitative audience research engages with audiences at length, perhaps asking them to keep diaries or interviewing them over a period of time; the focus is on understanding what, how and why. This type of analysis can be time-consuming and problematic. In 1995, the UK Broadcasting Standards Council's project, for instance, set out to gather disabled and non-disabled people's perspectives on the representation of disability. In the pilot research project, the researchers encountered a difficulty with getting respondents to talk about the topic and subsequently restricted the project to focus on just one text, in the hope that it would focus the respondents' answers (BSC, 1997).

The advantage of this approach is that it takes some of the 'guesswork' out of analysis, particularly if you are making claims about the 'effect' of texts, for example on attitudes towards impairment. However, as we will see, its disadvantage is that it results in rich but complex data sets which themselves have to be interpreted. Changes in the kind and level of engagement audiences have with television programmes (such as the ability to vote off contestants from reality shows) have also led researchers to reconsider the division between audience and text as well as what they mean by 'active' audiences (e.g. Tincknell and Raghuram, 2002, writing about *Big Brother*); this promises to add yet another level of complication, and fascination, to this area.

Case study: watching the soaps

Wilde's research (2004a, b, 2010) focuses on a specific medium (television) and a specific genre (soaps), and uses a specific critical approach (qualitative audience research). Wilde set out to 'examine issues of cultural identity and position through an exploration of the ways in which both disabled and non-disabled television viewers make sense of images and narratives of impairment, disability and "normality" within soap operas' (2004a:68). To do this, she met with seven 'discussion groups' over a six-month period. Twenty-one diarists were also recruited. The participants ranged in gender, age, education and impairment status. The texts discussed included *EastEnders* (1985 to the present) and *Coronation Street* (1960 to the present) – both long-running television soaps with new episodes at least twice a week, available on national UK television stations.

Soaps are an important genre, owing to their popularity and their ubiquity (ever-present nature) – so much so that they have been considered to be 'a valuable platform for addressing marginalised social concerns' (Wilde, 2004b:355). Finding out how audiences make sense of the texts is important in understanding whether and, if so, how soaps are, and could be, used to address attitudes towards disabled people, including how disabled people feel about themselves.

The nature of qualitative audience research means that short, simple findings are not the aim. Instead, Wilde (2004a, 2004b) presents in-depth analyses of the similarities and differences across the discussions and diary entries, which show that differences between disabled and non-disabled people's responses, as well as differences between genders, are not marked. However, general and tentative conclusions can be reached, such as the following: the disabled participants expressed dislike of the impairment and disability images in soaps (Wilde, 2004a); soaps in general are an alienating experience for men, whether disabled or not (Wilde, 2004b); and viewers make use of their personal experiences of impairment when making sense of the text, meaning that identification with the 'collective disability struggle' is minimal (Wilde, 2004a).

Interestingly, Wilde (2004a:77) also suggests that soaps create 'spectator positions which privilege (albeit exaggerated) forms of normality', and this enables viewers, whoever they are, to find positions from which to spectate the non-normal 'other'. For instance, she reports a disabled woman's homophobic response towards lesbian and gay characters, younger participants ridiculing older characters, and men criticising female characters as well as the 'feminine' genre of soaps. This neatly demonstrates the complexity of audience responses, and therefore the multifaceted nature of approaching texts through qualitative audience research methods.

Conclusion

Snyder and Mitchell (2006:201) have argued that 'textually based analysis is the *only* absolute remedy for the exhaustion of people-based research practices'. Similarly supporting texts as an important area of study, Haller (2010) suggests that content analysis of media is a useful and unobtrusive research tool. In conclusion to this chapter, we argue that Cultural Disability Studies offers an accessible (in terms of time, travel and money) way of approaching the study of disability but that *how* we choose to analyse (Mallett, 2009) is an important decision. Having an understanding of the components *of* and *in* a text means they are easier to break down (deconstruct) and therefore easier to approach. Once you can break down a text, you can then make informed decisions on what approach to use and what sort of analysis will follow.

In the next chapter (Chapter 5), we consider historical perspectives on disability and offer a way of contextualising attitudes and responses to disability within their wider circumstances. Where this chapter focused on *texts*, the next chapter focuses on social, cultural and political *contexts*.

Suggestions for Wider Reading

Haller, B. A. (2010) *Representing Disability in an Ableist World: Essays on Mass Media*, Louisville, KY: Advocado Press.

Rose, G. (2001) *Visual Methodologies: An Introduction to the Interpretation of Visual Materials*, London: Sage.

Thomson, R. G. (1997) *Extraordinary Bodies: Figuring Physical Disability in American Culture and Literature*, New York: Columbia University Press.

Chapter 5

Critical perspectives on disability and history

Introduction

The aim of this chapter is to explore the experiences of people labelled with impairments through the shifting *historical* conceptions of disability. The chapter will examine why it might be important to consider how responses to impairment and disability have changed over the decades and why researching disability history is not as simple as it may first appear. We begin with some time travel as we embark on a whistle-stop tour of disability in history.

Section 1: Time travelling through disability in history

Action Point: Before we start our time travel, can you think of any stops we are likely to make? What disability-related moments in history do you already know about?

In the space of a book chapter we will not attempt to offer a 'full history' of disability. There are many scholarly articles and even more books devoted to exploring specific historical times and places where impairment and disability mattered. In this first section, however, we offer a flavour of the work that has been undertaken in global North contexts as we embark on a whirlwind tour through time. If we stumble across a time period that particularly interests you, we hope these brief introductions will inspire you to seek out some of the more specific literature on the topic.

Many accounts of disability in history (e.g. Barnes and Mercer, 2001b; Braddock and Parish, 2001) begin with ancient Greece, where beliefs such as the desirability of killing babies born with 'deformities' are often attributed to contemporary writers such as the philosopher Aristotle (Rieser, 2006). However, the practice is thought to have been less widespread and more complicated than first thought. Garland (1995 cited in Braddock and Parish, 2001) described how, when infanticide (the killing of children) was practised, it was done for economic reasons (e.g. too many children to feed) and how the extent of the practice differed in different regions. Stiker (1999), adding to the complications, argues that infants with non-visible impairments (such as hearing, visual or cognitive impairments) were not considered 'deformed' and therefore were spared death.

In the early modern period (from the mid-fifteenth century to the eighteenth century), impairments (such as hearing impairments and epilepsy) were thought to be a sign of supernatural or demonic activity; indeed, possession by the devil was regarded as the primary aetiology (cause of disease) for mental illness, which resulted in individuals being 'treated' by exorcism (Braddock and Parish, 2001). The associated persecution of people deemed to be 'witches' on the basis of impairment has also been acknowledged. Rushton (1982:127) briefly notes 'attempts to associate deformity with witchcraft [...] on the basis of people's crooked shape or strange appearance', while Fabrega (1991) offers an extended analysis of the complicated overlaps of witchcraft, religion and psychiatric stigma.

Also within this time period, royal courts across Europe retained people of short stature as 'court jesters', or those who would be labelled today as having cognitive impairments and learning difficulties as 'fools'. Miles (2000:115) comments that there was little uniformity in the treatment received, stating that

> in a few times and places they [people of short stature] seem to have been regarded as personable human beings who could exploit an inherent talent for amusement; elsewhere they were merely exhibited as freaks or made to perform as buffoons.

Rush (2004:314) reports that 'at least into the 17th and 18th centuries', inmates of madhouses in England were controlled by chains or confined in small spaces, and 'wealthy people would visit them as one might a zoo, of entertainment and in thankfulness at being so different from them'.

During the nineteenth century, across Europe and North America such displays of difference had begun to take the form of the 'freak show', offering a 'formally organized exhibition of people with alleged physical, mental, or behavioral difference at circuses, fairs, carnivals, and other amusement venues' (Bogdan, 1996:25). Having their heyday in the mid- to late nineteenth century, freak shows exaggerated differences in impairment, race and gender by offering the (often white) middle classes a chance to gaze at exotic 'monsters'. Section 4 on p. 78 explores freak shows in more detail.

Key Issue: Rereading history

There has been some debate within Disability Studies as to whether people with impairments who were involved in freak shows should be considered victims or employees. While the general response to 'freaks' is a mixture of shock and sympathy, it has been shown that some performers enjoyed and courted the celebrity status they were afforded and sometimes earned extensive financial rewards (Bogdan, 1996; Patterson, 2011).

This example serves as a reminder that, as historians, we are looking back on history through our own perspective. While from our contemporary standpoint, performing in a freak show would be considered to be degrading and exploitative, we have to remember, in simple terms, that things were different then. The following section, Section 2, explores some of the issues that arise when rereading disability in history, and Section 3 suggests that *contextualising* our rereadings is one way to counter the problems.

In other areas of society, the response to difference was couched in terms of Christian charitable philanthropy and efforts to 'care for' unfortunate individuals. Benjamin (2006:28) discusses how in the mid-nineteenth century 'members of the public were invited to give a postage stamp to help sponsor the care of a nominated idiot child' who was being cared for within the increasing number of 'idiot' asylums. Benjamin (ibid.:31–32) goes on to argue that the introduction of universal schooling meant that mechanisms needed to be introduced for separating children into those who were deemed able to benefit from instruction and those who were not but 'could not be considered as idiots'. The formal categorisation of non-normative people, and the associated increase in state intervention, continued, with successive laws creating legitimate labels for use by statutory authorities. For instance, in the United Kingdom the Idiots Act 1886 refers to 'idiots' and 'imbeciles', and the Defective and Epileptic Children Act 1899 established the term 'feeble-minded' (Benjamin, 2006).

The rise of formal categorisation and the rise in institutions (which, over time, include workhouses, hospitals, madhouses, asylums and special schools) mean that the institutionalisation of people with impairments is a significant theme in the history of disability. Wright (2000:732) discusses the impact of amendments to the English Poor Law, in the mid-nineteenth century, on the 'residential provision, care and treatment for those deemed "idiot" or "imbecile"' as well as the provision, care and treatment of the 'insane' under the Lunacy Laws.

By 1913, the Mental Deficiency Act had given 'sweeping powers to local authorities in the United Kingdom to make certain individuals – idiots, imbeciles, the feeble-minded and moral imbeciles – "subject to be dealt with"' (Walmsley, 2001:65) in institutions or by being placed under supervision in the community. As Walmsley (2001) notes, the United Kingdom was not alone in enacting such laws: the United States, Canada and Australia also introduced regulations to control the 'feeble-minded'.

Before leaving the nineteenth century behind, we must make a stop at the Industrial Revolution. Occurring during the late eighteenth century and the early to mid-nineteenth, the Industrial Revolution, often spoken of as a transfer from rural feudalism to urban capitalism, marks a transition to mass-manufacturing processes supported by innovations in the use of coal as an energy source, an increasingly urbanised workforce, and state investment in infrastructure such as railways and canals. Some scholars have argued that the change marks a significant moment in the exclusion of disabled people from society. Arguing that how the means of production, and associated division of labour, are organised profoundly affects the meaning of disability, Finkelstein (1980) offers three phases of history, and he implies that it is in phase 2 that 'the creation of a new productive technology – large scale industry with production-lines geared to able-bodied norms' (ibid.:7) led to the exclusion of people with impairment from the workforce (Barnes, 1998) and therefore to the emergence of disability as an 'oppressive social relationship' (Finkelstein, 1980:7). Oliver (1990), Gleeson (1999) and Borsay (2005) have since furthered this focus on economics as a basis for disability history.

During the Second World War (1939–1945), 'the most structured and far-reaching attempt to eradicate the class of people with disabilities' (Evans, 2004:9) saw Nazi Germany use the idea of certain 'types' of people being unproductive to justify the segregation, sterilisation and, ultimately, the killing of those deemed 'useless' to the broader population. Section 5 (p. 81) will explore the Holocaust in further detail.

Read and Walmsley (2006) discuss the post-war period as particularly important for the development of special education for those deemed to be 'ineducable' or 'educationally subnormal'.

Continuing the legislative changes in the United Kingdom, 1995 saw the passing of the Disability Discrimination Act (DDA), which aimed to end discrimination on the basis of impairment. In 2001, the Special Educational Needs and Disabilities Act (SENDA) modified, and became Part 4 of, the Disability Discrimination Act 1995 (DDA), and in 2005 the DDA was amended further, in part by placing a duty on all public bodies to promote disability equality. By 2010, it was replaced by the Equality

Act, which sought to harmonise existing 'anti-discrimination' legislation across protected characteristics, summarised by Hepple (2010:16) as

> age, disability, gender reassignment (which is possibly narrower than gender identity), marriage or civil partnership, pregnancy and maternity, race (which includes colour, nationality and ethnic or national origins; caste may be added later by secondary legislation), religion or belief, sex (man or woman), and sexual orientation.

This places disability alongside, and on a par with, other categories for direct and indirect discrimination.

In more recent years, these legislative gains have been tempered by increases in hate crime. In her 2011 book *Scapegoat: Why We Are Failing Disabled People*, Katherine Quarmby discusses both her assumptions that legal rights had transferred into changing social attitudes and her dismay at 'uncovering' rising levels of violence towards disabled people. A short extract offers an insight into some of the cases she covers:

> [o]ver the last year [2010] I have travelled all over England – north, to Hartlepool, where Christine Lakinski was urinated on as she lay dying, and further north to Sunderland, where Brent Martin was kicked to death for a £5 bet. I have travelled to the Midlands, to the town of Barwell, near Leicester, where Fiona Pilkington and her daughter Frankie and son Antony were subjected to years of unrelenting abuse by neighbours. [...] And I visited the West Country, travelling to the tiny hamlet outside Bodmin where Steven Hoskins was born, and St Austell, where a young girl stamped on Steven's fingers until he fell from a railway viaduct 150 feet to his death.
>
> (Quarmby, 2011:3)

We end our whirlwind tour here to remind ourselves that the passing of time does not necessarily mean a march towards progress. Quarmby's (2011) book shows how disabled people and their friends, families, advocates and allies are working together to combat further incidents of hate crime, but, as Quarmby (ibid.:2) acknowledges, 'the motivation of the offenders was shaped by our common history and by the fears and prejudices that have fuelled violence against disabled people for over 2,000 years' – a common history that continues to be problematic and complex.

> **Action Point:** Choose one of the disability-related events mentioned in this chapter and do a literature search. What else can you find out about it? What sort of sources are you finding?

Section 2: Researching disability in history

Once disability is reframed as an important social experience of oppression and exclusion, one cannot help but ask why such experiences have not been more thoroughly documented. If you go to a history book, on the Middle Ages perhaps, you may find accounts of kings, priests and peasants; you may even find discussions of the role of women; but it would rare to find analyses of disability or considerations of the experiences of people with impairments. In this section, we look at why this might be and ask why disability has not been readily studied from an historical perspective. As the previous section gave a flavour of some of the disability-related events in history, we can also go on to think through some of the issues that arise when historical research into disability is undertaken, before giving some thought to the benefits of such research.

Lack of interest in disability/in history

In Borsay's (2002) consideration of disability history, she suggests some reasons why, in general, there has been a lack of interest in histories of disability, from both Disability Studies and History. She offers three main reasons:

1   *Disciplinary differences in approach.* Disability Studies (particularly in the United Kingdom) is generally seen as a subject area within the social sciences, and Borsay (2002) suggests that there are broad differences between how it and a humanities subject, such as History, would approach a topic of study. This she describes as the difference between a *nomethetic methodology*, which approaches a topic by looking at broad universal knowledges and themes (social science), and *idiographic methodology*, which approaches a topic by starting with particular and concrete instances or examples (humanities). While these methodologies are not representative of all the work carried out within these two disciplinary areas, the distinction does highlight why 'most historians do not deal readily with the conceptual strategies which are the stuff of sociology' (Borsay, 2002:100) and highlight why the work of historians 'may be inaccessible to social scientists trained to think in conceptual ways' (ibid.:100). It also offers an explanation as to why the early historical accounts of disability carried out by Disability Studies scholars, such as Finkelstein (1980) and Oliver (1990), focus on all-encompassing historical schemas.

2   *Social history is a relatively new specialism.* Borsay (2002) contends that in the early days of history as an established discipline, it was interested in matters of government, religion, legislation and the monarchy (including colonial rule). It was not until the 1960s that history started to pay attention to the social experiences of everyday life in the United Kingdom. Therefore, and quite simply, there has not been much time for a social history that considers disability to emerge – a situation which may be further explained by the third and final reason.

3   *Social discrimination in academia.* With the emergence of social history came a focus on socio-political inequalities. At first, this showed itself as an interest in the English working class and a commitment to 'rescue the poor' (Thompson, 1963 cited in Borsay, 2002:101). Since then, other 'disadvantaged' groups have been studied, with social histories of class, gender and race now available, but disability remains on the margins, with Borsay (2002:101) suggesting that '[s]ocial exclusion has been matched by intellectual exclusion'. This is echoed, but more encouragingly, by Buckingham (2011) when she comments that it is within the areas interested in the historical experience of marginalisation that histories of disability are emerging.

From an understanding of these reasons, it is easier to see that, whether you are an historian researching disability or a Disability Studies scholar using historical methods, the act of researching presents various issues.

Action Point: From your experiences of doing a literature search at the end of the previous section, did you come across any issues or problems when researching disability?

Issue: finding and capturing sources

The first issue is probably obvious by now: a lack of primary sources. We only have access to the past through the thoughts of others, so we rely on their efforts and are constrained by their interests. Many people whose thoughts we do have would not have been aware of a social approach to disability and, if they had been, would not have thought it an important matter to record. To a certain extent, it could be argued that looking for *disability* in historical accounts involves looking for something that isn't there, or at least isn't there in the ways we conceptualise it today.

What we are far more likely to find recorded in the historical record is *impairment* and the institutional records of people labelled with impairments, as the non-normal mind and body have been subjects of interest throughout the centuries. However, even here there are issues. Many diagnostic categories are relatively newly formed or have changed considerably over time, so we need to be careful about reaching back into history to reclaim people as affected by a particular impairment. In Chapter 8, we shall discuss the retrospective diagnosis of historical figures such as Dr Samuel Johnson and Albert Einstein. We argue that such diagnoses reveal an 'urge to know' an individual's impairment, but here we are more interested in how useful (or not) retrospective diagnosis is to the historical study of disability. Stiker (1999:65) is interesting here when he contends that maybe, at certain points in history, there is a lack of sources mentioning this subject because impaired people 'were spontaneously part of the world and of a society that was accepted as being multifaceted, diversified, disparate. [...] Normality was a hodge-podge, and no one was concerned with segregation, for it was only natural that there should be malformations'. Here he is talking about the Middle Ages, and although there is historical evidence that this is not strictly true (to which the fate of witches testifies), it does suggest that we should find ways to avoid 'the urge' to bring to historical accounts contemporary diagnoses, or even ideas, about the inevitable *oppression* of people with impairment. This all means care needs to be taken when reaching back into history to reclaim people as impaired and/or as disabled (Dodd *et al.*, 2004).

Of course, history is not just about the far-distant past, and there have been calls to ensure that we make efforts to 'capture' oral history from people with impairments who are alive today. This is often talked about in relation to experiences of the Holocaust (for more on this historical event, see Section 5, p. 81). Another example, smaller but equally important, is Dias *et al.*'s (2012) discussion of a project that worked with eight people with learning difficulties in Cumbria in the United Kingdom to record their memories of the Second World War. The article talks about how the project sought to 'fill in the gaps' in existing Cumbrian wartime history but also, and candidly, addresses the urgency with which we should capture experiences before they are lost for ever: '[w]e had to do the work quickly because otherwise, given the age group, the information would be lost forever. Anyone that was going to be of the target age would be in their eighties by now' (ibid.:36).

In a neat phrase, Buckingham (2011:426) asserts that 'disability is still young as an historical focus', and this is a useful way to think about the job of finding and capturing source materials. As 'disability' develops as an historical focus for study, we will become more skilled at securing historical records for the future as well as more experienced in interpreting the historical records we do have.

Issue: evaluating sources

When we do find sources, we need to be careful and make judgements about which we use. Bredberg (1999) calls for more critical awareness of the nature of sources and suggests that this would improve historical interpretations. She contends that one way to ensure we are more critically aware is to examine the *perspective* from which the material was produced.

Key Concept: Perspectives of historical sources
Bredberg (1999) delineates three main types of perspectives offered by historical sources. She notes that although these points of view sometimes exist together, one type will usual dominate, although she warns that the dominant perspective may change at different points within the same source. The three types are:

1 *institutional*: dominant and depersonalised (often associated within clinical 'expert' sources);
2 *vernacular*: non-institutionalised responses, more personalised;
3 *experiential*: personal accounts and other representations of the experience of impairment and disability.

Braddock and Parish (2001) note that, as the gold standard of historical research is the use of primary sources, quite a lot of disability history research has utilised *institutional* records which offer details of the delivery of services for people with cognitive impairments, such as Ferguson's (1994) examination of services for 'severely retarded' people in the United States between 1820 and 1920. The availability of these sorts of primary sources demonstrates the extent of the surveillance and bureaucracy to which impaired people's lives have been subjected. As Braddock and Parish (2001) go on to note, they were written from the viewpoint of professionals who delivered the services, therefore eclipsing the other views and leaving historians to interpret 'lived experiences' vicariously through the filter of professionals. It should also be remembered that as only a fraction of the disabled population lived within institutions, these sources only allow for a professional perspective on a section of the disabled community (ibid.). It is for these reasons that *vernacular* and, particularly, *experiential* sources are preferred by disability historians who are committed to describing the myriad of experiences disabled people have encountered through history.

A related issue here is the need to be careful when reading existing histories of disability and to be mindful of whether and, if so, how primary sources have been used. Martha Edwards' (1997a, b) work reviewing the primary sources available for the study of impairment and disability in ancient Greece has shown that, although some disability histories argue otherwise, deformity may not have been considered in absolute negative terms and has suggested that such a perspective was developed by historians in the nineteenth century who projected their particular views about deformity onto the ancient culture. Like the issue referred to earlier about bringing ideas about the *oppression* of disabled people to historical accounts, this reinforces the need to take care when reading existing histories and to be attuned to the values and ideas that may have influenced those interpretations.

Issue: interpreting change, cause and effect

Finally, when analysing sources there is the issue of how we research and write about *change*. Disability historians are often interested in why things changed, such as the demise of freak shows or the rise of segregated education. Foucault (1970), speaking about the subject of history in general, has warned against the way in which historical change is often dealt with. He argues that when changes occur and are evident, they should *not* be treated as:

* all being at the same level or of the same importance;
* inevitably leading to a single point (e.g. an event, moment, idea);
* having taken place because of the genius of an individual, or a new, all-encompassing collective spirit;
* having been because of the brilliance of a sudden and single discovery, invention or change in thought.

These points are particularly important to bear in mind in order to avoid simplifying history. In Section 3 (p. 76), we will argue that it is often more useful to investigate values, and changes in values, than it is to concentrate on facts. Studying values allows researchers to examine *how* things change, and doing so offers historians an understanding of the changing perceptions of people who are deemed different, as well as of how those perceptions affect the treatment such people received by society (e.g. how they were educated).

The benefits of considering disability in history

We have already hinted at some of the benefits of studying impairment and disability from an historical perspective. Buckingham (2011:420) suggests that in 'the context of the pressing everyday needs' of disabled people, 'historical research has seemed less urgent'. However, the benefits for Disability Studies, and for disabled people themselves, are increasingly being noticed and promoted.

Benefits for disabled people

The benefits for disabled people have been neatly summed up by Borsay (2002:114) when she concluded that 'knowing where we have been helps us to know where we are and where we are going'. This idea, that if we understand the past we can better understand the present and better plan for the future, will be returned to in Section 3 (p. 76), where we look at a particular methodology for understanding the general lessons history may offer us.

Specific histories of disability can offer alternative resources for positive disabled identities. These, in turn, can lead to increased individual and collective self-esteem (Borsay, 2002). Studies from a Disability Studies perspective into figures such as Helen Keller are revealing, as they offer a version of history markedly different from the dominant narrative. Crow (2000), for instance, has demonstrated how the image of Helen Keller as a little deafblind 'miracle child' eclipses the life of a woman who was a writer and radical activist, a suffragette and a socialist. Crow (2002) ends by speaking about how resistance is built up by the passing on of history and how, for her, researching Helen Keller became a reclaiming of her own story as part of disability history.

Dias *et al.* (2012:36) also talk about how the act of 'uncovering' hidden histories allowed those involved in their project to 'create a stronger sense of what people with learning difficulties have experienced as a group in the past' and how doing so helped 'people form a "group identity" ' in the present. (The benefits, and challenges, of establishing a 'group identity' based on impairment or disability will be further discussed in Chapter 6.) Likewise, Buckingham (2011:420) speaks of the power and potential of history to act as a 'tool of advocacy'. She argues that documenting past injustices can add weight to arguments for legislative and social change in the present, and, moreover, offers valuable insights into 'the contributions of people with disabilities to civic and political life and the historical roots of stigma and exclusion' (ibid.:427).

Honouring contributions of people with impairments can help to create public spaces for acknowledgement and reflective interaction with the past (Borsay, 2002). The 2001 unveiling of a new section of the memorial in Washington, DC, to the thirty-second president of the United States of America, Franklin Delano Roosevelt (FDR), is a good example. Unlike the original memorial, unveiled in 1997, a more recent addition adds a statue of FDR seated in a wheelchair, similar to the one he used during this lifetime (Parsons, 2012). Ott (2005:12) discusses how the National Park Service worked with disabled people and disability activist organisations on the design and fund-raising for the memorial, and comments on how 'the FDR memorial became a powerful tool for public awareness that sensibilities about, valuation of, and audiences for disability have changed dramatically in the last half century'.

Benefits for disability studies

The benefits of bringing a historical perspective to Disability Studies are also worth consideration. Borsay (2002) argues that placing experiences of impairment and disability into wider historical contexts undermines the 'taken-for-granted' nature of current ideas. It shows that ideas around impairment and disability are themselves contingent upon particular social and cultural contexts, and this can be extremely useful, especially in discouraging us from easy assumptions that as time passes, societies automatically develop more 'progressive' attitudes, and therefore automatically administer less oppressive practices, towards disabled people.

Another benefit of such historical study is work that seeks to document the emergence and practices of disability rights activism. As Kudlick (2003:776) is right to note, many historical studies of disability concentrate on the non-disabled response to impairment, and works such as Zames Fleischer and Zames' *The Disability Rights Movements: From Charity to Confrontation* (2001) offer welcome alternative histories of 'the historical agency of disabled people themselves'. (Also see Pfeiffer, 2005.) This is important, as it is part of the broader project of facilitating the voices of those who experience disability and is an example of how blurred the boundaries are between *academic* Disability Studies, *public* disability activism and *personal* lives of disabled people.

Benefits for history

The usefulness of Disability Studies to the discipline of history should also be considered. Buckingham (2011:427), speaking of Indian history, contends that the 'history of disability is a logical extension of the history of the body' and advocates the mutual benefits of firmly placing disability into a wider discussion of changing conceptions of, and responses to, 'different' bodies and minds. But it is Kudlick (2003:5) who is, perhaps, most bombastic in her advocacy for the significance of disability to historical analysis, stating:

> [j]ust as gender and race have had an impact well beyond women and people of color, disability is so vast in its import that it can force historians to reconsider virtually every concept, every event, every 'given' we have taken for granted.

In the next section we shall build on these ideas by arguing that the focus of study should be on contexts and values.

Section 3: Contextualising 'disability' in history: values rather than facts

Like Cultural Disability Studies (see Chapter 4), the study of disability history is predominantly Euro-American in its outlook and the focus. Buckingham (2011) has noted that these historical understandings have tended to assume that Judaeo-Christian ideas of stigma and exclusion are the same everywhere. Barnes and Mercer (2001b) acknowledge that Disability Studies has been slow to pay attention to non-Western, global South meanings of disability and, when it does, it often describes cultural differences at a superficial level. There is an attendant danger in assuming that non-Western societies and cultures 'represent traditional lifeworlds' (ibid.:528) which are either inferior to more progressive Western ways or superior to the ways of Western neo-liberal capitalism. Such judgemental assumptions can also leak into the study of disability history, where the meanings made of disability and impairment in the past, like those of the global South, are considered to be different and therefore 'not quite right'. A way of countering this problem is to *contextualise* historical analysis by concentrating on the historical values of the time rather than the historical facts of the situation. This is in line with the broader project of Disability Studies; as Burch and Sutherland (2006:129) have suggested, bringing a social perspective of disability means that the focus is 'often less about physical or mental impairments than it is about how society responds to impairments'.

One approach to this is to use the work of the French historian Michel Foucault and, in particular, his idea of *power*.

Key Concept: Power relations

Some histories describe power as flowing down, from government or monarchy, to the powerless citizens or subjects below. However, Foucault (1977) suggests that power can and does flow up and across as well as down. In his historical analyses, he argues that those generally considered 'powerful' and 'powerless' are engaged in *power relations* where no one has overall power and both rely on the other group for their existence. Here power is distributed (although unevenly) among the population and each group must play its part for the status quo to remain.

This conception of power changes how we approach history, and Foucault (1977) contends that to understand why a situation is as it is, we must, instead, ask *how* it is as it is. In other words, rather than search for a cause (e.g. an evil dictator or an inspirational inventor), we must focus on the *contingencies* that allow a situation to exist. When something is contingent on something else, it *relies* on it for its existence. For instance, the role of university lecturers is contingent on there being students to teach and a university to teach in. Similarly, the role of medical professionals can be said to contingent upon there being people labelled as 'impaired' and a medical system in which to 'treat' them. All involve a myriad of structures, institutions, bureaucracy and roles, and all rely on each other in order to make their existence make sense (for example, the existence of doctors does not make sense without there being patients).

Action Point: Think about a situation you are currently in. It could be as a student at university or an employee. Who has 'power'? What structures, institutions and/or systems support that power? Are there any possibilities for subverting or resisting that power, even in small ways?

You may be wondering why those considered 'powerless' do not just stop playing their part and 'bring down' the powerful. This is a good question, and the answers Foucault gives are surprising and quite shocking. Foucault (1977:27) asserts that 'power and knowledge directly imply one another', and therefore knowledge is power and power is knowledge. Borsay (2002) offers a disability-related example of this by describing the rise of the medical speciality of orthopaedics as an instance of the emergence of power/knowledge around physical impairment. Centres of clinical practice, such as the General Institution in Birmingham, as well as new therapies and charitable endeavours (e.g. the Central Council for the Care of Cripples), demonstrate how, from the start of the twentieth century onwards, physical impairment became increasingly medicalised. As Borsay's (2002) lengthy discussion shows, this did not happen because of one pioneering man or because of a scientific discovery, but because the *contingencies* present allowed certain power/knowledge coalitions to form and prosper. For example, the First World War gave orthopaedics an opportunity to grow: 'Between 1914 and 1918 World War I created additional clinical opportunities. Two-thirds of all casualties suffered locomotor injuries; and the treatment of fractures, gunshot wounds and nerve lesions all fell within the province of orthopaedics' (ibid.:109). Such growth, supported by an alliance with charity organisations (the only place from which funding was forthcoming) and coupled with 'a quest for professional power' (ibid.:110), led to an interest in the 'crippled' child and an ability to tap into contemporary concerns over child welfare.

More and more, medicine, and orthopaedics in particular, was gaining *power* over disabled children because it was widely seen as having the right and proper *knowledge* to do so. As Borsay (2002:111) notes, its unquestioned ability to oversee and intervene in the lives of children 'exposed many disabled people to painful and intrusive medical intervention. For by 1923 a minute to the Board of Education supporting a proposal for an orthopaedic hospital in Yorkshire was asserting that every disabled child required surgery (Bourke, 1996)'.

The *unquestioned* 'right and proper' knowledge/power of medicine was reinforced by other sections of early twentieth-century society, such as the Board of Education arguing that 'the proper treatment of "child cripples" was a "sound investment"' (Borsay, 2002:111) because it enabled those children to become useful members of society and thereby reduced the burden on families and the wider community. Therefore, to argue against medical intervention was to argue against the betterment of the nation; to do so would position you as a delinquent and place you within the reach of the increasing medicalisation of mental health and criminality. 'Crippled' children were expected to be grateful and compliant. Although Foucault (1988 cited in Borsay, 2002:111) insisted that 'we can never be ensnared by power; we can always modify its grip', the ability of children to resist was restricted to strikes against bad food or raids on the hospital orchard (Borsay, 2002).

In this example, understanding the values, beliefs and knowledges that permeated the society at the time helps us understand the contexts in which certain experiences occurred. Sadly, the values we have explored here are not dissimilar to those widely held at the beginning of the twenty-first century: deformity is better corrected and adults and professionals know best.

As Bredberg (1999) has noted, there is a distinct disadvantage to this approach to disability history. An emphasis on societal and institutional constructions of, and responses to, impairment is extremely useful in understanding broader contexts and contingencies, but it does under-represent accounts of the lived experience of disabled people. This sort of disability history, Bredberg (ibid.:192) suggests, 'in ironic consequences, seems to sustain the depersonalised and institutionalised representation of disabled people'. It may be that such historians are wary of returning to individual accounts for fear of reinscribing an individualised approach to the 'tragedy' of impairment, but, with care, the personal can be incorporated into analysis which focuses on historical values and how they were experienced.

What this approach does offer, above all else, is 'an understanding of exclusion as a construct rather than as a "natural" or inevitable consequence of disability' (Buckingham, 2011:427). This is incredibly useful and important if your starting point is 'disability' and not 'impairment'.

In the next two sections, we offer two extended examples of disability in history, using the approach outlined above. Section 4 will explore the rise and fall of freak shows in the nineteenth century and Section 5 will unearth a particularly painful event within disability history, the experiences of disabled children and adults in the Holocaust in mid-twentieth-century Europe.

Section 4: Exploring 'disability' in history: the rise and fall of freak shows

Although present in other parts of the world, freak shows are most often associated with North America and consist, in broad terms, of the commercial exhibition of human (and sometimes animal) oddities for public entertainment. They were at their peak in the mid- to late nineteenth century and were in decline by 1950 (Gerber, 1992), although some scholars have argued that elements of the freak show continue to exist in other forms such as television documentaries (Van Dijck, 2002).

Action Point: How do you feel about our using the word 'freak'? Should historians use other, less offensive words to describe people with impairments? Think back to Chapter 4: what might a *transgressive resignification* approach argue here?

In 1978, Leslie Fiedler published *Freaks: Myths and Images of the Secret Self*, a book to which, he later recounted, 'scarcely any of [his] academic colleagues responded positively' (1996:xiii). Although Fiedler believed that this response came about in part because the book dealt with 'sub-literature' (comic books, rock music and circus sideshows), it was also because he had 'insisted on calling the most exploited of my brothers and sisters not by a politely euphemistic name like "special people" or a presumably neutral scientific one like "*terata*" but simply "freaks"' (ibid.; italics in the original). Explaining his use of the words 'freak', 'midget', 'giant' and 'pinhead', another scholar of freak shows, Robert Bogdan, states: 'I use them here because individuals in the business used them' (1988:xi). For Bogdan, to do otherwise would be to implicate those terms as 'bad', 'negative' and thereby as 'unacceptable' *before* interpretation. Both Fiedler and Bogdan are attempting to *represent* the people in freaks show in ways that they feel are 'authentic'.

In Chapter 4, we introduced the idea of *transgressive resignification* as a way of avoiding a simple dismissal of unacceptable images and, in turn, of seeking to better understand and, even, embrace words such as 'freak' and events such as freak shows. This impulse to regain control and reclaim potentially harmful and hurtful ideas goes a long way to explain why there has been such an interest in freaks shows by scholars working on disability. Rather than dismissing them as a distasteful feature of history, researchers have used freak shows to help them 'develop understanding of past practices and changing conceptions of abnormality' (Bogdan, 1988:2). In this section, we will concentrate on analysis that charts the rise and fall of freak shows, and examine what this reveals about wider societal and cultural conceptions of disability and impairment.

We place our consideration within the approach described in Section 3, which argued that how we view people who are different has less to do with what *they* are than with who *we* are culturally (Bogdan, 1996). This approach enables us to argue that responses to 'differences' in bodies and minds have always depended on the historical time in which the response happened, and that those responses are often couched in terms of 'conceptions' or 'constructions' of certain sorts or types. There is a loose timeline here, and this section explores the move Monster → Freak and then suggests that the emergence of medical science meant the inevitable movement Freak → Medical Specimen and then → Patient (adapted from Bogdan, 1996).

As Bogdan (1996:24) suggests, 'while being extremely tall is a matter of physiology, being a giant involves something more'. His work on the 'social construction' of freaks argues that the something more is provided by the 'packaging', and describes four different categories of 'freaks' which were used in the business at the time (ibid.:24):

1 *'born freaks'*: 'people who, at birth, had a physical anomaly that makes them unusual, such as Siamese twins and armless and legless people';
2 *'made freaks'*, whose oddity was produced by means 'such as adorning their bodies with tattoos';
3 *novelty acts*: those who developed a particularly 'odd' talent or skill 'such as swallowing swords or charming snakes';
4 *gaffed freaks*: 'fake' or 'phony' freaks 'such as the armless wonder who tucked his arms under a tight-fitting shirt'.

As our interest is in the rise and fall of freak shows, we do not offer a detailed account of freak shows themselves. However, there is a wide range of literature that does; we have made some suggestions below and encourage you to explore this fascinating area.

Topic area	Suggested readings
Freaks shows in specific places or times	• Bogdan (1988) and Fiedler (1978) on the USA • Broome (1999, 2009) on Australia • Durbach (2010) on modern British culture • Semonin (1996) on early modern England • Stephens (2005) on the re-emergence of shows in the twenty-first century
Individual freak show 'acts'	• Browne and Messenger (2003) on Julia Pastrana ('Ape Woman') • Merish (1996) on Charles Stratton ('General Tom Thumb') • Pingree (1996) on Daisy and Violet Hilton ('Siamese twins') • McMillan (2012) and Reiss (1999) on Joice Heth ('Nanny to George Washington')
Freak shows and 'otherness'	• Lindfors (1996), Rothfels (1996) and Vaughan (1996) on racial otherness • Magubane (2001) on race/gender and the 'Hottentot Venus' • Frost (1996) on gender and imperialism

An interesting development in this area has been how historical research on freak shows has been used to explore its complex cultural legacy. There follow some sources you may find interesting if you wish to examine how conceptions of disability and non-normativity, perpetuated by freak shows, have had lasting and multifaceted impacts on continuing conceptions. This is a good example of how cultural perspectives on disability (see Chapter 4) can benefit from the types of historical analysis we are discussing in this chapter.

Freak shows, freakery and cultural texts	• Adams (1996) on Dunn's novel Geek Love • Birmingham (2000) on TV talk shows • Hawkins (1996) on the film Freaks • Clark and Myser (1996) and Van Dijck (2002) on medical documentaries • Tomlinson (2004) on the Olympics • Wardi (2005) on the film Beloved • Weinstock (1996) on science fiction • Yuan (1996) on Michael Jackson

Figure 5.1 Exploring freak shows: suggested academic sources.

He goes on to describe two specific 'strategies' of presentation (or packaging) that helped to display and emphasise the oddity of the 'freaks':

1   *Exotic presentation* 'appealed to people's interest in the culturally strange, the primitive, the bestial, the exotic' (Bogdan, 1996:28). Here, humans (and animals) were presented as objects from faraway places (e.g. darkest Africa) or exotic lands (e.g. a Turkish harem).
2   *Aggrandised status* laid claim to 'the superiority of the freak' (Bogdan, 1996:29) and packaged freaks as European or English aristocrats, often from 'normal' families.

What is interesting here is how these presentations position freaks as both inferior (exotic) and superior (aggrandised) to the viewing audiences. However, Bogdan (1996) shows how these presentations were not accidental or specific to individual freak-show owners, but were part of, and therefore reveal, wider historical contexts. It is here we can begin to examine the move from conceptions of people with impairments as Monsters → Freaks.

While extremely popular as places of amusement, entertainment and even education, by 1950 freak shows were in decline (Gerber, 1992). Hammer and Bosker (1996) relate this decline to the rise in medical science effecting a waning of audience interest as the conception of people with impairments moved from Freaks → Medical Specimens, and then → Patients. Likewise, Thomson (1996a:74), following Bogdan, links their demise to the medicalisation of disability, which sought to explain 'freaks' 'more and more in the ascending scientific discourse of pathology', thus moving away from a discourse of wonder.

Key Concept: Medical gaze

Often said to have its origins in the work of Foucault, the concept of 'gaze' was developed by Laura Mulvey (1975) in relation to film theory. It refers to structured ways of seeing and interpreting the socio-cultural world, and Mulvey's focus was on the 'male' gaze.

The idea of the 'medical gaze' refers to the dehumanising effect that comes from the separation of the body from the person during encounters between medical professionals and patients. Through medical examinations, bodies are 'gazed' at and become the site of symptoms, illnesses, disorders and deficits. In the process, the 'humanity' of the patient becomes marginalised. This 'way of looking' has since become one of the ways in which disabled people are generally viewed.

The emerging disciplines of science were increasingly present in freak shows, with professional 'expert' knowledge often being used to 'authenticate' the exhibits and showmen sometimes being introduced as 'lecturers' or 'doctors'. However, this attempt to utilise the increasing legitimacy of medicine is, for Bogdan (1996), the beginning of the end for freak shows. He argues that when the public started to look at the exhibits through a medical gaze, their taste changed. When people with impairments were packaged as 'freaks', they were wondrous. When people with impairments were packaged as 'medical specimens' and then, increasingly, as 'patients', they were to be pitied (because of their tragic circumstances) or feared (because of their dangerous conditions). Pity, compassion and danger were not something freak shows could easily 'sell' to a family audience, and their demise was sealed. In short, freak shows did not end because society became enlightened; they ended because conceptions of impairment and human difference became dominated by the medical professions.

In the next section, we explore another moment in disability history which reveals much about conceptions of impairment and human difference. In this case, the power and dominance of medical conceptions are all too obvious.

Section 5: Exploring 'disability' in history: the 'disability' Holocaust

The word 'holocaust' has a number of connotations and meanings, which include 'a religious sacrifice' or 'the total destruction of a race or group of people', sometimes known as genocide. However, as Garber and Zuckerman (1989:197) point out, the best-known use of this phrasing, *the Holocaust*, refers to 'what has come to be identified as the most horrific event of the Twentieth Century – the destruction of European Jewry by the Nazis'.

The events of the Holocaust are complicated and its scale is hard to imagine. An estimated 11 million people were killed in the concentration camps, the largest grouping of whom was six million Jewish people (Garber and Zuckerman, 1989). To many, this is *the* story of the Holocaust. However, among this number were an estimated 275,000 people with impairments, leading Suzanne Evans (2004:1) to comment that 'the vicious and systemic persecution of people with disabilities during the Nazi era has been overlooked and greatly underestimated in historical research and our collective remembrance of the Holocaust'. She is arguing here for a collective effort to remember and to document the experiences of people with impairments in Nazi Germany, which also includes an estimated 700,000 people who were sterilised as part of the Nazis' effort towards 'racial purity'. In this section, we suggest that a useful way of approaching this historical event is to contextualise it within wider eugenic concerns. Doing so, we argue, makes possible a more nuanced evaluation of the actual events. We end by considering the barriers to telling this particular historical story.

Eugenic justifications

Although it may be historical fact that between 1939 and 1945 the Nazis' 'euthanasia programmes' systematically killed hundreds of thousands of children and adults with impairments (Evans, 2004), it does not tell us much about *how* it happened. As we have discussed earlier, blaming one 'evil' individual (in this case Adolf Hitler) avoids asking the bigger questions such as *how* did murder on such a vast scale, involving so many people (as administrators, builders, doctors, etc.), continue for so long? As Section 3 suggests, examining the wider contexts often helps us better understand how such unimaginable events happened.

One of the wider contexts often discussed in relation to the Holocaust is *eugenics*.

Key Concept: Eugenics

Eugenics developed in Britain in the mid-nineteenth century when Charles Darwin's ideas about the role of natural selection in the process of evolution were extended to the human population. Sir Francis Galton (Darwin's cousin) coined the term 'eugenics' to refer to the idea that a person's breeding could be classified by measuring his or her anatomical features and that from those measurements, conclusions could be drawn as to whether that person was of superior or inferior breeding. These ideas were popular among academics in universities across Europe and North America. The British prime minister Winston Churchill is said to have been a proponent of eugenic theories in his younger years (Gray, 1999).

Eugenic thinking was underpinned by a developing interest in the use of mathematics and statistics for the monitoring and improvement of the health of nation-states (Davis, 1995).

Eugenic ideas quickly found their way into public life, with some US states enacting laws requiring the compulsory sterilisation of those held in custody who were deemed to have hereditary defects (Gray, 1999; Stubblefield, 2007). However, acknowledging the widespread 'belief' in eugenics is significant for us as it sets the historical scene for what was to happen in Germany, as it was in Nazi Germany that eugenic theories were most robustly adopted through national policy and legislation.

It was a specific interest in 'racial purity' that motivated much of what was to happen. The Nazis thought that the Aryan 'race' consisted of the quickest minds and the most able bodies, and therefore, in order to protect the future of the human race, all others in the population should be eradicated, ensuring that the 'purity' of the gene pool was secured

(Evans, 2004). The category of those to be eradicated included Jewish people, other ethnic groups such as Romany and Sinti traveller communities, homosexuals and people with impairments – all were deemed to be inferior, weak and dangerous. This is important, as we see here signs of the 'packaging' we discussed in Section 4. Here, particular categories of people were constructed and discussed as useless, burdens and threatening to the good of the majority, in order to justify their persecution and, ultimately, their death. Furthermore, as we discussed in Section 3, there were specific *contingencies* at work here which allowed certain power/knowledge coalitions to form and prosper. Eugenic thinking went *unquestioned* as 'right and proper' knowledge reinforcing the 'expertise' of medical professionals and supporting the actions of the elected Nazi government in its efforts to improve the lives of German citizens. As we suggested earlier, to argue against such practices was to argue against the betterment of the nation – a particularly impossible position.

Understanding the context of eugenics is a significant step in better understanding *how* the Holocaust was, as Ryan (2005:45) comments, 'overseen and administered by well-established and successful medical professionals, not by a handful of Nazi ideologues'. In the light of these eugenic justifications, we offer a brief overview of the three main components in the 'disability' Holocaust: the laws on sterilisation, the children's killing programme and the Adult T4 euthanasia programme.

The sterilisation law

In July 1933, within three months of coming to power, the newly formed 'Committee of Experts for the Population and Racial Policy' issued the 'Law for the Prevention of Progeny with Hereditary Disease' (Evans, 2004; Ryan, 2005). From this, compulsory, often forced, sterilisation was brought in for eight allegedly hereditary illnesses, including people with severe learning impairments, epilepsy, schizophrenia, hereditary blindness, deafness and physical impairments (Burleigh, 2000).

As was discussed earlier, the 'packaging' of these groups of people as inferior enabled the authorities to argue that allowing undesirable people to have children placed an unnecessary burden on the rest of the population, who would have to work harder and produce more in order to support these 'useless' people. To implement the new law, the German government established an elaborate bureaucracy in which doctors were required to register cases of genetic illness and recommend patients for sterilisations, which were then processed through one of a reported 181 genetic health courts (Proctor, 1988).

The children's killing programme

In the autumn of 1939, under the cloak of the Second World War, 'sterilization quickly turned to murder' (Evans, 2004:7) as Hitler issued a decree that all doctors, nurses, health officials and midwives were to report any children (up to the age of three) showing signs of physical deformity or intellectual incapacity. Registration forms were filled in for each child and reviewed by a panel of 'experts', who marked the forms 'with a plus sign if they believed the child should be killed' (ibid.:26). Those children were then transferred to nearby institutions before being killed. Letters were sent to parents of the children regretfully informing them that their child had died of influenza and that the child's body had been immediately cremated to prevent the spread of the disease. Evans (ibid.:26) reports that during the war years, 'at least 5,000 and perhaps as many as 25,000 children with disabilities were killed throughout Germany, Austria, Poland and other occupied territories'.

The T4 adult programme

The T4 programme began in 1940 and was headed by Hitler's personal physician (Evans, 2004). Six 'euthanasia' centres were created, often in converted hospitals, across Germany and the recently annexed Austria. At these centres, after a perfunctory medical check, people with impairments were led to gas chambers disguised as shower rooms and killed with carbon monoxide (Burleigh and Wippermann, 1991). Their corpses were buried in crematoria, whose ill-designed chimneys spread smoke over the surrounding countryside (ibid.). This smoke raised suspicions and the programmes were ended when a prominent clergyman, protected somewhat by his standing and reputation in the community, spoke out against the activities. However, the killings carried on, more secretly this time, in the concentration camp systems, only to end shortly before the people in those camps were liberated at the end of the war in 1945.

Telling the 'disability' Holocaust story

Action Point: What are some of the barriers and what are some of the solutions to the Holocaust story being told? Think about the issues with researching disability in history which we discussed earlier. How might they hinder or help the telling of this story?

1	The predominance of the Jewish story is understandable but can marginalise other stories, making them harder to tell.
2	Unlike Jewish culture, people with impairments are not necessarily part of families or wider communities who also have impairments and therefore do not necessarily identify with a collective disabled identity or a shared disability history.
3	Again, unlike the Jewish experience, because disabled people did not have access to a shared identity at the time of the Holocaust, their experiences were disparate and diverse, making attempts to write their stories a complex endeavour.
4	Many people who experienced events during the Second World War have already passed away, taking their memories and stories with them (Dias et al., 2012).
5	Passing memories to the next generation has been important for other groups, but the reality of sterilisation ensured that those who experienced that particular element do not have offspring who could pass on their experiences.
6	People with memories and experiences that could be captured are being missed because of a general lack of awareness and funding for historical research and publications in this area. Furthermore, there may be a lack of inclusive research methodologies which would support the inclusion of disabled participants (Ryan, 2005).
7	When stories are captured and artefacts are catalogued, many may not be identified as having an association with 'disability' (Dodd et al., 2004).
8	Museum curators may have anxieties and concerns about how to interpret, display and annotate these difficult and sensitive histories (Dodd et al., 2004).

Figure 5.2 Barriers to telling the 'disability' Holocaust story.

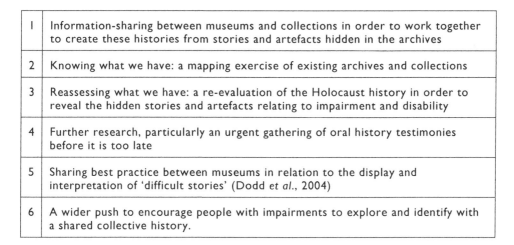

I	Information-sharing between museums and collections in order to work together to create these histories from stories and artefacts hidden in the archives
2	Knowing what we have: a mapping exercise of existing archives and collections
3	Reassessing what we have: a re-evaluation of the Holocaust history in order to reveal the hidden stories and artefacts relating to impairment and disability
4	Further research, particularly an urgent gathering of oral history testimonies before it is too late
5	Sharing best practice between museums in relation to the display and interpretation of 'difficult stories' (Dodd et al., 2004)
6	A wider push to encourage people with impairments to explore and identify with a shared collective history.

Figure 5.3 Suggested solutions to telling the 'disability' Holocaust story.

It has been argued that people with impairments were the first and the last 'victims' of the Holocaust (Evans, 2004). This makes the telling of their stories particularly important. However, capturing and telling the stories is a complicated and difficult process. We provide a summary of some of the barriers faced by researchers in this area (Figure 5.2) as well as some suggestions for possible ways of addressing those barriers (Figure 5.3). Exploring the Holocaust from a Disability Studies perspective also allows us to demonstrate many of the issues we discussed earlier, in Section 2.

Conclusion

> Literature and archival materials exist representing disabled people as productive members of their community's workforce, but this information has never been systematically compiled, leaving many stories untold.
>
> (Patterson, 2011:7)

It is often the case not that disability isn't present in our histories, but that it has not been noticed or adequately considered. This chapter has sought to bring a social perspective on disability and impairment to the study of history and explore the challenges, the benefits and the knowledge that can be gained by doing so.

Suggestions for Wider Reading

Burch, S. and Sutherland, I. (2006) 'Who's not yet here? American disability history', *Radical History Review*, 94, pp. 127–147.

Evans, S. (2004) *Forgotten Crimes: The Holocaust and People with Disabilities*, Chicago: Ivan R. Dee.

Thomson, R. G. (ed.) (1996) *Freakery: Cultural Spectacles of the Extraordinary Body*, New York: New York University Press.

Chapter 6

Critical perspectives on disability and identity politics

Introduction

The aim of this chapter is to explore disability in relation to identity politics. Identity politics is the term used when a person claims their identity as a member of an oppressed or marginalised group and uses this as a point of departure for political action (Woodward, 1997b). In this chapter, we consider the emergence of 'disabled' as a political identity, briefly explore the history of disability activism in the United Kingdom and acknowledge the emergence of 'biological citizenship' as an alternative to 'social model' identity politics. We then explore the ways in which the identity position of 'disabled person' is often complicated by the coexistence of other identities (such as those relating to gender and sexuality). Finally, we discuss the limits of identity politics and offer possible alternatives. We begin, at the beginning, by interrogating the concept of 'identity'.

Section 1: Questioning identity

Action Point: Which group identities do you identify with (e.g. student, academic, activist, male, female, practitioner, parent, carer, child, disabled?) Who or what decides whether you are a member of a group? Do any of your identities conflict with each other?

If you have thought about this Action Point, you will have realised that

> [i]dentities in the contemporary world derive from a multiplicity of sources – from nationality, ethnicity, social class, community, gender, sexuality – sources which may conflict in the construction of identity positions and lead to contradictory fragmented identities.
>
> (Woodward, 1997a:1)

As Woodward suggests, identity positions come from a wide variety of sources and owing to their 'multiplicity' it is not surprising that the question of identity can be complicated. In this first section, we explore the idea of 'identity' by unpacking what it means to hold a range of identities at the same time. The first element to note is that sometimes identities fit easily with one another and sometimes they are in conflict. That is to say that someone people hold identity positions which do not go well together. For example, in global North contexts, the economic system means that the identity of 'disabled person' is seen to conflict with the identity of 'employer', whereas the identity 'male' is compatible with the identity 'business manager'. This does not mean that a disabled person cannot be an 'employer', but it does mean that occupying both positions involves subtle negotiation within everyday encounters because the 'system' is not set up to accommodate both.

Identity is even more complex than this, because these 'conflicting' and 'compatible' identities are not fixed: they are in a constant state of flux, shifting and changing in different historical and geographical contexts. For instance, in 1950s Britain the identity positions of 'mother' and 'employee' might have been seen as conflicting, yet today women are expected to be both mothers and employees. Similarly, being a 'woman' involves different expectations and experiences in urban New York as compared with rural Kenya.

However, what tends not to change is that 'identity' is often defined in relation to its opposite, for example male/female, black/white, straight/gay, disabled/non-disabled (Woodward, 1997a). This is because the idea of 'difference' is crucial to understanding identity. 'Difference' is used to mark inclusion or exclusion within an identity category based on a shared characteristics such as skin colour or sexual orientation. In other words, identity is the category we cling to in order to decide who is 'us' and who is 'them' (Woodward, 1997a; Richardson, 2005). In this sense, identity is relational as it relies on something other than itself for its existence (Woodward, 1997b). The boundaries between what 'is' and what 'isn't' within the remit of a certain identity are often policed not by law enforcement arrangements but by everyday interactions. Supported by the everyday denial of any similarities between 'us' and 'them', shared practices such as mode of dress, language, food and music can all play their part in marking out 'us' from 'them'.

Deciding who is included in 'us' can be important in creating and sustaining a sense of belonging, as being in the 'us' category brings with it a sense of familiarity and trust. This is where identity can be confused with subjectivity. The terms are sometimes used to mean the same thing, but there is a difference, and teasing it out can be helpful. As Woodward (1997b:39) comments, subjectivity 'includes our sense of self. It involves the conscious and unconscious thoughts and emotions which constitute our sense of "who we are"', but 'we experience our subjectivity in a social context where language and culture give meaning to our experience of ourselves and where we adopt an identity [...] the positions which we take up and identify with constitute our identities'. In other words, identity can be thought of as the position we take up, or are placed into, and the personal experience we have of those positions can be thought of as our subjective, embodied experiences. In this way, it could be said that this chapter is mainly interested in the 'social' aspect, rather than the 'personal', subjective aspect, of identity. Crossley (2004:145) makes a useful distinction here:

> 'social identity' refer to forms of categorization which link individuals to a broader social grouping, for example, 'women' or 'the working class', whilst 'personal identity' refers to the various ways in which the individual demarcates their self, or is demarcated, as a unique being with a distinct body, biography, situation, and so on.

Studies into the subjective, embodied experiences of having an impairment and/or facing disabling barriers are outside of the remit of this chapter. However, you may want to explore work that considers disability using some of the insights of an area of sociology called symbolic interactionism, and particularly the work of Erving Goffman on 'stigma'. Some examples include Susman (1994), Ewing (2004) and Cahill and Eggleston (2005). Neither do we consider the psycho-emotional facets of 'identity'; some examples on that topic, which you may like to follow up, include Reeve (2002), Wilton (2003) and Watermeyer and Swartz (2008).

• Identities are **multiple** – they come from multiple sources and people hold multiple identities
• Identities can be thought of as **compatible** or they can be seen to **conflict**
• Identities are often **negotiated** in everyday encounters
• Identities are **historically specific** – they change over time
• Identities are **geographically specific** – they change depending on where you are
• Identities involve **inclusion** and **exclusion** based on shared characteristics
• Identities involve the identification of '**us**' and '**them**'
• Identities are **relational**
• Identities often involve **shared** everyday practices or experiences
• Identities involve **belonging** and give meaning to 'who' we are
• Identities are personal and subjective as well as **social** and **political**

Figure 6.1 Summarising 'identity'.

The 'essence' of identity?

Our 'social' identities matter because they are *our* identities; they locate us in the world and link us to the societies in which we live (Woodward, 1997a). Questioning 'identity' raises fundamental questions about where we 'fit', and yet the answer to the question of *where* identities come from (i.e. their origin) is highly contested. Some people argue that identity is determined by our biology, others that it is linked to history, while some people would argue that identity is part of our culture. However, the main debates about identity centre on whether identity is or is not predetermined by a pre-given *essence*.

There are two main theoretical standpoints on this issue (see Figure 6.2). Those who argue from an *essentialist* position 'regard identity as natural, fixed and innate' (Jagose, 1996 cited in Sherry, 2004:776). On the other hand, those who argue from a *non-essentialist* standpoint 'assume identity is fluid, the effect of social conditioning and avail-able cultural modes for understanding oneself' (ibid.). In Chapter 3 you were introduced to the Key Concept of *social constructionism*; this is related but is not exactly the same as non-essentialism, which is a broader concept. We shall return to these debates about the origins, and therefore the nature, of identity later in this chapter as it is a significant issue when it comes to political arguments and activities that aim to address equality. For instance, if you are arguing for the right for gay people to marry, you will be involved in an argument about the nature of sexuality and whether homosexuality should be acknow-ledged as on a par with heterosexuality, rather than as a medical deficit or a sinful act. This will involve either arguing that homosexuality is decided at birth by biology or genetics (essentialist) or that it is a legitimate sexual identity to choose (non-essentialist).

Because this is a highly contestable area, social identities have become a source of socio-political tension, action and activity. In the following sections, we shall examine the emergence of a certain sort of politics – identity politics – and explore it in relation to disability activism and biological citizenship.

Essentialism v.	Non-essentialism
Regards identity as ...	Regards identity as ...
fixed	fluid
permanent	changeable
natural	social and cultural
innate (given at birth)	able to be decided upon
trans-historical	relational and contextual
clear	messy
essential (within one's essence)	non-essential (not within one's essence)

Figure 6.2 Summary: essentialism versus non-essentialism.

Section 2: 'Disabled' as a political identity

In Chapter 1, we discussed the impact of the social model of disability on the disabled people's movement and on Disability Studies in the United Kingdom. We saw how the social model of disability has challenged what are described as medicalised, individualised and tragic perspectives on impairment. The emergence of the social model can be directly linked to the rise of a politicised disabled people's movement from the 1960s onwards (Barnes and Mercer, 2003). However, advocacy and activism, by and for disabled people, can also be seen as being underpinned by changes in wider social politics.

'New' social movements

As discussed in the previous chapter (Chapter 5), historical change does not happen overnight or out of nowhere. Instead, change occurs as a result of contingencies coming together to allow for new possibilities. A good example of this is the emergence of disability activism, which should be set in the broader context of the emergence of 'new social movements'. 'These "new social movements" emerged in the West in the 1960s and especially after 1968 with its peak of student unrest, peace and anti-war activism, especially anti-Vietnam war campaigns and civil rights struggles.' As Woodward (1997b:24) describes in this quotation, the time (the 1960s) and the place (the West) were experiencing many challenges to established powers. Traditional class allegiances were being questioned and/or resisted by increasing numbers of people (Woodward, 1997b). What is significant is how 'new' groups of people were being formed on the basis of shared characteristics (identities)

Key Concept: Identity politics
'Identity politics involve claiming one's identity as a member of an oppressed or marginalised group as a political point of departure and thus identity becomes a major factor in political mobilisation. Such politics involve a celebration of a group's uniqueness as well as an analysis of its particular oppression' (Woodward, 1997b:24).

Identity politics involves collective socio-political action, often in the form of activism, on behalf of a collectively oppressed social grouping. Academic studies in this area 'are interested in the ways in which identities are "defended" when attacked, built up and performed or enacted' (Crossley, 2004:144).

which cut across the established identities based on class or wealth, and the fact that these characteristics were seen to be the explanation for the group's disadvantage in society. That is to say, groups came together to express a 'collective' experience of marginalisation.

The 'new' in new social movements refers to the replacement of politics based mainly on class and stands in contrast to 'older' movements such as the labour movement. Examples of what are now not so 'new' social movements include the women's movement (feminism), the civil rights movement, the gay rights movement and the disabled people's movement.

Woodward (1997b) suggests that new social movements have a dual purpose: (1) to affirm, support and celebrate the group's uniqueness, while at the same time (2) to analyse and fight against the group's oppression and discrimination. As we will see, this is a fine line to follow, and the 'new' social movement we are particularly interested in is the disabled people's movement.

Although Barnes and Mercer (2003) trace the origins of the disabled people's movement to the 1960s, others suggest that the key date in the history of the disabled people's movement is 1981. This is because this was the United Nations' International Year of Disabled Persons (IYDP). The IYDP generated widespread dissatisfaction among disabled people at grass-roots level, particularly within Britain. This was because the IYDP was seen as an 'official response' to the problem of disabled people, as it was led by non-disabled people and generally considered to be rooted in 'welfarism' (Hasler, 1993): the view that disabled people needed welfare and support rather than to have the opportunity to voice their political concerns. However, the widespread dissatisfaction that resulted had the effect of galvanising existing, yet unofficial, movements among disabled people, leading to the inauguration of the British Council of Disabled People (BCODP) in November and the investiture of Disabled People's International (DPI) in December of that same year (1981).

As we saw in Chapter 1, the publication of *Fundamental Principles of Disability* (UPIAS, 1976), in which a crucial distinction was drawn between the biological and the social, was extremely important to the development of the disabled people's movement in Britain. It was 'an incentive for the growing number of new organisations to come together', as it offered the 'liberating message that, if disability was socially created, then it could also be overcome through a struggle for social change' (Davis, 1993:289). The principles were subsequently adopted by the BCDOP and DPI as *the* definition of disability. In Britain, the social model of disability became the idea around which the disabled people's movement grew and developed. From this idea came the notion of disabled people as an oppressed collective group, and this was their rationale for political action.

Disability activism in the United Kingdom

The danger in talking about the disabled people's movement is that it sounds like a unitary and coherent force, when in fact it is an umbrella term for the coming together of disabled people as a politically active grouping. The term 'disability activism' may be a more accurate term for more recent activity, which takes place on various scales, in a variety of forms (e.g. group or individual) and in response to a variety of concerns.

Although disability activism by groups in the United Kingdom is diverse, a key issue in all of it is whether the activity is by organisations *of* disabled people or organisations *for* disabled people.

Key Issue: Organisations *of* and *for* disabled people

The distinction made here is between user-led organisations such as People First Self-Advocacy (www.peoplefirstltd.com), which are run *by* people who identify as 'disabled', and organisations like Scope, the UK disability charity (www.scope.org.uk), which is run *for* disabled people but not exclusively by people who identify as 'disabled'.

This was a highly contentious issue in the early days of the disabled people's movement, as many existing organisations were being run by non-disabled people who held what could be called a medical-model conceptualisation of disability. Many of the first organisations within the movement were careful to be *by* disabled people, with UPIAS including a section in its 1974/1975 Policy Statement which noted that full membership was open to those with physical impairments, whereas non-disabled people were free to become 'associate members', stating, '[g]enuine supporters will recognise the need for us to control our own Union and so develop our powers of decision, organisation and action' (UPIAS, 1974/1975:7).

It is argued that organisations *for* disabled people aim to provide services and support to meet the needs that professionals have identified and defined, whereas organisations *of* disabled people aim to provide services and support to meet the needs that their members *themselves* have identified and defined (see Figures 6.3 and 6.4 for two examples). However, such a neat definition is not often maintained, as organisations *of* disabled people often work in collaboration with local governmental, national governmental and/or other voluntary organisations. Derbyshire Coalition for Inclusive Living (DCIL), for instance, draws on the social model of disability to support its work, and political action is based on what disabled people themselves have identified as key concerns in their live, but it works in conjunction with local authorities and some of its projects are funded by the Big Lottery Fund.

While DCIL is concerned with activism focused on addressing the self-identified needs of disabled people, other organisations focus their activism on lobbying for new laws and the extension of civil rights. Termed 'reformist' groups by Swain *et al.* (2003),

'At Leonard Cheshire Disability, we work for a society in which every person is equally valued. We believe that disabled people should have the freedom to live their lives the way they choose – with the opportunity and support to live independently, to contribute economically, and to participate fully in society.

'Leonard Cheshire Disability supports thousands of disabled people both in the UK and in more than 50 other countries. We help people with physical impairments, learning difficulties and long-term health conditions, as well as their carers, friends and families.

'The needs and aspirations of disabled people are at the heart of what we do. By providing services and helping everyone to understand disability and combat discrimination, we aim to remove the barriers that can stop people with disabilities from pursuing their goals and living their lives to the full.'

Leonard Cheshire Disability is run for, but not necessarily by, disabled people and as such is an organisation *for* disabled people.

Figure 6.3 Example of an organisation *for* disabled people: Leonard Cheshire Disability (source: *About Leonard Cheshire Disability*, www.lcdisability.org/?lid=32).

'Derbyshire Coalition for Inclusive Living (DCIL) is an organisation of disabled people. It works to apply disabled people's own ideas and experience to developing services and public policies. Derbyshire Coalition for Inclusive Living (DCIL) exists because disabled people realised that disability is caused by the way society is organised, and not by the way their bodies, senses or minds work.

'Derbyshire Coalition for Inclusive Living (DCIL) aims to provide independent, integrated living opportunities to disabled people through a range of services. This support is based on the seven needs identified by disabled people: Information, Counselling, Housing, Technical Aids, Personal Assistance, Transport and Access.'

DCIL is run *by* and for disabled people and is, therefore, an organisation *of* disabled people.

Figure 6.4 Example of an organisation *of* disabled people: Derbyshire Coalition for Inclusive Living (source: *About us* – www.dcil.org.uk/about-us).

these groups make alliances with 'non-representative' organisations – in other words, groups that do not directly represent the voices of disabled people. Such organisations may focus on a single issue and aim to work from within systems and organisations rather than from outside them (Oliver, 1990). An example of such an organisation is Independent Parental Special Education Advice (IPSEA) (www.ipsea.org.uk). IPSEA provides advice for parents or carers of children with special educational needs, helping them to access the services they need in education. IPSEA's work includes lobbying government for policy changes in education.

Swain *et al.* (2003) also noted the rise of what they call 'radical' organisations that take up overt political, sometimes called direct, activism. The focus on empowerment means that such organisations are often antagonistic to working in partnership with more mainstream or governmental organisations. Well-known historical examples from the United Kingdom of such direct action include the 1991–1992 Campaign for Accessible Transport's 'Stop the Bus' sit-downs in London's Oxford Street (Bowler and Rose, 2004; Hasler, 1993) and the 1992 demonstrations demanding the discontinuation of ITV's Telethon television programme (Barnes and Mercer, 2001a; Bowler and Rose, 2004).

More recent examples include action in January 2012 which involved disabled people launching a Twitter storm using the hashtag #spartacusreport. This culminated in the House of Lords rejecting the government's welfare reform bill (Butler, 2012). The Spartacus Report (S. J. Campbell *et al.*, 2012) criticised changes planned by the British government to disability benefits. Activists used #spartacusreport to keep the report 'trending' on Twitter so that a news story which had been largely ignored by the news media became the top-trending story of the day. Celebrities showed their support by re-tweeting and in the end the Department for Work and Pensions felt forced to defend itself from the criticism in the report by using #spartacusreport. Although a revised version of the bill was eventually passed into law, this is a remarkable example of radical political activism by disabled people using social media. In the United Kingdom, it is now against a backdrop of economic austerity that organisations *of* disabled people and organisations *for* disabled people are fighting for disability rights by campaigning against cuts to benefits and services. Organisations such as Disabled People

Against Cuts (www.dpac.uk.net) and The Hardest Hit (www.thehardesthit.wordpress. com) clearly draw on the political legacy of the social model to argue for the removal of oppressive barriers. However, as we shall discuss in Section 3, a social model approach to disability activism is not the only approach.

The benefits of social media are now well established for networking and sharing information among marginalised groups. Disabled people have been increasingly telling their own stories (Shakespeare, 2006), and access to social media has provided a space to get their message across (e.g. *Diary of a Benefit Scrounger*, www.diaryofabenefitscrounger. blogspot.co.uk). Indeed, disability activism has often used a range of media to get the message across, including disability arts. The disability arts movement in Britain is closely linked to political activism. The opportunity for disabled people to express their experiences and to communicate their feelings through the arts has 'played an important part in cementing the sense of a [disability] movement' (Hasler, 1993:282).

Action Point: Recent examples of activism include *Resistance on the Plinth*. Liz Crow, a disabled artist, activist and academic, sat on the fourth plinth in Trafalgar Square for an hour to draw attention to the hidden history of disabled people and to make links to the contemporary treatment of disabled people in society.

- Do an internet search for *Resistance on the Plinth* and see what you can find out.
- Do you think that disability arts are a valuable mechanism for political activism? What are your reasons?

Section 3: Evaluating disability activism

Social movements are formed with the purpose of *change* in mind, or, as Barton (2001:5) comments, 'they are concerned with what might yet be rather than uncritically accepting the way things are'. That being so, it should be pretty easy to evaluate whether they have changed what they set out to change. Campbell and Oliver (1996 cited in Barton, 2001:5) identify four criteria by which to judge a social movement:

1   'whether any new political or economic changes have resulted from its activities';
2   'whether any specific legislation has resulted';
3   'what changes in public opinion and behaviour have been produced';
4   'whether any new organisations or institutions have been created'.

They go on to identify three further criteria by which to judge the disability movement (Campbell and Oliver, 1996 cited in Barton, 2001:5):

5   'the extent of the consciousness raising and empowerment amongst disabled people';
6   'the extent to which disability issues are raised internationally';
7   'the promotion of disability as a human and civil rights issue'.

Action Point: From what you have read in this book and elsewhere, how would you judge the progress so far of the disabled people's movement against the above criteria?

So far, we have talked about disabled people's activism as 'one' entity and have there-fore assumed, for the purposes of discussion, that disabled people are a homogeneous group (i.e. they are all the same). However, this is clearly not the case. In Section 4 (p. 97), we are going to explore the ways in which the identity position of 'disabled person' is complicated by the coexistence of other identities (such as those relating to gender and sexuality). However, before we move beyond disability we want to explore some of the complications within disability activism. First, we explore the idea that not all disabled people consider themselves disabled, and second, we examine the idea that claiming disability solely on the basis of 'social oppression' is not the only way to 'fight' for disability rights.

Disabled as a non-political identity

Action Point: Think back to our discussions of the social model of disability and con-sider the following questions:

1　Is it possible to be 'impaired' and not consider yourself to be 'disabled'?
2　Is it possible to be 'disabled' and not consider yourself to be 'impaired'?

So far in this chapter, we have talked about 'disabled' as a political identity and, using social model ideas to do so, have talked about disabled people coming together to fight for their rights as a 'disabled' (i.e. socially oppressed) group. This raises an important question: do all disabled people consider themselves to be 'disabled? Here, it can be helpful to return to the social model and use its distinction between impairment and disability, where impairment is about biomedical matters and disability refers to social matters. This helps us argue that it is possible to be 'impaired' but not consider yourself to be socially oppressed. Watson's (2002) research explores this idea through interviews with 28 disabled men and women. He reported that '[d]espite daily experiences of oppressive practices, only three of the participants incorporated disability within their identity' (ibid.:514). For the others, although they did not deny their impairment, it did not play a large part in how they saw themselves, and they certainly did not self-identify with a collective 'disabled' identity. Such research supports the need to remember that, in this context, 'disabled' is a political term.

Returning to the social model also helps us to argue that it is possible to be 'disabled' (i.e. face social oppression) and not, yourself, be impaired. As Runswick-Cole (2007:316) has commented in relation to members of families that include a person with an impairment:

> [T]he term 'disabled families' is used here because it firmly locates the family within a social model framework and highlights disability as a form of social oppression which acts upon the whole family, not just the child with the label special needs or an impairment.

We shall return to this point in Chapter 7. However, here this leads to questions about the place of non-impaired people in the disabled people's movement. We explored this a little in Chapter 1 when we mentioned the tensions around the role of non–disabled people in disability research. These debates are ongoing and are further complicated by an increasing area of disability activism which is based on essentialist understandings of bodies and minds and, therefore, involves 'impairment' being claimed as a 'political' identity.

Impairment as a political identity: biological citizenship

Basing disability activism on essentialist understandings of bodies and minds refers to activism which claims that there are very *real* biological differences between 'types' of human beings and that those differences can and should form the basis of group formation and advocacy for rights and resources for disabled people. Hughes (2009) characterises this approach to activism as 'biological citizenship', whose adherents he contrasts with 'social model stalwarts'. *Biological citizens* see impairment, genetics and biomedical diagnosis as central to their identity (ibid.); they have created supportive communities based on such an identity and have informed advocacy in the sphere of social policy for health, care, benefits and interventions.

This essentialist approach involves disabled people locating the 'difference' *in* their bodies and/or minds. By drawing on well-established and accepted 'medical' ways of knowing, they sidestep the complexity and 'fluidity' of many of the identity discussions we will explore in Section 4. It could be argued that at a time of economic austerity, with the talk of scarce resources, such appeals to 'real' and 'legitimate' biological differences are not surprising.

Although it began before the most recent global economic crisis, the neurodiversity movement represents one example of this essentialist approach to politics and activism. The neurodiversity movement is founded on two claims:

1   There are neurological (brain wiring) differences in the human population, of which autism is one.
2   Autism is a natural variation among humans – not a disease or a disorder, just 'a difference' (Jaarsma and Welin, 2012).

Judy Singer, a sociologist who identifies with the label of Asperger syndrome (which is described as a form of autism), is widely credited with introducing the phrase 'neurodiversity' in an article 'Why can't you be normal for once in your life?' (1999 cited in Ortega, 2009). She argues for a 'politics of neurodiversity' in which the 'neurodiverse' population constitutes a political grouping comparable to those of class, gender or race (Jaarsma and Welin, 2012).

***

Key Concept: Neurodiversity

The terms 'neurodiverse' and 'a politics of neurodiversity' are most often associated with people labelled with autism but are also claimed by those with other neurological differences, including attention deficit hyperactivity disorder, bipolar disorder, developmental dyspraxia, dyslexia, epilepsy and Tourette syndrome (Baker, 2011). Neurodiversity is constructed as a biopolitical category concerned with the rights of, and discrimination against, people who are neurologically different from the 'neurotypical' (or non-autistic) population.

The key point to notice here is that while those belonging to the neurodiverse community claim that there are 'real' brain wiring differences between populations, they argue that these should not be considered as deficits, simply differences (Runswick-Cole, 2012b). So, the neurodiversity movement goes beyond simply claiming rights and anti-discriminatory practices for neurodiverse people and argues for *recognition* and *acceptance* of (valuable) difference. In so doing, autistic self-advocates reject research that focuses on cures for autism, criticising such research as oppressive and diverting much-needed resources from the lives of neurodiverse individuals (Kapp *et al.*, 2012).

A focus on recognition and acceptance of biological difference means that the phrases 'autist', 'Aspie' and 'autistic' are preferred to the term 'people with autism', as autism is regarded as an inseparable aspect of the individuals' identity (Ortega, 2009). As Jim Sinclair (1993:n.p.) says:

> Autism isn't something a person *has*, or a 'shell' that a person is trapped inside. There's no normal child hidden behind the autism. Autism is a way of being. It is *pervasive*; it colors every experience, every sensation, perception, thought, emotion, and encounter, every aspect of existence. It is not possible to separate the autism from the person – and if it were possible, the person you'd have left would not be the same person you started with.

The neurodiversity movement has also campaigned for acceptance of difference by hijacking what could be described as the 'tools of the oppressor'. For example, the Institute for the Study of the Neurotypical (ISNT, 1998:n.p.) uses satire to describe 'neurotypical syndrome' as 'a neurobiological disorder characterized by preoccupation with social concerns, delusions of superiority, and obsession with conformity'.

A key feature of the neurodiversity movement has been to emphasise the value of self-advocates' insider accounts by suggesting that experience best qualifies autistic individuals to lead attempts to remove socio-political barriers and to enable equal opportunity (Baker, 2011). In 1992, Jim Sinclair and Donna Williams, autism rights activists, founded the Autism Network International and in 1996 the first autistic retreat, 'Autreat', took place in the United States. Autreat is 'a retreat-style conference run by autistic people, for autistic people and our friends' (Autreat, 2012:n.p.). It provides an environment that focuses on the positive aspects of autism in an 'autism-friendly environment' (i.e. no pressure to interact, no sensory overload, no crowded environments).

Action Point: Amanda Baggs is an autism rights activist. In January 2007, she published a video on YouTube entitled *In My Language* describing her experiences as an autistic person.

Search for, and watch, this video on Youtube. How effective do you think this video is as a form of political advocacy?

We will briefly return to these ideas in Chapter 8 when we further discuss the place of 'impairment' in Disability Studies, but now we want to move to wider fields of identity so that we do not mirror a criticism that has been levelled at disability activism by not taking into account the multiple identity positions held by many disabled people. As we saw in Chapter 1 (in Challenge 5 to the social model, p. 14), acknowledging the inter-sections between identities is not unique to disability activism: the neglect has also been mirrored within Disability Studies.

Section 4: Intersecting identities

> Already a complex construct, identity becomes even more so when exploring the experiences of individuals in multiple minority groups.
>
> (Caldwell, 2010:n.p.)

As we demonstrated in Section 1, each of us has multiple, shifting and interconnecting identities, and yet this multiplicity is not always reflected in disability activism or Dis-ability Studies. In this section, we focus on the moments when identity positions, such as those associated with gender and sexuality, intersect with and affect the lived experi-ence of disabled people. We start by thinking about why it took some time for Disabil-ity Studies to acknowledge these multiplicities.

Disabled people = assuming white heterosexual males

> When I helped research and write *The Sexual Politics of Disability* between 1994 and 1996, it was striking that issues of sexuality had a low profile in the British disability movement, and in the developing field of disability studies.
>
> (Shakespeare, 2006:167)

One of the reasons why Shakespeare found few references to issues of sexuality and dis-ability in the field of Disability Studies may be that a disabled identity and a sexual identity have widely been seen as conflicting. However, there may have been broader reasons too. It has been argued that the Marxist, materialist origins of British Disability Studies (see Chapter 1) may also be part of the reason why Disability Studies has paid little attention to the intersections between disability and other minority identities. Shakespeare (2006:167) identifies '[t]he divide between the public and the private, which feminists had also identified, as the key factor explaining the neglect of issues of sex and identity within disability politics'. It has been the case that while the public and material aspects of disabled people's lives have been the focus of debate within disability activism and Disability Studies, their private lives were not seen as being of equal concern and might, indeed, distract attention from what is seen as the primary aim of advocating for an end to discrimination in education and work (Shakespeare, 2006). In other words, a strategic choice was made to focus on 'public' issues and, as Shakespeare (ibid.) goes on to suggest, ending poverty and social exclusion was, rightly or wrongly, probably prioritised as a matter of urgency above the need to campaign for disabled people to have a good sex life. Acknowledging that there may have been pragmatic reasons for this exclusion hints at one of the limits of 'identity politics', and we shall return to this in Section 5 (p. 102).

While this pragmatic approach goes some way to explain the avoidance of the *per-sonal*, it is difficult to maintain support for such a stance once one realises how it led to the particular marginalisation of certain 'sorts' of personal lives. Jenny Morris (1989, 1993) and Carol Thomas (1997, 1999) were among the first to offer British 'feminist accounts' of disability and in doing so acknowledged both the exclusion of disabled people from feminist analysis and the exclusion of women from disability theories and research. Morris (1991) highlights how the dominance of men in the disabled people's movement (especially the academic section of it) results in the prioritising of 'work' (*paid* employment) over issues of sexuality, motherhood and personal relationships. Lloyd (2001:726) goes further, suggesting that although the social model 'has been essential to the success of the disability movement up to this point in time', it has achieved this position by prioritising the interests of 'white, middle-class, professional, physically disabled men'.

The mention of 'physically disabled' is worth noting here. As we saw in Chapter 1 (in Challenge 6 to the social model, p. 14), the social model of disability, and therefore the disabled people's movement, has been accused of failing to include all people with impairments. It has been argued that people with learning difficulties (Chappell *et al.*, 2001) and people who use mental health services have often been excluded from mainstream Disability Studies and activism. Indeed, there is a debate about whether there is a need for a separate model of madness and distress distinct from the social model of disability (Beresford *et al.*, 2010). One of the consequences of this is that when 'rights' are being fought for, it may be that a narrow concept of 'rights' is being used (for example, fighting for the right to 'work' often focuses on the need for physical access and ignores the need to challenge inflexibility of working hours or high-pressure working environments).

A recognition that disability activism and Disability Studies have often assumed a 'male', 'middle-class', 'professional', 'heterosexual', 'physically impaired' and 'global North' subject is at the heart of the work which has been done in this area. There is now an increasing body of literature that explores the lived experiences of people with impairments who also hold other identities. We are going to focus on the work which considers the intersections of disability, gender and sexuality.

Living multiple 'minority' identity positions

Action Point: Consider the following questions:

1   Do men or women have more power in society?
2   Do non-disabled people or disabled people have more power in society?
3   Do disabled men or disabled women have more power in society?
4   What are the reasons for your answers?

Here 'power' refers not only to the holding of positions of authority and esteem but also levels of wealth, freedom to determine life decisions, perceptions of value to society and having a 'voice' that is generally listened to.

In a discussion about gender and disability, we need to be clear about why we are using the term 'gender' rather than 'sex' to talk about identity. 'Sex' is usually understood as relating to the biological and physiological ideas about bodies and minds, whereas 'gender' is understood as the social and cultural interpretation of sexed bodies. This takes us back to the key debate referred to earlier about the origins of identity being rooted in the essentialist/non-essentialist positions. We will return to this debate shortly, but for now we explore the lived experience of disabled women.

In their chapter, which provides a useful overview of disabled women and girls, Frohmader and Meekosha (2012) offer the following observations (to do this they cite a range of international non-governmental sources – for full details please refer to the chapter). We can estimate that there are 325 million women and girls with impairments in the world, most of whom live in rural areas of the global South. Worldwide, less than 25 per cent of disabled women are in the workforce and, regardless of the country, the employment rates of disabled women are significantly lower than those of their male peers. When they are employed, disabled women earn less than their male counterparts. Worldwide, the literacy rate for disabled women is estimated at 1 per cent. Neglect, lack of medical care and less access to food and related resources have resulted in a higher mortality (death) rate for girls with impairments. Disabled women are two to three times more likely to be victims of physical or sexual violence. They also tend to be subject to violence over a longer period.

Frohmader and Meekosha's (2012) work is just one of many studies which seem to suggest that disabled women face a 'double disadvantage' because of their membership of two oppressed identity groups: women and disabled people. As Morris (1993:9; emphasis in the original) says:

> [t]he fact that dependence is a key part of the social construction of gender for women *and* of the social construction of disability means that women's powerlessness is confirmed by disability. In contrast, a man who is disabled will experience a conflict between the two roles and may attempt to use masculinity as a way of resisting the disabled role.

The term 'double disadvantage' refers to the idea that being in two or more oppressed identity groupings has a cumulative effect. However, Morris (1992) has argued that while it may be evident, using the term 'disadvantage' simply reinforces negative ideas of disabled people and, instead, disability research should challenge such beliefs. In a similar vein, Stuart (1992) considers whether a black disabled person can be said to experience 'double oppression' and concludes that black disabled people in his research reported a singular experience and that 'simultaneous oppression' is a more accurate term. Caldwell notes the use of 'additive' (double oppression) and 'interactive' (simultaneous oppression) but argues that whichever term is used, the important point is that people who find themselves 'located at these intersections often find themselves in/visible' (2010:n.p.). Caldwell's comment mirrors the increasing interest in the concept of 'intersectionality' as a useful way of framing these discussions.

Key Concept: Intersectionality

Intersectionality refers to an interdisciplinary methodology (way of studying) which is interested in the intersections between different social identities, especially between collective groups of minorities and the systems of oppression and discrimination with which they live. It has its roots in feminist sociology (Crenshaw, 1991; McCall, 2005) but has broadened its focus to other minorities based on race, sexual orientation, class and disability. Its main insight is that conceptualisations of oppression which focus on only one identity (such as sexism, racism, homophobia or disablism) do not adequately address or examine the complex forms of oppression that result from intersecting minority identities.

An area where this need to consider 'intersectionality' is particularly significant is where disability and gender meet sexuality. Anne Finger (1999 cited in Shakespeare, 2006:168) has commented that for disabled women

> [s]exuality is often the source of our deepest oppression: it is often the source of our deepest pain. It's easier for us to talk about [...] discrimination in employment, education and housing than to talk about our exclusion from sexuality and reproduction.

As an identity position, 'sexuality' has a dual meaning. It refers to being sexual as well as being a specific sexuality (e.g. homosexual, heterosexual or bisexual). This distinction is useful because, unlike in the case of many other minority groups, being seen as a sexual being (regardless of which 'sort' of sexuality) can be a significant challenge for some disabled people. As Goodley (2011:40) notes:

> a key area of activism for people with the label of intellectual disabilities has been around their sexual autonomy, fertility and their right to parent (Booth and Booth, 1994, 1998). They have clashed with professionals and service providers who, for a variety of reasons ranging from paternalism to risk-avoidance, maintain asexual and incompetent views of their clientele (Varela, 1978).

The significance of recognising, and then discussing, sexuality in the lives of disabled people is highlighted when we consider sexual abuse. We have already noted that disabled women are two to three times more likely to be victims of physical or sexual violence (Frohmader and Meekosha, 2012). Citing a study by Kvam, Stalker and McArthur (2012) note that the incidence of childhood sexual abuse reported by deaf men in Norway was more than three times that reported by hearing men, and the level of abuse was more serious than for the general population. Taking sexuality seriously in the lives of disabled children and adults is about more than a good sex life: it also involves access to good sex education and being on the agenda during conversations around child protection.

Having said all this, we also note that taking sexuality seriously includes also taking asexuality seriously. Kim (2011) has discussed how claims for the sexual rights of disabled people mistakenly target asexuality and celibacy, and in doing so uphold universal and normative ideas of sexual pleasure and desire which exclude those who do not identify as sexual. We would not want to mirror such mistakes here.

One area of study that has tried to deal with the 'fluid' nature of a/sexual identities is 'queer' theory. Although primarily concerned with sexuality, ideas from queer theory have been borrowed by those interested in theorising other identities, including disability. The word 'queer' is used

> rather than other terms such as 'gay' or 'lesbian', in order to include a range of sexual practices which lie outside the mainstream, but which may not be labelled 'homosexual'. For instance, the category 'queer' could comprise not only gay, lesbian, transgender, and intersexed people, but also those who engage in sadomasochism, public sex, those with certain fetishes (such as leathermen) and sex workers.
>
> (Sherry, 2004:771)

By attempting to cover all sexual identities that do not fall within the 'normal' sexual identity (monogamous heterosexuality), 'queer' enables a very broad category of people to be considered, all of whom share, to larger and lesser extents, non-normal sexualities.

Key Concept: Queer theory

Queer theory is a relatively new branch of study and knowledge. It has political commitments as well as academic connections and has been called a 'provocative offsring' of lesbian and gay studies (Segal, 1997:214). Queer theory centres on the significance of sexuality and gender and their interrelationships. It challenges the dominance and ubiquity of heteronormativity (the presumption that heterosexuality is the normal or best form of sexuality). Queer theory owes a debt to feminism, especially in separating biology from the social (sex from gender), as well as to the work of Foucault. Queer theory rejects any fixed or stable notions of 'essentialist' identities (sexuality, gender, disabled) and advocates 'constructionist' ideas of identity as being in constant formation. Judith Butler (1990, 1993) is perhaps the area's most famous scholar.

A good example of how useful 'queer' can be is Sherry's (2004) discussion of the intersections between the experiences of queer and disabled individuals. These include:

1   *Familial isolation*. A queer or disabled family member may be the only person with that identity in the family and this can lead to isolation, loneliness and denial.
2   *High rates of violence*. Both queer and disabled people have been the victims of hate crime and violence towards them on the basis of their identity.
3   *Intolerance*. Both groups experience prejudice and discrimination in key areas of social life such as the workplace and within education.
4   *Stereotypes*. Both groups are the victims of harmful stereotyping (e.g. being unfit parents).
5   *In/ability to pass*. The ability to 'pass' refers to those people who are able to hide their impairment or sexuality in order to appear 'normal'.
6   *Concerns over gene identification (eugenics)*. Both groups are the subjects of a 'race' to find relevant gene(s) relating to the 'condition' of certain impairments or certain sexualities. If such genes were identified, this could lead to the attempted eugenic elimination of disabled and queer people.
7   *Rejecting pathologisation*. Both groups have to challenge their designation as medically 'abnormal'. In 1973, the American Psychiatric Association declared that homosexuality was no longer a 'disorder'. Before then, homosexuality was judged to be an inherent feature of a 'disorder' and was duly treated by medical intervention. While no longer sanctioned by the medical authorities, this view of homosexuality still exists.

As Sherry's (2004) discussion demonstrates, exploring how minority identities intersect not only can shed light on the lives of individuals who are negotiating multiple identities, but also develops understandings of those lived experiences by borrowing and adapting ideas. For instance, queer theory and Disability Studies both problematise the taken-for-granted ideas of 'normal', and oppose process and structures that demand 'normal'. Within feminism and queer theory, this is sometimes called 'heteronormativity' or 'compulsory heterosexuality'; McRuer (2006) has talked about 'compulsory ablebodiedness' in the same terms.

Intersecting disability with...	
Age	Jönson and Larsson (2009) on older adults in Sweden Priestley (2006) on 'old age' and disability Slater (2012, 2013) on 'youth' and 'young people' Riach and Loretto (2009) on unemployed 'working'-age adults
Pregnancy and maternity	Booth and Booth (1993, 1999) on parenthood for with the label of learning disabilities Finger (1999) on pregnancy and birth Thomas (1997) and Grue and Lærum (2002) on motherhood
Race (which includes colour, nationality and ethnic or national origins)	Bell (2006) introducing 'White' Disability Studies Stuart (1992, 1993) on race/disability as a double oppression Harris (2003) on the experiences of disabled refugees and asylum seekers in the UK Islam (2008) on young disabled Pakistani and Bangladeshi people in the UK Goodley et al. (2013) on British Pakistani families and disabled children
Religion or Belief	Miles (1995) on historical perspectives of disability in eastern religions Treloar (2002) on disabled people and families in evangelical Christian churches

Figure 6.5 When disability intersects with other 'protected characteristics': suggested academic sources.

In Chapter 5, we noted that the United Kingdom's Equality Act 2010 harmonised existing 'anti-discrimination' legislation across nine 'protected characteristics'. Although not all of the 'protected characteristics' are the focus of social movements, some of them have been researched as identities that intersect with disability. Using Hepple's (2010) summary as a guide, and as we have considered 'sex' (man or woman) and 'sexual orientation', Figure 6.5 offers suggested sources for further reading in some of these areas.

Section 5: Identity politics: the problems with 'groups'

So far in this chapter, we have considered disability as a social identity and explored some of the interconnections between a disabled identity and other 'minority' identities. In the United Kingdom, these identity issues are often discussed under the term 'equality and diversity'; indeed, the Equality Act 2010 sought to harmonise existing legislation across protected characteristics. However, there are two particular difficulties with this approach.

The first difficulty with this 'harmonising' approach is that there are critical tensions between the agendas of 'minority' groupings. Consider, for instance, the case of abortion. Sharp and Earle (2002:137) discuss

> the tension that exists between the feminist principle that a woman's right to control her own body must entail the right to terminate an unwanted pregnancy, and the concerns of the disability movement that to permit the abortion of foetuses on the grounds of suspected impairment is tantamount to endorsing an anti-disability eugenics.

They conclude that, on the issue of abortion, feminist identity politics and disability identity politics 'remain in fundamental opposition' (ibid.:144). Similar, although not so fundamental, differences exist between queer and disability politics over the importance of the built environment and the 'cult of "body beautiful"'' (Corbett, 1994:345). While debates are ongoing there is hope that solutions can be found, but there is a more serious concern.

The second difficulty with this approach is the more significant. While 'equality' implies sameness ('we are all equal' implies that we are all the same), 'diversity' implies difference (on the basis of age, class, disability, ethnicity, gender, race, religion and sexuality). When this disparity is mirrored in identity politics, it results in paradoxical arguments that argue for equal rights (sameness) based on a recognition of diversity (difference). At times, identity politics has responded to this paradox by denying, or downplaying, difference. For example, the gay rights movement has argued that lesbian and gay men are 'normal' citizens and are the *same* as everyone else: they want to go to work, fall in love, access education, like everyone else. Yet at a corporeal level, a distinct 'homosexual body' is identified as *different* from, but no lesser than, the heterosexual biological norm (Richardson, 2005), and that allows the movement to highlight where changes need to be made (i.e. in the laws on marriage) to accommodate the difference.

However, at the heart of the problem of identity politics is the fact that it depends on the creation and the maintenance of the categories of 'us' and them' (Woodward, 1997a). This is a reminder of a point made in Section 1: that all identities exist because of difference and exclusion of those who are 'not'. While one can acknowledge that those categories ('us' and 'them') are built on oppressive concepts of 'heteronormativity, compulsory able-bodiedness, and institutional racism' (Richardson, 2005:170), and that it is the 'them' category which is subjected to prejudice and oppression, it leaves little room for political manoeuvre. It can be argued, therefore, that identity politics is limited in what it can achieve for minority groups because it only engages in redrawing the boundaries of 'us' and fails to trouble the very existence of categories of 'us' and 'them'. Whenever the boundary of 'us' is redrawn, the boundary of 'them' is also redrawn and re-enforced. There are many instances where this is evident, such as calls for employers to be positive towards disabled applicants because 'disabled people just need to be given a chance'. When this argument is made, it is attempting the redraw the boundary of 'us' (those who work) to include disabled people, but in doing so it does not challenge neo-liberal working practices that demand high levels of flexibility and autonomy. This, in turn, leaves those excluded by such practices in the 'them' category and succeeds in including only some disabled people.

The problem here, then, is that even a widened category of 'us' is always dependent on the construction of 'them'. We have mentioned, at various points, how people labelled with learning disabilities and/or mental health issues have been marginalised within disability activism. These are examples of an us/them divide *within* a minority group. This also happens within minority studies: Kate Caldwell (2010:n.p.) has described how queer theory does its own work of exclusion, as:

> [q]ueer theory is particularly problematic from a bisexual perspective. Although the theory is intended to provide a unified sexual citizenship, in practice it reconstructs the same binary in a way that is more politically advantageous for the homosexual community and more palatable to heterosexuals. The primary contributing factor and consequence of this phenomenon is bisexual in/visibility.

So if, as we are suggesting, identity politics is limited in what it can achieve for disabled people, then perhaps we need to look for alternatives.

Beyond identity politics?

> Disability studies can provide a critique of and a politics to discuss how all groups, based on physical traits or markings, are selected for disablement by a larger system of regulation and signification.
>
> (Davis, 2002b:29)

Lennard Davis (2002b) has contended that we should pay attention to the unstable nature of the categories we have come to know concerning 'the body', including disability and impairment, in order to explore a new ethics of the body. A new ethics of the body should, he suggests, start with the disability (rather than end with it).

If the limits of identity politics come from trying to make all identities (black/white, man/woman, gay/straight, dis/abled) equal, independent and autonomous by simply trying to widen the category of 'us', then, he argues, our aim should be, instead, to question the 'us' and 'them' and to create a new category based on the 'dismodern' subject. For Davis (2002b:30), the 'dismodern subject' is 'the partial, incomplete subject whose realization is not autonomy and independence, but dependency and interdependence'. He asks us to imagine that rather than subjectivity being about our sense of self or the conscious and unconscious thoughts and emotions which constitute our sense of *who we are*, we should look at *inter-subjectivity* and concentrate on who we are in relation to others. He asks us to think about how *we* could constitute *us*.

> **Action Point:** What would a dismodern society look like? How would it be organised? How useful is it to think beyond what we know and 'imagine' alternatives?

For other critics, such as Nancy Fraser, 'identity politics' regrettably 'signalled a retreat from a vision of a "just social order", and a shift away from struggles over redistribution' (Barnes and Mercer, 2003:130). She argues for a 'transformative' politics that is allied to a deconstruction of those binary categories and is not unlike Davis's (2002b) call for the dismodern subject.

A more radical alternative is offered by James Overboe. Overboe (2012:123) disputes the need to fight for recognition and advocates 'moving away from the incessant need for disabled people to claim or carve out a place for their personhood to be legitimised and recognised by themselves or "able" others'. His alternative involves engaging in the 'politics of imperceptibility', and he goes on to detail 'how impersonal singularities affirm impairments and can lead to a fuller life expressed through the vitality of disability' (ibid.:113). Such an affirmation of impairment does not involve a return to medical science, such as the biological citizenship we discussed earlier (in Section 2), but rather involves a radical questioning of contemporary notions of 'personhood' and their reliance on liberalism and humanism. As Agamben (1996 cited in Overboe, 2007:122) states, '[t]he concept of people pretends to be inclusive with no remainder. While simultaneously an exclusive concept known to afford no hope.' With our ideas of what it is to be afforded a 'personhood' questioned, Overboe (2012) urges us to move beyond the 'human' and, in doing so, move beyond dis/ability, to stop fighting for recognition to come out from the 'normative shadows' (Overboe, 2007) and, instead, 'allow for the generative source of impairment to flourish as a life' (Overboe, 2012:119).

Conclusion

The slogan 'Nothing about us without us' communicates the idea that nothing should be decided about any group(s) without the direct participation of members of the group(s) affected. It is often used in reference to the making and implementation of social policy and has become associated with disability activism, particularly since James Charlton's (2000) book of the same name. In this chapter, we have focused on the 'us' by exploring disability, identity and politics. We have explored the central debates surrounding the nature of an 'us' identity: essentialism and non-essentialism. We considered the historical and present-day role of disability activism in the United Kingdom and explored the interconnections between 'us' identities. We revealed the limitations of identity politics (which is based on an 'us') and offered some alternatives. Following Davis (2002b), we asked *you* to imagine how 'we' might constitute 'us' and, following Overboe (2012), we suggested that perhaps an 'us' shouldn't matter.

Suggestions for Wider Reading

Humphrey, J. C. (1999) 'Disabled people and the politics of difference', *Disability and Society*, 14, 2, pp. 173–188.

Sherry, M. (2004) 'Overlaps and contradictions between queer theory and disability studies', *Disability and Society*, 19, 7, pp. 769–783.

Woodward, K. (ed.) (1997) *Identity and Difference*, London: Sage/Open University Press.

Part III

Critical issues

Chapter 7

Critical issues

Researching disabled children in the social world

Introduction

In Chapter 1, we set out nine challenges to the social model of disability. Here we reflect again on challenge 7: *the social model has little to say about disabled children*. In Chapter 3, we focused on critical approaches to the sociology and psychology of dis/abled childhoods. Our aim in this chapter is to respond to challenge 7 and to bring a Disability Studies lens to focus on the lives of disabled children in the social world – that is, in families, in education, at play and in leisure. Finally, we explore some of the issues involved in working with disabled children in research and draw on an example of a recent research project carried out with disabled children and families to do so.

Section 1: Disabled children in families

We start by talking about disabled children in families. This is a controversial approach. As we have seen in Chapter 3, children are no longer considered to be the property of their parents or carers in law, in services or in research. There has rightly been a shift in emphasis to listening to the voice of the child, rather than talking to the child's proxies, including parents or carers and professionals (Lewis, 2011).

And yet, writings from the field of Disability Studies often discuss disabled children and their families together. This is not because Disability Studies researchers share the assumptions of developmental psychologists who mesh together children's development with their mothers' parental capacity (as we saw in Chapter 3); rather, it is because researchers in Disability Studies are responding to how disablism affects not only the child, but the whole family. As we mentioned in Chapter 6, this is why families with disabled children living in them are often referred to as 'disabled families'. Not surprisingly, this phrase is not accepted universally and is seen as controversial, because some view the use of the term as implying that it is the child that has 'disabled the family'. Indeed, Dowling and Dolan (2001:22) argue against use of the term, saying that it is not 'a common anti-oppressive term'. However, we use the term 'disabled families' here in order to highlight the ways in which discriminatory and oppressive practices act on the whole family, not just the child with an impairment (Runswick-Cole, 2007). It is not the child who has disabled the family, but the social arrangements that result in the oppression of disabled families.

There is a plethora of research about the lives of disabled families. Much of this research has been underpinned by models of disability that view the birth of a disabled child as a 'tragic' occurrence for the family (Bruce and Schulz, 2002). Stalker and

Connors (2007:19) tell us that '[t]he social model of disability has paid little attention to disabled children', and analyses of disabled families' lives, like that of Bruce and Schulz (2002), seem to suggest that this is the case. And yet, in many ways the social model of disability has had a big impact on the lives of disabled children. For instance, there has been a welcome shift in the research literature away from stories of tragic families with disabled children living in them towards more affirmative analyses of the lives of disabled families (see Derbyshire, 2013, and Haraldsdóttir, 2013, for some examples of more affirmative stories).

Much of the research in this area has been written from a Disability Studies perspective that has drawn on the social model of disability (Beresford, 1994; Read, 2000; McLaughlin et al., 2008). Not surprisingly, then, this research has often focused on the material disadvantages and barriers disabled families face. For example, a recent study funded by the UK-based charity Scope (Pyer and Bush, 2009) summarises some of the ways in which disability, or social oppression, affects the whole family in material ways:

- Thirty-two per cent of disabled families felt that they were accepted within their local communities, compared to 48 per cent of families with non-disabled children.
- Parents of disabled children reported difficulty in accessing paid employment because of caring responsibilities and a lack of accessible child care.
- Over a third of disabled families felt that their home was quite unsuitable or very unsuitable. By comparison, 90 per cent of families of non-disabled children reported that the family home was quite suitable or very suitable for their needs.
- Fifty-two per cent of disabled families said they had enough money only some of the time, rarely or never.

Research in England has consistently shown that poverty has a major negative impact on the lives of disabled children (Sloper and Beresford, 2006; EDCM, 2007), so much so that it almost appears as if there is an inevitable link between disability and poverty. However, this link is not a necessary outcome of living in a family with a child with an impairment, as while there is poverty among disabled families in England, this is not universally the case within global North countries. Bjarneson (2010) describes the economic differences between disabled families in Iceland and other countries. In Iceland, the economic gap between disabled families and other families is not as great as it is in England. This is because of the difference between the two countries' social arrangements, including the difference in the numbers of mothers in paid work in Iceland, where child care is more affordable and accessible, in comparison to the number of mothers of disabled children in paid work in England.

Living in poverty clearly affects the life chances of children, and disabled children in England are among the most disadvantaged children in terms of their economic status. In the United Kingdom, it is often said that education is the route out of poverty for children, and so access to good-quality education for disabled children is a key issue. It is to the education of disabled children that we now turn.

Section 2: Disabled children in education

The question of where and how disabled children should be educated has been the subject of passionate debate in global North countries. In England, the debate has been raging since the 1944 Education Act, which identified 11 categories of handicapped children: blind, partially sighted, deaf, delicate, diabetic, educationally subnormal, epileptic, maladjusted, physically handicapped and those with speech defects.

Currently, disabled children's education is most often discussed under the banner of inclusion (Runswick-Cole, 2008, 2011a). The Enabling Education Network (1998) sets out the principles of inclusive education as follows:

- It acknowledges that all children can learn.
- It acknowledges and respects differences (age, gender, ethnicity, language, disability, HIV status, etc.).
- It enables education structures, systems and methodologies to meet the needs of all children.
- It is part of a wider strategy to promote an inclusive society.
- It is a dynamic process that is constantly evolving.
- It need not be restricted by large class sizes or shortage of material resources.

Inclusive education has become a 'global agenda' (Pijl *et al.*, 1997) enshrined in international laws. The *UN Convention on the Rights of the Child* (UNICEF, 1989) states that inclusive education should be the goal for education of 'children with disabilities', and *The Salamanca Statement and Framework for Action on Special Needs Education* (UNESCO, 1994) requires signatory nations to ensure that all their educational policies stipulate that disabled children attend the neighbourhood school that would be attended if the child did not have a 'disability'.

Traditionally, debates in the global North about inclusive education have focused on *where* a child is educated – in 'mainstream' provision with non-disabled peers or in 'special' provision with disabled peers. In the United Kingdom, since 1978 the policy has been that special education should 'wherever possible' take place within mainstream settings (DES, 1978:150; DfES, 2004). However, inclusion is about more than the type of school placement for children labelled with special needs. In part, inclusion is as much about race, gender, sexuality and poverty as it is about dis/ability (Culham and Nind, 2003), and the complex intersectionalities that occur within education should always be attended to. Moreover, inclusion involves schools and practitioners challenging cultures to ensure that no one is left out (Allan, 2012). Erevelles (2011:66) reminds us that such cultures are often 'met with a complacency that accepts these enactments of power and erasure as natural and normative'. It is in challenging the manifestations of 'normative' cultures that the work of inclusion is to be done, as Barton (1997 cited in Runswick-Cole, 2011a:113) tells us:

> inclusive education is not about 'special' teachers meeting the needs of 'special' children in ordinary schools (Ballard 1995). It is not merely about placing disabled pupils in classrooms with their non-disabled peers; it is not about 'dumping' pupils into an unchanged system of provision and practice. Rather, it is about how, where and why, and with what consequences, we educate *all* pupils.

Inclusion is described as an ongoing 'journey' (Culham and Nind, 2003). Education systems are inevitably in a constant state of flux as priorities change and cultural influences come to bear; the aim of attaining equity in education is not something that will simply be achieved, it is always something that will be striven for (Naylor, 2005). In this sense, inclusion is always a process and never an end point.

Barriers to inclusion

Many individual nation-states have, as we have seen, signed up for inclusion at the level of international law. However, as is often the case, the gap between the policy rhetoric and the everyday experiences of disabled children remains. It is certainly the case that barriers to children's participation in schools remain. Inevitably, in the global North, as we saw in Chapter 3, ever-narrowing definitions of 'normal' childhoods and 'achievement' work to marginalise disabled children within mainstream education. These narrow definitions are used at all stages of the education system and can be clearly seen within prospectus and on websites for higher education institutions, which utilise ideas around 'able', ultimately 'employable' and future-focused students (Radcliffe, 2013), and, in doing so, marginalise students who would not easily fulfil such prescriptive expectations.

This marginalisation is supported and compounded by the increasingly market-orientated nature of the education system (Runswick-Cole, 2011a). In England, schools compete with each other for the 'best' pupils and the 'best' results. Their results are published and ranked in league tables. The aim is to raise standards of teaching and learning in schools by forcing schools to compete with each other in the local market-place, where parental choice is influenced by the schools' academic standing. Narrowly defined academic attainment has become *the* marker of a 'good school' (ibid.). The operation of market forces has meant that schools are increasingly looking for ways to attract 'motivated' parents with 'able' children (Apple, 2010 cited in Runswick-Cole, 2011a). An agenda that pushes for the inclusion of children whose academic attainment is considered to be 'low' sits uncomfortably alongside a marketised education system (Runswick-Cole, 2011a).

Debating Point: Is it time to end the bias towards inclusion?
Read the following section and then visit the website for the Alliance for Inclusive Education: www.allfie.org.uk. Make a list of arguments for and against inclusive education.

Despite the continuing barriers to inclusion, in England there has been a significant discussion about the inclusion agenda. Indeed, the Special Educational Needs and Disability Green Paper *Support and Aspiration: A New Approach to Special Educational Needs and Disability – A Consultation* promised to 'remove the bias towards inclusive education' (DfE, 2011:5). The Green Paper stated that '[n]o one type of school placement (such as full inclusion in mainstream provision, special schools, or specialist units in a mainstream setting) is the most effective at meeting children's SEN [special educational needs]' (DfE, 2011:20).

While the policy shift was welcomed by many who felt that the inclusion project had failed, it also angered groups of disabled people, and parents and carers of disabled children, who continued to advocate for inclusion. As the proposed Children and Families Bill, which sets out provision for children with special educational needs, passes through Parliament, it seems that the legislative framework for inclusion in England will not be altered.

While inclusion is often discussed in the context of schooling, it is important to consider the inclusion of disabled children beyond education and in their communities. And it is to these experiences that we turn next.

Section 3: Disabled children at play and being creative

When we think about disabled children's participation in their communities outside of schools, it is clear that social model thinking has impacted in some ways on children's lives. In the areas of play and leisure, social model approaches to disability have made a considerable impact on the drive to promote inclusive play environments (Dunn and Moore, 2005; John and Wheyway, 2004). A focus on structural barriers to the participation has increased disabled children's participation in play and leisure (John and Wheyway, 2004; Play Safety Forum, 2002) and has underpinned calls for disabled children's rights to be asserted (Goodley and Runswick-Cole, 2010a). In addition to identifying the physical barriers to children's play, John and Wheyway (2004) have identified social and institutional barriers to disabled children's play, including health and safety concerns. It is now agreed that

> [a]ll children both need and want to take risks in order to explore limits, venture into new experiences and develop their capacities, from a very young age and from their earliest play experiences. [...] Children with disabilities have an equal if not greater need for opportunities to take risks, since they may be denied the freedom of choice enjoyed by their non-disabled peers.
>
> (Dunn and Moore, 2005: 334–335)

Sadly, despite these positive developments, disabled children are still more likely than non-disabled children to be offered segregated activities in highly surveilled environments (John and Wheyway, 2004; Hodge and Runswick-Cole, 2013). Pyer and Bush's (2009) research demonstrates the limited impact of these changes on the lives of disabled families. They found that 80 per cent of families with non-disabled children found it easy to access leisure activities, whereas only 58 per cent of families with disabled children said it was easy for them to access leisure activities.

A consequence of the psychologisation of childhood that we saw in Chapter 3 is that for disabled children, day-to-day experiences become sites for therapeutic assessment and intervention. In other words, the response to the identification of difference in childhood is to offer therapy. Papatheodoru (2006) explains that play-based assessments enable adults to identify children whose development is thought to differ from the norm and to develop appropriate interventions. There is a tendency for such assessments to create 'monologues *about* children's bodies and minds rather than pedagogies of hope and potential *with* children' (Goodley and Runswick-Cole, 2010a:503; emphasis in the original). Play therapy may or may not be enabling for disabled children, but it is also one of the mechanisms of surveillance that construct the image of the disabled child. As Goodley and Runswick-Cole (2010a) suggest, a number of recurring themes emerge. Disabled children are viewed as:

- playing differently from other children (if they are seen to play at all);
- doing play that is either generally lacking or specific to their impairment (only children with a particular impairment play that way);
- being in need of intervention to correct and to normalise their play.

In the global North, play is valued as a positive end in itself and as something that children should be allowed to enjoy freely and spontaneously (John and Wheyway,

2004). However, in the lives of disabled children in particular, play is most often a site for surveillance and a mechanism for intervention; there is little time for disabled children to 'get dirty, and to scrape their knees' (Goodley and Runswick-Cole, 2010a:509).

Rethinking creativity

Disabled children's participation in creative activity has also been presented through a medicalised lens (Goodley and Runswick-Cole, 2011a). Disabled children's creativity is often seen as a facet of their impairment. Children labelled with autism who are judged to be gifted are labelled 'autistic savants' (Young and Nettlebeck, 1995). As we saw with play, participation in the arts has also been framed in terms of its *therapeutic* value for disabled children (Goodley and Runswick-Cole, 2011a). It is not, perhaps, surprising that opportunities for creative activity for disabled children are often only to be had in the context of rehabilitation and intervention. Disabled children are offered drama therapy (e.g. Chesner, 1995 cited in Goodley and Runswick-Cole, 2011a), where the focus is on the therapeutic aspects of the performance rather than opportunities for creativity and participation in cultural life. This is regrettable, not least because when disabled children are given the opportunity to participate in creative activities, this can create spaces for them to challenge negative images of their lives and to increase their participation in their local communities (ibid.).

So far, we have focused on the disabled children's participation in schools and their communities by drawing on research findings that are underpinned by social oppression theories of disability in order to demonstrate the ways in which such analyses might contribute to the lives of disabled children. We now turn to consider some of the complex and exciting challenges posed for researchers wishing to carry out research with disabled children drawing on affirmative analyses of disabled children and their families.

Section 4: Disabled children in research

Traditionally, the terms 'child' and 'disabled' have both suggested notions of vulnerability and passivity. Certainly, research 'on' disabled children underpinned by such notions has contributed to the further marginalisation of disabled children (Goodley and Runswick-Cole, 2012a). However, changes in the new sociology of childhood and in national and international law have changed approaches to listening to children. Indeed, the *Convention on the Rights of the Child* (UNCRC) (UNICEF, 1989), Article 12, asserts the right of children to give their opinions about issues that affect them and asserts that these views must be heard regardless of ability.

Despite these welcome changes in approaches to research with disabled children, it remains the case that the meaningful involvement of children within a research process can be difficult to establish and to sustain (Goodley and Runswick-Cole, 2012a; Greenstein, 2013). Lewis and Porter (2004) describe children's participation as being on a continuum (Figure 7.1).

At one end of the spectrum, children's participation is low and research is done 'on' disabled children; at the other end of the continuum, children's participation is high and research is carried out 'with' disabled children. Despite the changes in approach to childhood research, there is still sometimes a reluctance to include disabled children as participants in research.

Research *on* children

- Children not participants, subjects
- Children's competence is not presumed

Participatory ◄──► Non-participatory

Research *with* children

- Children competent social agents
- Children set the research questions
- Children guide the conduct of the research
- Children take part in research
- Children involved in data analysis
- Children involved in dissemination

Figure 7.2 Participation continuum (Adapted from Lewis and Porter, 2004 cited in Goodley and Runswick-Cole, 2012a).

However, there is a growing acceptance that *all* children (who want to) are able to participate in research. Morris (2003) sets out useful guidelines for those wishing to work with disabled children in research in which she proposes the following principles to underpin research with disabled children:

- to treat children as experts and agents in their own lives;
- to use multi-methods in recognition of the different 'voices' or languages of children;
- and to seek to establish a climate of listening.

(Adapted from Goodley and Runswick-Cole, 2012a)

Issues of anonymity and consent take on a further layer of complexity in research with disabled children, not least because of the role that parents or carers play in allowing their children to participate in research. While parents or carers must give their consent for their child to participate, children must also 'assent'. 'Assent' is the term used to describe the child's agreement to participate when 'consent' has been given by their parent or carer (Lewis, 2002). Gaining 'assent' is not a one-off activity; rather, researchers have to check with the child each time they meet that the child is happy to continue to participate, and to check during the meetings that the child is happy to continue.

Recently, childhood research has been enhanced by the use of new and innovative methods. Early years practitioners have been at the forefront of developing multiple methods to elicit children's views (Clark *et al.*, 2003; Runswick-Cole, 2012a). Tours, modelling and map-making are among the multiple methods childhood researchers have employed (Clark *et al.*, 2003; Greenstein, 2013). However, a variety of tools alone may not be enough to enable disabled children's participation, and researchers must be reflexive and adapt research tools to match each child or young person (Morris, 2003). Finally, it is worth remembering that despite the many and varied attempts to listen to disabled children, it is the case that '[a]dult researchers may have less insight into the daily lives of children than they think they have' (Save the Children, 2004 cited in McLaughlin *et al.*, 2008).

The case study example in the next section offers one approach to research carried out with disabled children and draws on the participatory, emancipatory and ethical approaches outlined in this chapter.

Section 5: Case study: disabled children and resilience

This case study describes one aspect of a research study undertaken by researchers at Manchester Metropolitan University (Katherine Runswick-Cole, Dan Goodley and Rebecca Lawthom) in collaboration with Scope, the UK disability charity, from September 2011 to October 2012 (for further details of the research project, visit http:// disabilityresilience.wordpress.com/2013/06/23/disability-resilience/). The specific aims of the research project were:

- to explore what resilience means to disabled people at different stages across the life course;
- to explore how resilience, or a lack of it, has affected disabled people's ability to negotiate challenges and make the most of opportunities in their lives;
- to understand what works in building resilience among different groups of disabled people;
- to develop a toolkit for use by Scope's policy and services functions that outlines what Scope means by resilience, what does or doesn't work in supporting people to become resilient, and what we can do to build resilience in disabled people throughout the life course.

Here, we present one of the children's stories. Peppa (a pseudonym chosen by Peppa) is five years old and is labelled with global developmental delay, speech and language disorder and severe learning difficulties. Peppa communicates using signs and a communication booklet.

Peppa took part in the life-story phase of the research. Life-story approaches have often been used in research with disabled people (Booth and Booth, 1998; Goodley *et al.*, 2004; Goodley and Runswick-Cole, 2011a; Runswick-Cole, 2007). Life-story approaches assume that the narrators, in this case disabled children, are experts in their own lives and hence life-story work draws on the principles of emancipatory disability research.

Key Concept: Emancipatory disability research
Emancipatory disability research is underpinned by the principles of the social model of disability. It aims to disrupt the usual power relationships within research by taking power away from professional academic researchers and giving power to disabled people to shape and control the research agenda (Barnes, 2003).

The research team took the view that disabled children who want to can participate in research (Goodley and Runswick-Cole, 2012a). The team also wanted participants to shape and to be actively involved in the research process and so participants were encouraged to tell their story about the things in their lives that they felt were important (Runswick-Cole and Goodley, 2012). Life stories can offer detailed accounts of people's lived experiences, often offering unique insights into personal worlds. However, they are not only personal stories: they also tell us about the contemporary social, political, policy, service, community and familial contexts in which the stories occurred (ibid.).

Participants in the project were recruited from throughout the North-West region of England and from a range of urban and rural locations between November 2011 and

March 2012. Information about the research was disseminated via a range of organisations, including disability-specific support organisations, pan-disability organisations,
parents' groups and carers' groups, and via disability mailing lists and word of mouth
(Runswick-Cole and Goodley, 2012). Peppa's mother had heard about the project
through a social networking site. She talked to Peppa and to the rest of the family about
being involved in the research.

As we have seen, it is imperative to listen sensitively to children in research (Morris,
2003). The research team sought to do this by responding to children's different communication styles and needs in the interviews. They used pictures, tours and drawings
to support the interview process (Clark *et al.*, 2003). Some children chose to be interviewed with their parents, carers or siblings. Where this is what a child wanted, the
research team aimed to combine – ethically, sensitively and carefully – the perspectives
of the child with those of significant others in their lives whom the child had invited
into the interview. The researchers called this a 'distributed' methodology.

This approach is potentially controversial and the research team was cautious. Primarily the researchers were concerned that by interviewing disabled children with their
parents and siblings, the voice of the disabled child might be drowned out. The difficulties of interviewing disabled children, including examples of where parents dominate the interview, are sensitively described by Abbott (2013), drawing on his work
with young men with Duchenne muscular dystrophy. In the resilience project, the
research team sought to minimise the danger of others dominating the interviews by
using multiple methods. The use of the child's drawings and photos, as well as tours led
by the child, opened up opportunities for children to shape the interviews and to be
heard. And so, although the research team acknowledged the limitations of their study,
they hoped that the richness of narratives was further enhanced through the bringing in
of distributed but interconnected voices to tell the story.

Key Concept: Ethical research in action

A member of the research team (Katherine) met the family twice. As a research team,
Dan, Rebecca and Katherine saw ethics as an active process rather than as something that
is signed off at the start of the research project (Cocks, 2006). This meant that each time
Katherine met with the family, she checked that all family members, and Peppa in particular, were happy to assent to the interview (ibid.). Doing so involved paying careful
attention to Peppa to see whether she was tired or fed up, checking with her and with her
family that everyone was happy to continue and that the interviews were carried out as
clearly and sensitively as possible.

It was important for Katherine to ask Peppa's family for guidance about the best way to
communicate with Peppa, using her communication aid and signing system. After the
interview, Peppa and her family commented on the story and were given their own copy
to keep. Peppa's mother said that she would like to share it with Peppa's teachers at
school.

Figure 7.2 shows Peppa's story written by Peppa and her family: Mum, Dad, Kagome
(her sister), and Mr Bob (her brother). (Pseudonyms were chosen by the family
members.) Peppa is five years old and is labelled with global developmental delay,
speech and language disorder, and severe learning difficulties. Peppa communicates
using signs and a communication booklet.

My name is Peppa, I am five years old and I go to a special school. I live with my mum, dad, sister, Kagome and brother, Mr Bob. People say that I am cheeky and funny and have a great sense of humour. I can be very determined and very stubborn. I am always busy and I never sit still and I never stop.

One of my favourite jokes at the moment is to say 'no' when I mean 'yes'! That is a very funny joke! It makes me laugh!

Eating is one of my favourite things to do. I love biscuits, pasta, peaches, apples, pears and fruit cake.

I like to play rough and tumble with my dad and to chase around and bounce on the trampoline. I like reading books. My favourite book is *The Tiger who came to Tea.*

My perfect day would mean getting up and having cake for breakfast. I would watch *Peppa Pig* on tv. Then I would go to the adventure playground and perhaps for a swim and if there was time I would go to the shops and I would walk around holding my mum or dad's hand – that would be a very exciting thing to do! I would have spaghetti bolognese for my tea and my brother would read me lots of stories – again and again and again.

If you want to get to know me, there are a few things you need to know:

- you need to learn about the things I like and I don't like;
- you need to keep me safe by watching I don't fall over and helping me down the steps;
- you need to keep an eye on me when I am eating – just in case I choke;
- if we go somewhere new, you have to check to make sure I will be safe;
- please don't talk about me when I am in the room as if I'm not there – I understand a lot more than you think!
- please use my communication book;
- learn how I say yes and no;
- learn the signs I use.

Thank you, Peppa x

Figure 7.2 Peppa's story.

Peppa's story also allows us to reflect on the process of carrying out research with children. First, Peppa's story reminds us of the importance of listening to *all* disabled children in research, including those who are labelled with 'severe global developmental delay' and who use communication aids. Peppa's story encourages to us to reflect on the extent to which is it possible sensitively to involve disabled children in research and to draw on the voices of others without drowning out the voice of the child. We end this section on research with disabled children by sounding a note of caution. As we have seen, the research team used a variety of approaches to listen to Peppa. As Clark *et al.* (2003) point out, there is a danger in using imaginative methods in listening to children that we may intrude on their private worlds. We have already noted the high levels of surveillance that disabled children are subjected to in schools and at play and in leisure. Researchers need to be mindful of the fact that they too might be adding to that intrusion (Goodley and Runswick-Cole, 2012a).

Conclusion

In this chapter, we have focused on the lives of disabled children and their families in the social world. We have looked at the lives of disabled children in families, in education, in play and in creativity. We have made links to the social model of disability by drawing attention to the discriminatory attitudes and barriers that disabled children face. Finally, we have explored the complex issues involved in working with disabled children and their families in research.

Suggestions for Wider Reading

Clark, A., McQuail, S. and Moss, P. (2003) *Exploring the Field of Listening to and Consulting with Young Children*, Research Report 445, London: DfES.

Cocks, A. (2006) 'The ethical maze: Finding an inclusive path to gaining children's agreement to research participation', *Childhood*, 26, 13, pp. 247–266.

Morris, J. (2003) 'Including all children: Finding out about the experiences of children with communication and/or cognitive impairments', *Children and Society*, 17, pp. 337–348.

Chapter 8

Critical issues

Theorising bodies in the social world

Introduction

In Chapter 1, we introduced the issue of the body within Disability Studies. We did so, first, in relation to the claim that social model thinkers have written the body out of Disability Studies (see Challenge 4), and then by focusing on feminist accounts that called for a recognition of disabled people's subjective experiences of their bodies (Morris, 1996; Thomas, 1999). We suggested that social theory approaches to impairment create ways to reclaim the discussion of the body from medicine and to talk about the disabled body more positively (Tregaskis, 2002) and more productively. In this chapter, we return to the question of the body. We do so because the body is currently a highly contested area of Disability Studies. We are mindful that opinions on this current issue are diverse and, as Goodley (2011) suggests, fraught and fractious. However, that also makes this issue particularly interesting and important.

We start by exploring a moment in the history of Disability Studies in the United Kingdom when disputes about bodies were brought to the forefront: the publication of Shakespeare's (2006) book *Disability Rights and Wrongs*. We focus here on the differences and discrepancies in various claims made about the 'reality' of bodies and explore the implications for disability activism, disabled people and the field of Disability Studies.

Section 1: Arguing about 'real' bodies

The fraught and fractious nature of debates about bodies is clearly illustrated by the publication of, and reaction to, Tom Shakespeare's 2006 text: *Disability Rights and Wrongs*. Shakespeare made a number of claims that were seen as startling and, perhaps, 'heretical' (Goodley, 2011) in the context of British Disability Studies (see Chapter 1 to remind yourself of the distinguishing features of this field). As Sheldon *et al.* (2007:210) point out:

> [w]ithin the first five pages of the book, Shakespeare claims the British disability movement 'appears to have stagnated' (p. 1), the 'social model version of Disability Studies has reached a dead end' (p. 2) and the social model of disability 'should be abandoned' (p. 5).

Indeed, on p. 28 Shakespeare (2006) claims that Disability Studies 'would be better off without the social model' and by p. 53 he claims boldly that 'the social model [of disability] is wrong' and, indeed, politically dangerous. Given that the social model of disability has been hailed as the disabled people's movement's 'big idea' (Hasler, 1993) and has underpinned teaching, research and writing in British Disability Studies for more than 30 years, these were shocking claims.

Not surprisingly, the book provoked passionate and vigorous responses from within the Disability Studies community. In particular, 'strong social modellists' (Shakespeare, 2006) – people who adhere closely to the social model of disability – criticised Shakespeare both for misrepresenting the social model and for damaging the disabled people's movement and Disability Studies (Sheldon *et al.*, 2007). On the one hand, Shakespeare stood accused of failing to pay attention to the ways in which the social model has developed over time to include feminist perspectives and the perspectives of people with the label of learning difficulty and mental health service users (ibid.) (see Chapter 1). On the other hand, he was attacked for failing to pay attention to the perspectives of people with the label of learning difficulties and mental health service users within his own book (ibid.). His approach to prenatal testing and end-of-life issues also raised alarm within the Disability Studies community. However, despite the range of criticisms aimed at this book, it is worth noting that it was welcomed by academics from outside British Disability Studies, including from medical sociology (Edwards, 2008) and Nordic Disability Studies. While many of the issues Shakespeare raised in his book are worthy of consideration and debate, it was perhaps his views about the body that caused the most controversy, and these are our focus here.

One of Shakespeare's key concerns and criticisms of the social model and British Disability Studies is that 'the problematic reality of biological limitation' has been ignored (2006:40). As we saw in Chapter 1, the social model rests on a distinction between impairment (the body) and disability (a form of social oppression imposed upon, and done to, people with impairments). However, Shakespeare (2006) challenged this view and argued that impairment is a *necessary* cause of the socially created difficulties that disabled people experience. In other words, he put forward the view that the presence of an impairment *necessarily* contributes to a disabled person's experiencing difficulties such as discrimination and exclusion. This was a direct challenge to the social model view that there is no *necessary* link between impairment and disability and that by altering the social arrangements that disadvantage disabled people, disability could be eliminated, and impairment alone would remain. In rejecting this view, Shakespeare also insists that '[i]mpairment *is* a predicament and *can* be tragic' (Goodley, 2011:28).

Shakespeare's focus on the 'reality' of the biological nature of disability is seen by many as a regressive and unhelpful step. The fear is that by focusing on the 'biological limitations' of disabled people, Shakespeare runs the risk of undoing the political advances made by the disabled people's movement and by Disability Studies in advocating for barrier removal and equality for disabled people. The concern is that his work will herald a return to individualised, medicalised and charity models of disability (see Chapter 1). However, although Shakespeare wants us to pay attention to the 'limitations of the body', he acknowledges the benefits of the social model in shifting attention away from individuals with 'deficits' to the way in which 'society includes or excludes' (2006:29). Shakespeare is drawn to social relational approaches to disability (see Chapter 2), in which disability is characterised as a mismatch between the individual (and his or her body) and the environment. Despite the many and impassioned criticisms levelled against Shakespeare from social modellists, Shakespeare is interested in disability as a sociological, not simply a biological, phenomenon. However, in contrast to social oppression approaches to disability, he views the *interaction* between the biological and the social as crucial.

Key Concept: Critical realism

Critical realism is often associated with the work of Roy Bhaskar (1979). While realists are theorists who believe that social phenomena exist in the form that they appear to the observer (they are directly knowable), critical realists take the view that although social phenomena exist independently of the observer, there are different *interpretations* of those pre-existing phenomena.

It is Shakespeare's critical realist approach to the 'reality' of impairment that is of primary interest here. His discussion of impairment reveals a degree of confusion. On the one hand, he insists that 'an impairment is real and may have a biological basis' (2006:71). He seems to be taking a straightforwardly realist, biomedical approach to impairment. Interestingly, he makes this claim in relation to a particular impairment: autism (2006). Yet at the same time, he argues that impairment is 'always and already social' (ibid.:35). To illustrate this argument, he gives the example of another impairment, dyslexia, which he says 'may not become a problem until society demands literacy of its citizens' (ibid.:35). There is a confusion created by presenting one impairment, 'dyslexia', as socially constructed and another, 'autism', as 'real'. And yet Shakespeare insists that autism is an impairment that has a 'pervasive and devastating impact on both the child and the family' (ibid.:72). Shakespeare's confusion stems, in part, from the failure of the book to explore the criticisms of the critical psychology and critical psychiatry movements in relation to medical and biological approaches to mental health issues (Sheldon *et al.*, 2007). The absence of reference to such literature is particularly regrettable in relation to his discussion of autism, not least because a number of writers have offered powerful accounts of the ways in which autism has been produced in cultural and historical contexts (Molloy and Vasil, 2002; Nadesan, 2005; McGuire, 2011, 2013; Timimi *et al.*, 2011). Whatever the merits or otherwise of the idea that impairments are socially constructed categories rather than biomedical 'truths' (a question we shall return to), Shakespeare (2006) fails to account for why he describes some impairments as 'real' and others as 'socially constructed'.

Section 2: The place of impairment in disability activism

While Shakespeare may have drawn the wrath of the UK disabled people's movement, which is wedded to the social model of disability, his call to take impairment seriously chimes with developments within other forms of disability activism. As we saw in Chapter 6, Hughes (2009) identifies groups of disability activists who, rather than organising under the banner of the social model, organise as 'biological citizens'. Biological citizens are disability activists who are intent on influencing policy, practice and thinking about people with particular *medical conditions*. Nikolas Rose (2001 cited in Hughes, 2009) describes these new social movements in the following ways:

- They form around biological conditions and diagnostic labels.
- They challenge stigmatisation of people with the condition.

- They use stories about their lives to challenge negative and exclusionary attitudes.
- They demand civil and human rights.
- They demand recognition, respect, resources, research and control over medical and technical expertise.

In contrast to social model stalwarts and groups that form on the basis of a shared experience of oppression and discrimination (see Chapter 6), biological citizens, as Hughes (2009) describes them, see impairment, genetics and biomedical diagnosis as central to their identity. The emergence of such groups certainly supports Shakespeare's call to pay attention to impairment.

So far, we have seen how Shakespeare (2006) has challenged the distinction between impairment and disability upon which the social model is premised. Meanwhile, Hughes (2009) has revealed that the disabled people's movement, drawing on the social model, does not have a monopoly on political action and that disabled people are organising around their impairment labels and diagnoses as 'biological citizens'.

Biological citizens organise themselves in the belief that impairment and diagnosis are biomedical facts – the approach Shakespeare takes to autism. They seek to minimise stigma and discrimination but they argue that their impairments are a biological limitation that is relevant to the struggle for disability equality. This stance, as we have seen, stands in direct opposition to that taken by proponents of the social model, who view impairment as irrelevant in the struggle for disability equality. Biological citizens see impairments as real and relevant, whereas social model stalwarts see impairments as real but irrelevant.

In contrast to both the positions outlined above, although we agree that impairment is very relevant to the field of Disability Studies, we suggest that, rather than impairment being 'real, biological truth', it is a socially and culturally constructed category. Indeed, we would wish to extend the position Shakespeare sets out in relation to dyslexia to all impairment labels. In the next section, we set out what is, perhaps, a radical position: that impairment is relevant but not 'real'.

Section 3: The relevance of impairment in disability studies

The arguments we are making may seem theoretical and complex. If they are to be worthwhile in the field of Disability Studies, which is premised on the struggles of disabled people for rights and equality, then these arguments must have relevance for disabled people's lives. In this section, we set out to justify why we argue that it is relevant and, indeed, important to talk about theories of impairment in Disability Studies and in the lives of disabled people.

Snyder and Mitchell (2006:11) have remarked that disabled people frequently encounter 'journalists who seem to believe that gaining access to one's disability [i.e. impairment] label somehow delivers the truth of one's social identity'. The belief that knowledge of an impairment label somehow delivers the truth about a person's identity and motives is far from uncommon. In fact, it underpins some branches of academic study and, as we shall see, is evident in contemporary popular culture. In academia, 'literature and medicine', a sub-discipline of medical humanities (Jones, 2013), introduced the study of literary works into US medical schools. Using archival research, some scholars in this area work to label authors and literary characters with contemporary medical diagnoses and then to reread the texts they have written, or in which they appear, in the light of this new knowledge. In other words, the discipline seeks to know the impairment status of the author or character in order to better understand the text (Mallett and Runswick-Cole, 2010).

A good example of scholarly attempts to diagnose the author is that of Dr Samuel Johnson. Murray (2003:372) claims that 'over 80 physicians' have subsequently written about Johnson. In an earlier article, Murray (1979:1610) comments:

> [t]here are excellent accounts of the scrofula (the King's Evil) he suffered as a child, unsuccessfully treated by the Royal Touch of Queen Anne; the recurring depression that plagued him like 'a black dog of melancholy'; his tics and gesticulations; the stroke that left him aphasic but able to write; his death in 1784; and his necropsy.

An example of attempts to diagnose a literary character is that of Bashir *et al.* (2004:1435), who ask: 'Tolkien's character Gollum is certainly disturbed, but is he physically or mentally ill?' The character, from *The Hobbit* (Tolkien, 1937) and the three-volume *The Lord of the Rings* (Tolkien, 1954a, 1954b, 1955), receives formal diagnosis in the conclusion: 'Gollum displays pervasive maladaptive behaviour that has been present since childhood. [...] He fulfils seven of the nine criteria for schizoid personality disorder' (Bashir *et al.*, 2004:1436). Frith (2003) also indulges in retrospective diagnosis in her book *Autism: Explaining the Enigma*. In a chapter entitled 'Beyond enchantment', she suggests that the fictional character Sherlock Holmes may have had a form of autism.

Retrospective diagnosis is not limited to authors and fictional characters: historical figures have also been subjected to retrospective labelling. For example, in his book *Autism and Creativity*, Michael Fitzgerald (2004) diagnoses autism in historical figures including George Orwell, Isaac Newton, Albert Einstein and Andy Warhol. Adelman and Adelman (1987) also cite Hans Christian Andersen, Charles Darwin, Winston Churchill and Leonardo da Vinci as people who have been posthumously labelled with 'learning disabilities'. Having reviewed the available evidence for Albert Einstein's having 'learning disabilities', Thomas (2000) concludes that despite there being little evidence to support these claims, their continued repetition can be explained by a desire to believe that 'even geniuses can suffer from learning disabilities' (Adelman and Adelman, 1987 cited in Thomas, 2000:157).

A similar preoccupation with impairment is evident in contemporary culture. In 2009, a series of popular radio programmes, *Robert Winston's Musical Analysis*, allowed Professor Robert Winston, who is well known in the United Kingdom as a fertility expert and television and radio broadcaster, to explore 'the relationship between the music and the medical conditions of composers who suffered mental and physical illness' (BBC, 2009:n.p.). In the series of programmes on BBC Radio 4, Professor Winston explored how Schumann may have 'suffered from bipolar disorder', how Mahler's 'marital problems may have led him to consult Freud' and how Ravel's dementia 'trapped the music he created in his head' (ibid.). Winston's exploration of the impairments is a reflection of a common assumption that an audience would understand the music more fully by knowing the impairment status of its composer.

Elsewhere, we have discussed what we describe as a pervasive 'urge' for people to 'know' a disabled person's impairment label – an urge we suggest is not limited to the fields of literature, historical analysis or popular culture but directly affects the lives of disabled people and their families (Mallett and Runswick-Cole, 2010). Two stories from our own lives illustrate this point:

Story 1

In a lift, I was asked that question, prefaced as it always is, with a caveat: 'I hope you don't mind me asking but ... what's wrong with you?' I replied, 'Nothing.' I took less than a second but it took some thinking about. Knowing I was to leave the lift at the next floor and therefore only had time to state a label, and knowing that mine is a diagnosis without a media profile, I also knew that the label on its own would not answer the question.

(Author's personal encounter, *c*.2003)

Story 2

At a conference, a colleague and I gave a presentation on care in which I mentioned that I was the parent of a disabled child. Over lunch, a woman I didn't know approached me and briefly said she was interested in the presentation and then asked, 'What is your son's problem?' I replied: 'He doesn't have a problem, he is disabled.' She countered, 'Yes, but what is his disability?' I said I'd prefer not to say.

(Author's personal encounter, *c*.2011)

As the stories above illustrate, being asked about impairment is a mundane and everyday experience for disabled people and their families. As we mentioned in Chapter 1, such encounters have been described as a form of psycho-emotional disablism and they not only limit where disabled people and their families can go, but also negatively affect how disabled people see themselves (Thomas, 1999; Reeve, 2002, 2006).

Section 4: The implications of impairment-specific research

Discussion of impairment *within* the discipline of Disability Studies is important precisely because it is seen as important *outside* the discipline, whether in literary and historical studies, in contemporary culture or in disabled people's social interactions in their day-to-day lives. As the previous section showed, the discussion is more complex than a simple argument over whether impairment is 'real or not', and in this section we offer some words of caution about how this discussion might develop.

By appealing to Disability Studies to take impairment seriously, Shakespeare (2006) has implicitly commended a shift in approaches from research that focuses on barrier removal for *all* disabled people, regardless of their impairment label, to more research focused on meeting the particular needs of people with specific impairments. A number of academics who follow a social model approach to disability have also embraced impairment-specific research (for examples, refer to Edwards and Boxall, 2010, on cystic fibrosis and employment, and Madriaga *et al.*, 2008, on Asperger syndrome and education), claiming that their research is focused on removing the barriers for people with particular types of impairment but maintaining that the 'problem' lies in the attitudes to and barriers all people with impairments face rather than with the impairment itself. For us, this turn to impairment-specific research, whether premised on medical or social approaches to disability, is problematic in a number of ways.

First, it is problematic because, as Shakespeare (2006) acknowledges, a hierarchy of impairments exists (Deal, 2003). The notion of a hierarchy of impairments suggests that some impairments are more significant or worthy of attention than others. The consequence for disability research is that some impairments attract more research and funding than others. For example, as we have noted elsewhere (Mallett and Runswick-Cole, 2012), currently autism is an impairment that attracts a great deal of attention within the academy, including research conferences, research centres, research journals and publications on autism; and qualifications for practitioners in autism. This fascination with autism is echoed in cultural texts, with the impairment becoming the subject of films (e.g. *Rain Man*, 1998; *Snow Cake*, 2006), novels (e.g. Haddon, 2003), autobiographies (e.g. Grandin, 1996; Lawson, 2000), museum exhibitions (e.g. *Welcome to Our World … Living with Autism*, 2011) and newspaper articles (e.g. McNeil, 2009; Alleyne, 2010). As Murray (2008:xvii) suggests, autism is, in some ways, considered to be 'compellingly attractive in the way it presents human otherness'. Thanks to high-profile campaigns by well-organised and well-funded voluntary organisations, autism is known across the globe (see, for examples, www.autism.org.uk (UK), www.autismspeaks.org (USA), www.autism.my (Malaysia) and www.autisminiran.com (Iran)). On the other hand, other impairments have much lower public and global profiles, and people labelled with those impairments struggle to attract research interest and funding. For example, neurofibromatosis is still a relatively little-known condition, and it was only in the last two decades of the twentieth century that systematic medical research began (Huson *et al.*, 1988). A focus on impairment-specific research will inevitably result in some 'losers' and 'winners'. Some people with impairments will be 'lucky' enough to be the focus of research; more than likely, it will mean that those people with impairments that are more widely diagnosed and with effective impairment organisations to campaign with and for them will attract more research interest.

However, those very same people may, willingly or not, find themselves defined by their impairments. Our second worry about a turn to impairment-specific research is that the 'truth' about their identity will be summed up by knowledge about their diagnosis or impairment. In *Disability Rights and Wrongs*, Shakespeare (2006) challenges the disabled people's movement to accept that not all people with impairments identify as disabled people. He argued, as have others (Watson, 2002), that many people do not see their disabled identity as their primary identity status. In a similar vein, we would argue that not all people with impairments wish to organise around their biological citizenship or to see their impairment as *the* most important thing about them or as the piece of information that delivers the *truth* of their social identity. A related word of warning here is that, just as disability research that focuses on barrier removal has been criticised for treating all disabled people as a homogeneous group, ignoring differences of race, class, gender and ethnicity and, of course, living with different impairments and their effects, impairment-specific research also needs to pay attention to these differences. After all, people with impairments do not experience their impairments in the same way, and these differences will be created as much by social and cultural factors, such as housing, education and family support, as by 'real' biological differences between individuals.

Third, and pragmatically, we worry that in dividing disability research into different impairment silos, learning will be lost or work repeated. For example, a communication passport is an effective form of removing the barriers to communication whatever the aetiology of the person's speech impairment. A ramp removes the barriers for people with mobility impairments regardless of their diagnosis, and a visual timetable that informs pupils of the structure of their day is simply good practice for all children, rather than of being of exclusive benefit for children labelled with autism. Again, we worry that impairment-specific research reinforces another layer of difference, when finding commonalities would be more pragmatic, beneficial and ethical for all.

By this point, you may be wondering whether we are arguing against common sense. You may be thinking that people experience impairments and that while people may experience the same impairment differently, there are still some basic (sometimes called 'brute') facts that are universal (the same everywhere) and should be accounted for. In the next section, we advance the idea the impairment is always experienced and therefore cannot be meaningfully removed from the social and cultural sphere within which it is being experienced.

Section 5: Social and cultural contexts of impairment

Impairment is, then, relevant to the field of Disability Studies. So, in what sense are we problematising its 'realness'? After all, Shakespeare (2006) insists, as we explored earlier, that impairment *is* a predicament and *can* be tragic. He argues that there is 'a danger of ignoring the problematic reality of biological limitation' (ibid.:40). Analyses of disability and abnormality must, according to Shakespeare, take seriously the experiential realities of 'impaired bodies' (ibid.:54).

We argue that impairment is relevant to the field of Disability Studies but, we would suggest, not in the way that Shakespeare and others (Shakespeare and Watson, 2001; Shakespeare, 2006) have presented it. They suggest that 'real' bodies exist independently of culture, and it is this point that we want to challenge. Our view is that it is not possible to talk about, or experience, the body outside of culture. We dispute the views of Shakespeare and others about the 'givenness' or 'already there' nature of a body. Following Braidotti (2003), for us the body is neither a biological nor a sociological category, but an interface, a threshold, a field of intersecting material and symbolic forces; a surface on which multiple codes (sex, class, age, race, etc.) are written (Goodley and Runswick-Cole, 2012b). Simply, bodies cannot exist outside of culture, and therefore they reveal much about deeply held cultural discourses around disability (ibid.). We argue that when Shakespeare (2006) suggests that impairment *is* tragic and *is* a predicament, he cannot do so in a vacuum; those judgements have been made in a cultural, social and political context. In order to explain this point further, we offer some examples.

A few thoughts on faeces

> Sorry to bring this up but last summer it was horrendous and that's all because he [son labelled with autism] wouldn't have a poo at school.... I hate it, it's just like, poo up the carpet, the walls, on the fingers on toes, it's just horrible for anybody to have to deal with that and you're having to carry him upstairs and constantly asking 'have you had a poo, do you need a poo? Do you need a poo poo or do you need a wee wee?' You know, because I don't want him to do it in his pants!
>
> (Angela, mother of a disabled child cited in Goodley and Runswick-Cole,
> 2012b:14)

Angela's story is a story about faeces; it is, as she says, 'horrendous' and 'horrible'. It is uncomfortable to read, as it must have been to tell (Runswick-Cole, 2011b). While Disability Studies stands accused of having little to say about bodies, it has, perhaps, even less to say about leaky bodies (Ogden, 2013). Reeve (2010) describes the absence of analyses of leaky bodies as a form of ableism within Disability Studies itself. There is, then, a need for Disability Studies to engage with faeces, but as well as being about faeces, this story is also about a host of cultural values. Embedded within this brief account are assumptions about the age at which a 'normal' child should be in control of his bowels and a 'good enough' mother should have taught her child to poo in the loo. The story about faeces is situated in its cultural context and set against a backdrop of expectations of 'good' mothering and typical development in global North countries, as well as being framed by (in this brief account hidden) 'variables' such as race, class, socio-economic status and access to support services. As this story reveals, it is impossible to talk about the body outside of the wider cultural context (Runswick-Cole, 2012b) – poo isn't just poo – and this further suggests that Angela cannot experience her son's poo without also being within, and feeling the force of, those cultural expectations. Perhaps the story is 'horrendous' and 'horrible' not because of the 'reality' of poo but because specific cultural standards have not been upheld and, therefore, shame, guilt and embarrassment have been invoked.

For philosopher and historian Michel Foucault (1980), such expectations of what bodies should and should not do are instances of 'disciplinary power'. For Foucault, power is not located in the hands a few elite individuals (e.g. the monarchy or prime ministers) and exercised upon the majority (e.g. subjects or citizens) through propaganda or ideology. Instead, power is *productive*: its effects are produced through interactions which are often daily and mundane. As Crossley (2004:24) states, 'What matters, Foucault argues, is not what people think but how they behave habitually, and how the prerequisites of liberal order become engrained in their habits' – prerequisites such as knowing where to, and where not to, poo. Benson (1997:129) agrees, pointing out that 'our physical bodies are always, everywhere, social bodies'. Using the work of Marcel Mauss, Benson states that 'all those activities which we think of as "natural" – walking, swimming, sitting or squatting, eating, sleeping, having sex or giving birth – are in fact acquired techniques' (ibid.:129) – acquired, Foucault would argue, through technologies of power such as schools, teachers, prisons, doctors, even families. We are encouraged to acquire these techniques in order to avoid shame, guilt and embarrassment.

Debating Point: Our bodies are sites of control?
Take a few moments to consider who and what has control over your body. Do you have a say in everything that happens to your body? Are you in complete control of what you think of your own body? Do any external forces exercise power over your body? Do you ever feel pressure to think or feel things about your own body? Are there things you do *only* to avoid embarrassment? Think about the influences of education, family, medicine and celebrity culture.

For us, the need to pay attention to how contexts create 'naturalness' is all the more important in moments when 'facts' are involved. It may be easier to accept that poo has a myriad of cultural values attached to it than it is to think of impairment categories, such as dyslexia or Down syndrome, as also being constituted through social and cultural meanings.

A few thoughts on facts

Over the past few decades, our genetic DNA has replaced blood and hereditary lines as an explanation and a root cause for the apparent differences between us such as race, gender and impairment. But even these seemingly most basic of 'facts' cannot be considered to be devoid of social and cultural construction.

Davis (2002b:14) discusses how 'so far no one has been able to identify a person as belonging to a specific "race" through DNA analysis' and how this raises questions when we are told that 'various "races" and ethnic groups have differing genetic markers for disability, defect, and disease' (ibid.:15). Davis (ibid.:14) argues that rather than *discovering* pre-existing categories, since the mid-nineteenth century science and medicine have established and given legitimacy to categories of 'difference' through the circulation of 'medicalized, scientificized discourses'.

Contradictions and discrepancies such as this one are not new to the age of genetics. Homosexuality, for instance, was considered a legitimate psychiatric diagnosis, with 'treatments' being administered to those 'suffering' from the condition (Sherry, 2004). In the global North, this categorisation of homosexuality has widely been discarded, although, as Sherry (ibid.) is at pains to point out, the idea that homosexuality can be treated (or even cured) remains in circulation. The same can be said of hysteria, sometimes called 'feminine distress', which in the late nineteenth century was attributed to physiological and psychological weaknesses in women (Benson, 1997).

In relation to the establishment and legitimatisation of a specific impairment category, Davis (2008) charts the establishment of obsessive compulsive disorder (OCD), while Bumiller (2009:875) charts the 'dramatic change in the social construction of autism from a psychiatric disorder to a genetic disease'. Compared with Timimi *et al.* (2011:63), who do argue that 'the "evidence" for autism and its spectrum having a strong biological and genetic basis [...] is no more than vapid rhetoric', Bumiller (2009) is less interested in discrediting the science. Instead, along with Melendro-Oliver (2004) and Nadesan (2005), Bumiller (2009) is interested in the process of 'geneticisation': the ways in which 'discoveries' of 'new' genetic truths are encouraged, accepted, funded and used in activism. She sees it as part of moves within wider social and political spheres to extend the reach and influence of science as a source for both explanation and resolution of the 'problem' of autism. In doing so, she too is arguing that the meanings of scientific 'facts' and scientific 'progress' are mediated through specific contexts, opening up some spaces and closing others down. For instance, despite 'little professional and public acknowledgement that [neurobehavioural disorders like autism] are far more complicated than originally conceived by molecular geneticists' (ibid.:891), genetic autism discourses remain extremely powerful and largely unchallenged.

So far, we have suggested that the meanings of bodily processes and scientific facts cannot be divorced from their contexts. However, both of these could be considered as somewhat external to the body, or, in other words, as meanings that could be stripped away to reveal a 'real' body beneath. We finish this chapter by trying to address this and asking whether pain, something often considered as being fundamental to our individual experience of our own bodies, can also be considered to be socially and culturally mediated.

Section 6: Experiencing pain

When discussing the 'reality' of impairment, pain is often raised as an experience that cannot be theorised away as socially or culturally constructed. It is argued that the body feels pain, that it is unpleasant and signals that the person experiencing it should stop what they are doing (e.g. remove their hand from a flame) or should seek medical attention as it may be a sign of internal breakdown, blockage or damage (e.g. a heart attack). During discussions over whether being disabled can be a positive experience, impairments and illnesses that are associated with long-term (chronic) pain are often mentioned as a reason why being impaired should, sometimes, be considered to be undesirable.

Debating Point: All pain is bad?
Take a few moments to stop and think about our common understanding of pain as unquestioningly bad. Is it always bad? Is all pain the same? Is all pain equal? Is all pain to be avoided? Is any pain pleasurable?

Following sociologists and anthropologists who have theorised 'pain', and just as we have been arguing in relation to impairment, we contend that the meaning of pain is bound up with historical, spatial and cultural contexts, so much so that one cannot talk about, or even experience, pain without its meaning being constructed through those contexts. Pain is, indeed, 'a small word with many implications' (Morris, 1989:175), and we argue here that depending on the 'pain' discourses available to you in your context, you will *experience* pain in different ways. In this section, we will explore this geographically, historically and culturally.

Geographically – is all pain the same?

Honkasalo (1998:37) suggests that 'pain as an embodied experience is constituted in the knots of existential, social and cultural structures, as well as bodily processes' and shows how by paying attention to the language of pain, we can better understand how Western medical practices (such as administering 'painkillers') work to shape the meanings of what she calls 'Western pain'. By carrying out an ethnographic study in a pain clinic in Finland, which included talking to patients, Honkasalo demonstrates how pain is located in certain places, '*here* instead of *there*' (ibid.:43), how pain physically restricts and emotionally isolates the person experiencing it, how pain is positioned as an external force that has intruded across bodily boundaries and must be removed, and how pain is talked to, argued and reasoned with as if it has its own agenda and could, if it wished, leave at any time. In contemporary Western societies, all of these ways are culturally available when one talks about and, crucially, when one experiences pain.

Differences are not always found across continents: the meaning of pain can also differ in difference places. For examples, in contrast to Honkasalo's (1998) study, Bridel (2010, 2013) explores how participants in Ironman Triathlons talk about negotiating 'positive' and 'negative' kinds of pain during a race, suggesting that pain experienced in a medicalised setting may be different – be experienced and talked about differently – from pain felt in a sporting event.

It is important to reiterate that by arguing that how pain is experienced can depend on *where* you are, we are not arguing that people with different nationalities inherently have different pain thresholds. This would be reducing the argument once more to *essential* biological differences and, as Trnka (2006) argues in her study of state-funded clinics in Fiji, even apparent biological differences can be culturally explained. Trnka (ibid.) explores the processes that lead to some patients being labelled as 'complaining of, but not actually experiencing, physical pain'. Noticing that they were often Indo-Fijian women, she suggests that the category of 'unreal' pain used by the medical professionals is constructed through a complex web of cultural meanings related to gender, nationality as well as occupation. Trnka (ibid.) points to an interesting conclusion: that for the Fijian physicians, not all pain is the same; some pain was more worthy of attention and, therefore, more worthy of treatment.

Historically – is all pain equal?

Other research points to the idea that although pain may be universal, it is not universally a problem. Illich (1976 cited in Bendelow and Williams, 1995:152) suggests that in traditional cultures, 'pain was recognised as an inevitable part of the subjective reality of one's own body' and was not considered a 'problem'. In contrast, as industrial Western society grew and medical technology such as anaesthesia advanced, Illich (1976 cited in Bendelow and Williams, 1995) argues that individuals lose awareness of self and are more likely to find pain distressing. In other words, when there is technology for, and an expectation of, pain relief, individuals are more likely to articulate a need for pain relief.

It is also worth remembering that the experience of pain can alter over time and space. In an interesting study, Johansen (2002) spoke to Somali women who had left Africa as refugees and were now living in Norway about the practice and the pain of female genital mutilation. In their Somali surroundings, as Johansen (ibid.:312–313) describes, 'female circumcision, although overwhelmingly painful, is regarded as intrinsic to women's lives, as part of being a woman, of growing up'. It is argued that while the immediate experience of pain may not be affected by culture, perceptions of that pain are. In Somalia, the experience changed with maturity, time and healing to become 'a necessary experience, since it accompanies or accomplishes the transformation of the child to the woman' (ibid.:331). However, living in exile apart from many of their wider family and community members and 'in a society and culture that both morally and legally condemn the operation' (ibid.:313), the women had started to reflect, voice and confront their experiences, leading to shifts in their perception of that pain. Johansen's study sought to 'analyse pain as a complex web of physical, cultural/symbolic, and personal/emotional experiences' (ibid.:313) and demonstrates that cultural meanings influence our memories of pain as well as our experiences.

Culturally – is all pain avoided?

The avoidance of pain is often considered to be a given. However, acts of body modification, such as piercings and tattoos, involve choosing to experience pain. In the global North, such acts were once considered to be counter-cultural and the preserve of those who wanted actively to resist the norms of (Western) society, but, as Pitts (1998) highlights, some such practices have been absorbed into mainstream Western culture, and this shift is another indication that pain is not always something which is avoided. Bikini-line waxes and Botox injections are other examples where pain is suffered willingly.

Pitts (1998:71) also highlights the *reclaimative* nature of some such acts and extends her discussion to the (far less mainstream) practice of scarification, in this case by women who wish to reclaim their bodies by engaging in 'planned, self-directed rituals aimed at achieving a transformation of the self's relation to the body in response to a specific situation of bodily oppression'. She offers the narratives of six women who use body modification to rewrite themselves, using painful processes such as marking, cutting and bleeding to reclaim their bodies from previous painful experiences. Pain here is experienced as escape, recuperation and renewal.

Culturally – is any pain pleasurable?

The idea that some pain is pleasurable is hard to comprehend, but sadomasochism (S/M) presents a particularly significant challenge to the idea that all pain is bad. It has been usefully defined by Wiseman (cited in Bauer, 2005 as cited in Kolářová, 2010:51) as 'the use of psychological dominance and submission, and/or physical bondage, and/or pain, and/or related practices in a safe, legal, consensual manner in order for the participants to experience erotic arousal and/or personal growth'. The use of pain for sexual pleasure takes the argument one step further. In the previous discussions, pain could still be considered as being 'suffered through' even though it was invited and consented to. Here, though, pain is the means and the end of the pleasure.

Katerina Kolářová (2010) explores one example of pain as pleasure being used to redefine disability. She examines the work of performance artist Bob Flanagan and his partner Sheree Rose. Often dubbed the pain artist, Bob Flanagan lived with cystic fibrosis (CF) and enjoyed S/M, using it in his performances to resignify pain. In Chapter 4, we introduced the idea of *transgressive resignification*, where meanings are turned inside out and challenged in order to rewrite them. Kolářová (2010) outlines how Flanagan's best-known and biggest installation, *Visiting Hours*, sought to transgress norms such as sick (disabled) bodies being exhibited, rather than kept in private, and expectations that would position sick (disabled) people as desiring relief and cure. She further suggests that Flanagan's work highlights that 'pain is not located solely in/on the individual body, but, in contrast involves interaction between those who are *in* pain and those who are *out* of pain' (ibid.:46). Again we are returned to pain's being situational and contextual as well as embodied: pain as a 'body in situation' rather than a situation of the body' (ibid.:50).

If this is so, it also opens up possibilities of rethinking pain and, therefore, of inventing, and making available, alternative 'pain discourses'. In 1984, Hilbert (cited in Bendelow and Williams, 1995:154) suggested that 'the main problem for those with chronic pain is that they are bereft of adequate cultural resources for organising their experience'. Taking seriously the assertion that bodies are far more than biology allows us to radically attend to the productive possibilities of alternative ways of being, not only in relation to pain but also in relation to the reminders of pain (and often medical intervention) such as wounds and scars. Kuppers (2007) explores how (disabled) visual and performance artists are seeking to explore and resignify scars, and through this, reimagine bodies and their relationship with medical practices.

Conclusion

The importance of discussion of the body in Disability Studies is that it reveals the ways in which bodies are shaped by and, indeed, shape the socio-cultural contexts in which they are to be found; they are bodies-in-the-world (Goodley and Runswick-Cole, 2012b). The particular significance for us is that by insisting that social and cultural contexts are relevant, we are refusing to allow 'bodies' to be returned to the realm of medical knowledge.

Suggestions for Wider Reading

Goodley, D. and Runswick-Cole, K. (2012) 'The body as disability and possability: Theorising the "leaking, lacking and excessive" bodies of disabled children', *Scandinavian Journal of Disability Research*, 15, 1, 1–19.

Hughes, B. (2009) 'Disability activisms: Social model stalwarts and biological citizens', *Disability and Society*, 24, 6, pp. 677–688.

Mallett, R. and Runswick-Cole, K. (2012) 'Commodifying autism: The cultural contexts of "disability" in the academy', in Goodley, D., Hughes, B. and Davis, L. J. (eds) *Disability and Social Theory: New Developments and Directions*, Basingstoke: Palgrave Macmillan, pp. 33–51.

Part IV

Conclusion and future directions

Chapter 9

Conclusion

Final thoughts and future directions

Introduction

In this final chapter, we reflect on our journey through critical approaches, issues and perspectives in Disability Studies and use this process of reflection to look towards future developments. We start at the very beginning, with the book's front cover.

During the course of writing this book, an event happened which shocked and angered us both. A few months later, we were involved in organising the fourth annual Theorizing Normalcy and the Mundane conference. We chose to acknowledge this tragic event within the conference programme and at the conference launch as follows:

> We are dedicating this conference to the memory of 'LB', bus fanatic, ticket collector, and much loved dude. 'LB' died on 4th July 2013 in a hospital bath – alone. In remembering 'LB', we hope that all the Normalcy conference delegates will play their part in exposing and rejecting the mundane disablism that has such catastrophic consequences for the lives of disabled people and their families.
> (Dedication – Theorizing Normalcy and the Mundane conference, 2013)

The front cover of this book uses one of LB's artworks, called *Colour*. We are extremely honoured that his family gave us permission to use this dynamic and joyful piece of art here and we do so as a way to pay tribute to a life that was cut short too soon. We also consider LB's story to be an important reminder of the reasons why Disability Studies matters. The chapters in this book discuss lived experiences, often within the realm of theoretical concepts. However, we do not intend that these discussions remain, exclusively, within such a realm. When matters of life and death are at stake, we must always remember that how we choose to *approach* impairment and disability always has significant consequences for the lives of disabled people and their families. Our aim in this book has been to offer approaches to impairment and disability which are sensitive to these consequences and which can be useful in the process of creating societies in which all disabled children and adults are cared *about*, cherished and valued.

Disability: present and possible futures

Bearing in mind all that we have said above, we turn now to a recap of the book as a springboard for considering the avenues Disability Studies may wander down in the near future.

Approaching disability

In Chapter 1, we described Disability Studies' development and its link to activism in the United Kingdom. The social model of disability has emerged as the 'big idea' (Hasler, 1993) in Disability Studies, dominating much of the discussion and, indeed, the research in the field of disability, as well as influencing both policy and practice agendas. However, we also saw that the social model has been challenged in a number of ways, and we returned to these challenges as we progressed through the book.

In the light of Chapter 1, Chapter 2 provided an important and timely reminder that Disability Studies is not just a UK-centric discipline, nor indeed solely located in the global North. By considering an overview of Disability Studies in different cultural locations, we also explored how Disability Studies is often carried out in transdisciplinary spaces. As we noted in Chapter 1, the emergence of Critical Disability Studies suggests that Disability Studies will continue to occupy the 'spaces between' disciplines and approaches.

One of the most exciting areas of current work is that around 'ableism' (Goodley, 2014). An important aspect of this work, for us, is that it contends that '[w]e all live and breathe ableist logic' (Campbell, 2012:212). In this way, the concept is not interested in blaming (able-bodied) 'individuals'; rather, it focuses on *ableist* systems and practices we are *all* implicated within. Collective responsibility for changing the lives of those deemed to be 'impaired' sidesteps the 'them'/'us' divide and fosters practices that are nearer another concept introduced in Chapter 2, the idea of *ubuntu* – interconnectedness.

Critical perspectives

In Chapter 3, we explored disabled childhoods in relation to the 'new sociology of childhood' and developmental psychology. These discussions revealed that the 'tyranny of the norm' (Walkerdine, 1993) overshadows the lives of disabled children and their families. This led us to consider future directions for constructing children and childhoods that move away from approaches premised on assumptions of 'norms' and 'ableism'. We pondered on how, in the future, disabled childhoods could be reconstructed in ways that recognise and value their potential.

In Chapter 4, we offered a range of ways in which cultural representations of disability, impairment and disabled people could be analysed. We argued that *how* we choose to analyse (i.e. which methods to use) is an important decision. By providing detailed guidance on how to break down (deconstruct) a cultural text, we hoped to enable you to make informed decisions on which approaches to use and, therefore, what sort of analysis will follow. We also argued for the importance of cultural perspectives and suggested that Cultural Disability Studies offers an accessible way of researching disability issues.

If *how* we choose to analyse directly affects *what* the resulting analysis will be like, and remembering, as we mentioned in Chapter 1, that our language choices have material impact upon the lives we all lead (Titchkosky, 2001), then *how* we analyse is highlighted as an important moment of decision in all areas of Disability Studies. In the light of our reminder at the start of this conclusion – that how we choose to *approach* impairment and disability always has significant consequences for the lives of disabled people and their families – it is worth dwelling on this point for a moment longer.

Following Titchkosky's (2008) call to watch our watchings and read our readings, Goodley and Runswick-Cole (2012c:57) have offered four 'readings' of Rosie (a disabled girl with whom they have worked) in an attempt 'to challenge grand, overarching, totalising narratives' of disabled children within which 'quirky quality, creative and personhoods of disabled children are merely understood as signs, symptoms and signifiers of pathology' (ibid.:64). Juxtaposing readings that use the autism canon, an orthodox social model approach to disability, the Nordic relational model of disability and a socio-cultural lens, they offer another important demonstration that *how* we choose to read matters. In their conclusion, Goodley and Runswick-Cole (ibid.:64) directly address the reader, as follows:

> [w]e end the paper by asking you, the reader, about your relationship with knowledge, children and disability: How do you read disability and children? When do your readings of disability and children stifle or enable? At what moments do we use and refuse our varied readings?

Acknowledging the relationship between *how* we analyse and the results of our analysis highlights once more the ethical and political dimensions of Disability Studies and of doing disability research. In Chapter 4, we made this point in relation to Cultural Disability Studies, but here we argue that it should be considered by everyone.

In Chapter 5, we moved from cultural to historical perspectives and examined the changing conceptions of disability over time. We examined the importance of this area of study and considered some of the barriers to researching 'disability' from a historical perspective. We also argued that studying the *contexts* of events enables us to better understand *how* people with impairments have been on the receiving end of oppression, exploitation and genocide, and that this provides opportunities to better understand our contemporary society. Kudlick (2003:764) has suggested that disability history

> helps historians ask and attempt to answer the overarching questions central to our mission as scholars and teachers in the humanistic disciplines: what does it mean to be human? How can we respond ethically to difference? What is the value of a human life? Who decides these questions, and what do the answers reveal?

For us, the potentials of the cultural and historical study of disability, stemming from the humanities, have not yet been fully realised and we expect these to be a burgeoning area of interest over the coming decades.

Chapter 6 set out the important role that disability politics has played in the lives of disabled people. It focused on the intersections between disability and other identity categories, as well as unpacking the concept of 'identity' itself.

While the sense of belonging and mutual support have been immensely important, the complexities and limitations of identity politics are all too obvious. This led us to consider the possibilities of moving beyond the (paradoxical) 'collective' calls for equality, independence and autonomy for 'individuals' and towards a politics that recognises the connections between people and their *interdependencies* as positive and productive relationships in their lives. Challenges for the future organisation of society include the possibility of placing the 'dismodern' subject (Davis, 2002b) at the centre and/or a 'politics of imperceptibility' in order to enable 'a fuller life expressed through the vitality of disability' (Overboe, 2012:113). The questioning of what it means to be 'human' is also an area we expect to be developed in coming years.

Critical issues

In Chapter 7, we returned to the lives of disabled children and explored their experiences of exclusion in education, in access to play and creativity, and, indeed, in research. In this chapter, the future possibilities of working with disabled children and their families in research were considered, but the challenge remains in listening to disabled children in ways that are meaningful to them and in giving them a say in the way they live.

Chapter 8 returned to the highly contested nature of the place of the body in Disability Studies. Arguments continue about the 'real' and 'constructed' nature of the body and how Disability Studies should respond to the issue of impairment and impairment effects. We debated these issues in relation to faeces and pain, but while we refuse to allow bodies to be returned to the realm of medical knowledge, we recognise that this debate has not been resolved.

This is an interesting point at which to pause and highlight again the importance of interdisciplinary work. An area we suggest could be particularly important is the *historical* analysis of impairment categories. Discussing psychological categories in particular, Geoff Bunn (2011:146) argues that a 'historical approach to psychological categories is necessary precisely because its categories are not empirical discoveries; they are historical constructs that have effects (Smith, 2005)'. Some work has already been done, for instance by Nadesan (2005) and Timimi *et al.* (2011) on autism, and Davis (2008) on obsessive compulsive disorder (OCD).

The benefits of bringing knowledge and methods of inquiry from history, the philosophy of ideas (through Foucault), psychology and critical psychiatry, cultural studies and sociology all to bear on 'impairment' in order to examine how entities which are often taken 'to have a solid biological foundation – a "natural kind"' (Bunn, 2011:145) can be understood as social, cultural, historical and political products is an exciting future direction. This is certainly an area of debate that will run and run.

Finally...

> There is something liberating about being able to say in a tutorial: 'I don't know; but this is how I would begin to think about it, how I would set out the issues, pose questions.'
>
> (Game and Metcalfe 1996:156)

In the Preface to this book, we suggested that approaching Disability Studies can be challenging or even daunting as long-held beliefs are challenged, reconsidered, replaced or, perhaps, reaffirmed. We hope, however, that this book will in some small way have brought wider dimensions to your thinking, to your advocacy and/or to your practice. As Game and Metcalfe (1996) suggest above, the most important thing is to begin.

References

Abbott, D. (2013) 'Who says what, where, why and how? Doing real world research with disabled children, young people and family members', in Curran, T. and Runswick-Cole, K. (eds) *Disabled Children's Childhood Studies: Critical Issues in a Global Context*, London: Palgrave Macmillan, pp. 39–56.

Adams, R. (1996) 'An American tail: Freaks, gender, and the incorporation of history in Katherine Dunn's *Geek Love*', in Thomson, R. G. (ed.) *Freakery: Cultural Spectacles of the Extraordinary Body*, New York: New York University Press, pp. 277–290.

Adelman, K. A. and Adelman, H. S. (1987) 'Rodin, Patton, Edison, Wilson, Einstein: Were they really learning disabled?', *Journal of Learning Disabilities*, 20, pp. 270–278.

Albrecht, G., Seelman, K. D. and Bury, M. (2001) 'Introduction: The formation of Disability Studies', in Albrecht, G., Seelman, K. D. and Bury, M. (eds) *Handbook of Disability Studies*, London: Sage, pp. 1–10.

Allan, J. (2012) 'Failing to make progress? The aporias of responsible inclusion', paper presented at Difference in Policy and Politics, Seminar Series in Education, 2011–2012, Education and Social Research Institute, Manchester Metropolitan University, 7 March.

Alleyne, R. (2010) 'Brain scan could diagnose autism early', *Daily Telegraph*, 8 January. Online at: www.telegraph.co.uk/health/healthnews/6951699/Brain-scan-could-diagnose-autism-early.html [accessed 2 December 2013].

Ariès, P. (1962) *Centuries of Childhood*, London: Cape.

Aubrecht, K. (2012) 'Disability Studies and the language of mental illness', *Review of Disability Studies: An International Journal*, 8, 2, pp. 31–44.

Auslander, G. K. and Gold, N. (1999) 'Disability terminology in the media: A comparison of newspaper reports in Canada and Israel', *Social Science and Medicine*, 48, 10, pp. 1395–1405.

Autreat (2012) What *is* Autreat? Online at: www.autreat.com/autreat.html#INTRO [accessed 15 December 2013].

Baffoe, M. (2013) 'Stigma, discrimination and marginalization: Gateways to oppression of persons with disabilities in Ghana, West Africa', *Journal of Educational and Social Research*, 3, 1, pp. 187–198.

Baker, B. (2002) 'The hunt for disability: Eugenics and the normalization of school children', *Teachers College Record*, 104, 4, pp. 663–703.

Baker, D. L. (2011) *The Politics of Neurodiversity: Why Public Policy Matters*, Boulder, CO: Lynne Rienner.

Barker, C. (2010) 'Interdisciplinary dialogues: Disability and Postcolonial Studies', *Review of Disability Studies*, 66, 3, pp. 15–34.

Barnes, C. (1991) *Disabled People in Britain and Discrimination: A Case for Anti-discrimination Legislation*, London: Hurst/BCODP.

Barnes, C. (1992) *Disabling Imagery and the Media: An Exploration of the Principles for Media Representations of Disabled People*, Halifax, UK: BCODP/Ryburn Publishing.

Barnes, C. (1998) 'The social model of disability: A sociological phenomenon ignored by sociologists', in Shakespeare, T. (ed.) *The Disability Reader: Social Science Perspectives*, London: Continuum, pp. 65–78.

Barnes, C. (2003) 'What a difference a decade makes: Reflections on doing emancipatory disability research', *Disability and Society*, 18, 1, pp. 3–17.

Barnes, C. (2008) 'Disability and the academy: A British perspective'. Online at: http://disability-studies.leeds.ac.uk/files/library/Barnes-paris-presentation.pdf [accessed 1 December 2011].

Barnes, C. (2009) 'Disability in a majority world context: A materialist account', paper presented at the Disability and Economy Conference, Manchester Metropolitan University, 29–30 April. Online at: www.leeds.ac.uk/disability-studies/archiveuk/Barnes/majority%20world%202.pdf [accessed 29 November 2010].

Barnes, C. and Mercer, G. (2001a) 'The politics of disability and the struggle for change', in Barton, L. (ed.) *Disability, Politics and the Struggle for Change*, London: David Fulton, pp. 11–23.

Barnes, C. and Mercer, G. (2001b) 'Disability culture: Assimilation or inclusion?', in Albrecht, G. L., Seelman, K. D. and Bury, M. (eds) *Handbook of Disability Studies*, Thousand Oaks, CA: Sage, pp. 515–534.

Barnes, C. and Mercer, G. (2003) *Disability*, Cambridge: Polity Press.

Barton, L. (ed.) (1997) *The Politics of Special Educational Needs*, Lewes: Falmer.

Barton, L. (2001) 'Disability, struggle and the politics of hope', in Barton, L. (ed.) *Disability, Politics and the Struggle for Change*, London: David Fulton, pp. 1–10.

Bashir, N., Ahmed, N., Singh, A., Tang, Y. Z., Young, M., Abba, A. and Sampson, E. L. (2004) 'A precious case from Middle Earth', *British Medical Journal*, 329, pp. 1435–1436.

BBC (2009) *Robert Winston's Musical Analysis* [radio programme, Radio 4].

Beauty and the Beast [film] (1991) Directed by Gary Trousdale and Kirk Wise.

Bell, C. (2006) 'Introducing White Disability Studies: A modest proposal', in Davis, L. J. (ed.) *The Disability Studies Reader*, New York: Routledge, pp. 275–282.

Bendelow, G. A. and Williams, S. J. (1995) 'Transcending the dualisms: Towards a sociology of pain', *Sociology of Health and Illness*, 17, 2, pp. 139–165.

Benjamin, S. (2006) 'From "idiot child" to "mental defective": Schooling and the production of intellectual disabilities in the UK 1850–1944', *Educate*, 1, 1, pp. 23–44.

Benson, S. (1997) 'The body, health and eating disorders', in Woodward, K. (ed.) *Identity and Difference*, London: Sage/Open University Press, pp. 121–182.

Beresford, B. (1994) *Positively Parents: Caring for a Severely Disabled Child*, London: HMSO.

Beresford, P., Nettle, M. and Perring, R. (2010) *Towards a Social Model of Madness and Distress? What Service Users Say*, York: Joseph Rowntree Foundation.

Berghs, M. (2010) 'Coming to terms with inequality and exploitation in an African state: Researching disability in Sierra Leone', *Disability and Society*, 25, 7, pp. 861–865.

Bérubé, M. (2005) 'Disability and narrative', *PMLA: Publications of the Modern Language Assocation of America*, 120, 2, pp. 568–576.

Bettleheim, B. (1967) *The Empty Fortress: Infantile Autism and the Birth of the Self*, New York: Free Press.

Bewick, M. (2005) 'Smile, you're on TV', *Lifestyle*, 48, pp. 28–33.

Bhaskar, R. (1979) *The Possibility of Naturalism: A Philosophical Critique of the Contemporary Human Sciences*, London: Harvester Press.

Biklen, D. (1987) 'Framed: Print journalism's treatment of disability issues', in Gartner, A. and Joe, T. (eds) *Images of the Disabled, Disabling Images*, New York: Praeger, pp. 79–98.

Birmingham, E. (2000) 'Fearing the freak: How talk TV articulates women and class', *Journal of Popular Film and Television*, 28, 3, pp. 133–139.

Bjarneson, D. (2010) *Social Policy and Social Capital: Parents and Exceptionality 1974–2007*, New York: Nova Science Publishers.

Bogdan, R. (1988) *Freak Show: Presenting Human Oddities for Amusement and Profit*, Chicago: University of Chicago Press.

Bogdan, R. (1996) [1991] 'The social construction of freaks', in Thomson, R. G. (ed.) *Freakery: Cultural Spectacles of the Extraordinary Body*, New York: New York University Press, pp. 23–37.

Booth, T. and Booth, W. (1993) 'Parenting with learning difficulties: Lessons for practitioners', *British Journal of Social Work*, 23, 5, pp. 459–480.

Booth, T. and Booth, W. (1998) *Growing Up with Parents Who Have Learning Difficulties*, London: Routledge.

Booth, T. and Booth, W. (1999) 'Parents together: Action research and advocacy support for parents with learning difficulties', *Health and Social Care in the Community*, 7, 6, pp. 464–474.

Borsay, A. (2002) 'History, power and identity', in Barnes, C., Oliver, M. and Barton, L. (eds) *Disability Studies Today*, Cambridge: Polity Press, pp. 98–119.

Borsay, A. (2005) *Disability and Social Policy in Britain since 1750: A History of Exclusion*, Basingstoke: Palgrave Macmillan.

Bowler, E. and Rose, D. (2004) 'A Q and A on the notorious DAN: The UK's direct action activist group', *OUCH* news bulletin, 8 March. Online at: www.bbc.co.uk/ouch/news/btn/danqa.shtml [accessed 6 December 2005].

Boydon, J. (1990) 'Childhood and the policy makers: Comparative perspectives on the globalisation of childhood', in James, A. and Prout, A. (eds) *Constructing and Reconstructing Childhood: Contemporary Issues in the Sociological Study of Childhood*, Basingstoke: Falmer Press, pp. 187–210.

Braddock, D. L. and Parish, S. L. (2001) 'An institutional history of disability', in Albrecht, G. L., Seelman, K. D. and Bury, M. (eds) *Handbook of Disability Studies*, Thousand Oaks, CA: Sage, pp. 11–68.

Braidotti, R. (2003) 'Becoming woman: Or sexual difference revisited', *Theory, Culture and Society*, 20, 3, pp. 43–64.

Branfield, F. (1998) 'What are you doing here? Non-disabled people and the disability movement: A response to Robert F. Drake', *Disability and Society*, 13, 1, pp. 143–144.

Branfield, F. (1999) 'The disability movement: A movement of disabled people: A response to Paul S. Duckett', *Disability and Society*, 14, 3, pp. 399–403.

Bredberg, E. (1999) 'Writing disability history: Problems, perspectives and sources', *Disability and Society*, 14, 2, pp. 189–201.

Briant, E., Watson, N. and Philo, G. (2011) *Bad News for Disabled People: How the Newspapers Are Reporting Disability*, Project Report, Strathclyde Centre for Disability Research and Glasgow Media Unit, University of Glasgow.

Bridel, W. F. (2010) '"Finish … whatever it takes": Exploring pain and pleasure in the Ironman Triathlon: A socio-cultural analysis', unpublished PhD thesis, Queen's University Belfast, Kingston, ON.

Bridel, W. (2013) 'Not fat, not skinny, functional enough to finish: Interrogating constructions of health in the Ironman Triathlon', *Leisure/Loisir*, 37, 1, pp. 37–56.

Brolan, C. E., van Dooren, K., Taylor Gomez, M., Fitzgerald, L., Ware, R. S. and Lennox, N. G. (2013) '*Suranho* healing: Filipino concepts of intellectual disability and treatment choices in Negros Occidental', *Disability and Society*, 29, 1, pp. 71–85.

Broome, R. (1999) 'Windows on other worlds: The rise and fall of Sideshow Alley', *Australian Historical Studies*, 29, 112, pp. 1–22.

Broome, R. (2009) 'Not strictly business: Freaks and the Australian showground world', *Australian Historical Studies*, 40, 3, pp. 323–342.

Browne, J. and Messenger, S. (2003) 'Victorian spectacle: Julia Pastrana, the bearded and hairy female', *Endeavour*, 27, 4, pp. 155–159.

Bruce, E. and Schulz, C. (2002) 'Non-finite loss and challenges to communication between parents and professional', *British Journal of Special Education*, 29, 1, pp. 9–13.

BSC (Broadcasting Standards Council) (1997) 'The disabled audience: A television survey', in Pointon, A. and Davies, C. (eds) *Framed: Interrogating Disability in the Media*, London: British Film Institute/Arts Council of England, pp. 193–205.

Buckingham, J. (2011) 'Writing histories of disability in India: Strategies of inclusion', *Disability and Society*, 26, 4, pp. 419–431.

Bumiller, K. (2009) 'The geneticization of autism: From new reproductive technologies to the conception of genetic normalcy', *Signs*, 34, 4, pp. 875–899.

Bunn, G. (2011) 'Historical analyses', in Banister, P., Bunn, G., Burman, E., Daniels, J., Duckett, P., Goodley, D., Lawthom, R., Parker, I., Runswick-Cole, K., Sixsmith, J., Smailes, S., Tindall, C. and Whelan, P. (2012) *Qualitative Methods in Psychology: A Research Guide*, 2nd edn, Maidenhead: Open University Press/McGraw-Hill Education, pp. 143–162.

Burch, S. and Sutherland, I. (2006) 'Who's not yet here? American disability history', *Radical History Review*, 94, pp. 127–147.

Burleigh, M. (2000) *The Third Reich: A New History*, London: Pan Books.

Burleigh, M. and Wippermann, W. (1991) *The Racial State: Germany 1933–1945*, Cambridge: Cambridge University Press.

Burman, E. (2001) 'Beyond the baby and the bathwater: Postdualistic developmental psychologies for diverse childhoods', *European Early Childhood Education Research Journal*, 9, 1, pp. 5–22.

Burman, E. (2008) *Deconstructing Developmental Psychology*, London: Routledge.

Burman, E. (2010) 'Beyond "emotional literacy" in feminist and educational research', *British Educational Research Journal*, 35, 1, pp. 137–155.

Burman, E. and Parker, I. (1993) 'Introduction: Discourse analysis and the turn to text', in Burman, E. and Parker, I. (eds) *Discourse Analytic Research: Repertoires and Readings of Texts in Action*, London: Routledge, pp. 1–17.

Burton, G., Sayrafi, I. and Srour, S. A. (2013) 'Inclusion or transformation? An early assessment of an empowerment project for disabled people in occupied Palestine', *Disability and Society*, 28, 6, pp. 812–825.

Bury, M. (1997) *Health and Illness in a Changing Society*, London: Routledge.

Butler, J. (1990) *Gender Trouble*, London: Routledge.

Butler, J. (1993) *Bodies That Matter: On the Discursive Limits of 'Sex'*, London: Routledge.

Butler, P. (2012) 'How the Spartacus welfare cuts campaign went viral', *The Guardian* (London), 17 January. Online at: www.theguardian.com/society/2012/jan/17/disability-spartacus-welfare-cuts-campaign-viral [accessed 2 December 2013].

Cahill, S. E. and Eggleston, R. (2005) 'Reconsidering the stigma of physical disability', *Sociological Quarterly*, 36, 4, pp. 681–698.

Caldwell, K. (2010) 'We exist: Intersectional in/visibility in bisexuality and disability', *Disability Studies Quarterly*, 30, 3/4. Online at: http://dsq-sds.org/article/view/1273/1303 [accessed 8 December 2013].

Campbell, D. J., Coll, N. and Thurston, W. E. (2012) 'Considerations for the provision of prosthetic services in post-disaster contexts: The Haiti Amputee Coalition', *Disability and Society*, 27, 5, pp. 647–661.

Campbell, F. K. (2001) 'Inciting legal fictions: Disability's date with ontology and the ableist body of the law', *Griffith Law Review*, 10, pp. 42–62.

Campbell, F. K. (2008) 'Refusing able(ness): A preliminary conversation about ableism', *M/C Journal*, 11, 3, pp. 1–15.

Campbell, F. K. (2009) *Contours of Ableism*, Basingstoke: Palgrave Macmillan.

Campbell, F. K. (2012) 'Stalking ableism: Using disability to expose "abled" narcissism', in Goodley, D., Hughes, B. and Davis, L. J. (eds) *Disability and Social Theory: New Developments and Directions*, Basingstoke: Palgrave Macmillan, pp. 142–163.

Campbell, J. (1990) 'Developing our image: Who's in control?', paper presented at the Cap-in-Hand Conference. Online at: http://disability-studies.leeds.ac.uk/files/library/Campbell-DEVELOPING-OUR-IMAGE.pdf [accessed 3 March 2014].

Campbell, S. J., Anon., Marsh, S., Franklin, K., Gaffney, D., Anon., Dixon, M., James, L., Barnett-Cormack, S., Fon-James, R., Willis, D. and Anon. (2012) *Responsible Reform: A Report on the Proposed Changes to Disability Living Allowance: Diary of a Benefit Scrounger.* Online at: www.ekklesia.co.uk/files/response_to_proposed_dla_reforms.pdf [accessed 26 February 2014].

Carson, G. (2009) *The Social Model of Disability*, Belfast: TSO@Blackwell.

Chappell, A. L. (1992) 'Towards a sociological critique of the normalisation principle', *Disability, Handicap and Society*, 7, 1, pp. 35–50.

Chappell, A. L., Goodley, D. and Lawthom, R. (2001) 'Making connections: The relevance of the social model for people with learning difficulties', *British Journal of Learning Disabilities*, 29, 2, pp. 45–50.

Charlton, J. I. (2000) *Nothing about Us without Us: Disability, Oppression and Empowerment*, Berkeley: University of California Press.

Chataika, T. (2012) 'Disability, development and postcolonialism', in Goodley, D., Hughes, B. and Davis, L. J. (eds) *Disability and Social Theory: New Developments and Directions*, Basingstoke: Palgrave Macmillan, pp. 252–269.

Chemers, M. M. (2004) 'Mutatis mutandis: An emergent disability aesthetic in *X-2: X-Men United*', *Disability Studies Quarterly*, 24, 1. Online at: http://dsq-sds.org/article/view/874/1049 [accessed 7 December 2013].

Cheu, J. (2002) 'De-gene-erates, replicants and other aliens: (Re)defining disability in futuristic film', in Corker, M. and Shakespeare, T. (eds) *Disability/Postmodernity: Embodying Disability Theory*, London: Continuum, pp. 198–212.

Cheyne, R. (2013a) '"She was born a thing": Disability, the cyborg and the posthuman in Anne McCaffrey's *The Ship Who Sang*', *Journal of Modern Literature*, 36, 3, pp. 138–156.

Cheyne, R. (2013b) 'Disability studies reads the romance', *Journal of Literary and Cultural Disability Studies*, 7, 1, pp. 37–52.

Church, D. (2006) '"Welcome to the atrocity exhibition": Ian Curtis, rock death, and disability', *Disability Studies Quarterly*, 26, 4. Online at: http://dsq-sds.org/article/view/804/979 [accessed 7 December 2013].

Clark, A., McQuail, S. and Moss, P. (2003) *Exploring the Field of Listening to and Consulting with Young Children*, DfES: Research Report 445, London: The Stationery Office.

Clark, D. L. and Myser, C. (1996) 'Being humaned: Medical documentaries and the hyperrealization of conjoined twins', in Thomson, R. G. (ed.) *Freakery: Cultural Spectacles of the Extraordinary Body*, New York: New York University Press, pp. 338–355.

Cobley, D. S. (2012) 'Towards economic empowerment: segregation versus inclusion in the Kenyan context', *Disability and Society*, 27, 3, pp. 371–384.

Cocks, A. (2006) 'The ethical maze: Finding an inclusive path towards gaining children's agreement to research participation', *Childhood*, 13, 2, pp. 247–266.

Cooper, H. (2013) 'The oppressive power of normalcy in the lives of disabled children: Deploying history to denaturalize the notion of the "normal child"', in Curran, T. and Runswick-Cole, K. (eds) *Disabled Children's Childhood Studies*, Basingstoke: Palgrave Macmillan, pp. 136–151.

Corbett, J. (1994) 'A proud label: Exploring the relationship between disability politics and gay pride', *Disability and Society*, 9, 3, pp. 343–357.

Coronation Street [television series] (1960–present) Created by Tony Warren: ITV (UK).

Crabtree, S. A. (2007) 'Family responses to the social inclusion of children with developmental disabilities in the United Arab Emirates', *Disability and Society*, 22, 1, pp. 49–62.

Crenshaw, K. (1991) 'Mapping the margins: Intersectionality, identity politics, and violence against women of color', *Stanford Law Review* 43, 6, pp. 1241–1299.

Crossley, N. (2004) *Key Concepts in Critical Social Theory*, London: Sage.

Crow, L. (2000) 'Helen Keller: Rethinking the problematic icon', *Disability and Society*, 15, 6, pp. 845–859.

Culham, A. and Nind, M. (2003) 'Deconstructing normalisation: Clearing the way for inclusion', *Journal of Intellectual and Developmental Disability*, 28, 1, pp. 65–78.

Cumberbach, G. and Negrine, R. (1992) *Images of Disability on Television*, London: Routledge.

Curran, T. and Runswick-Cole, K. (eds) (2013) *Disabled Children's Childhood Studies: Critical Approaches in a Global Context*, Basingstoke: Palgrave Macmillan.

Da Vinci Code, The [film] (2006) Directed by Ron Howard.

Darke, P. (1998) 'Understanding cinematic representations of disability', in Shakespeare, T. (ed.) *The Disability Reader: Social Science Perspectives*, London: Cassell, pp. 181–197.

Darling, R. B. (2003) 'Toward a model of changing disability identities: A proposed typology and research agenda', *Disability and Society*, 18, 7, pp. 881–895.

Dauncey, S. (2012) 'Three days to walk: A personal story of life writing and disability consciousness in China', *Disability and Society*, 27, 3, pp. 311–323.

Davidson, I. F. W. K., Woodill, G. and Bredberg, E. (1994) 'Images of disability in 19th century British children's literature', *Disability and Society*, 9, 1, pp. 33–46.

Davis, J. (1998) 'Understanding the meanings of children: A reflexive process', *Children and Society*, 12, 5, pp. 325–335.

Davis, J. and Watson, N. (2001) 'Where are the children's experiences? Analysing social and cultural exclusion in "special" and "mainstream" schools', *Disability and Society*, 16, 5, pp. 671–688.

Davis, K. (1993) 'On the movement', in Swain, J., Finkelstein, V., French, S. and Oliver, M. (eds) *Disabling Barriers – Enabling Environments*, London: Sage/Open University Press, pp. 285–292.

Davis, L. J. (1995) *Enforcing Normalcy: Disability, Deafness and the Body*, London: Verso.

Davis, L. J. (1997) 'Enabling texts', *Disability Studies Quarterly*, 17, 4, pp. 248–251.

Davis, L. J. (2002a) 'Crips strike back: The rise of disability studies', *American Literary History*, 11, 3, pp. 500–512.

Davis, L. J. (2002b) *Bending Over Backwards: Disability, Dismodernism, and Other Difficult Positions*, New York: New York University Press.

Davis, L. J. (2006) [1995] 'Constructing normalcy: The bell curve, the novel, and the invention of the disabled body in the nineteenth century', in Davis, L. J. (ed.) *The Disability Studies Reader*, 2nd edn, New York: Routledge, pp. 3–16.

Davis, L. J. (2008) *Obsession: A History*, Chicago: University of Chicago Press.

Deal, M. (2003) 'Disabled people's attitudes to other impairment groups: A hierarchy of impairments', *Disability and Society*, 18, 7, pp. 897–910.

Deng, M. and Holdsworth, J. C. (2007) 'From unconscious to conscious inclusion: Meeting special education needs in west China', *Disability and Society*, 22, 5, pp. 507–522.

Derbyshire, L. (2013) 'A mug or a teacup and saucer?', in Curran, T. and Runswick-Cole, K. (eds) *Disabled Children's Childhood Studies*, Basingstoke: Palgrave Macmillan, pp. 30–35.

DES (Department of Education and Science) (1978) *Special Educational Needs: Report of the Committee of Enquiry into the Education of Handicapped Children and Young People* (the Warnock Report), London: HMSO.

DfE (Department for Education) (2011) *Support and Aspiration: A New Approach to Special Educational Needs and Disability: A Consultation*. Online at: http://webarchive.nationalarchives.gov.uk/20130401151715/https://www.education.gov.uk/publications/eOrderingDownload/Green-Paper-SEN.pdf [accessed 27 February 2014].

DfES (Department for Education and Skills) (2004) *Removing the Barriers to Achievement: The Government's Strategy for SEN*, London: DfES.

Dias, J., Eardley, M., Harkness, E., Townson, L., Brownlee-Chapman, C. and Chapman, R. (2012) 'Keeping wartime memory alive: An oral history about the wartime memories of people with learning difficulties in Cumbria', *Disability and Society*, 27, 1, pp. 31–50.

Dodd, J., Sandell, R., Delin, A. and Gay, J. (2004) *Buried in the Footnotes: The Representation of Disabled People in Museum and Gallery Collections*, Leicester: Research Centre for Museums and Galleries.

Dos Santos, M. P. (1997) 'Brazilian concepts of special education', *Disability and Society*, 12, 3, pp. 407–415.

Dowling, M. and Dolan, L. (2001) 'Families with children with disabilities: Inequalities and the social model', *Disability and Society*, 16, 1, pp. 22–35.

Drake, R. F. (1996) 'A critique of the role of the traditional charities', in Barton, L. (ed.) *Disability and Society: Emerging Issues and Insights*, London: Longman, pp. 147–167.

Drake, R. F. (1998) 'What am I doing here? "Non-disabled people" and the disability movement', *Disability and Society*, 12, 4, pp. 643–645.

Duckett, P. (1998) 'What are you doing here? "Non-disabled" people and the disability movement: A response to Fran Branfield', *Disability and Society* 3, 4, pp. 625–628.

Dunn, K. and Moore, M. (2005) 'Developing accessible play spaces in the UK: A social model approach', *Children, Youth and Environments*, 15, 1, pp. 331–353.

Durbach, N. (2010) *Spectacle of Deformity: Freak Shows and Modern British Culture*, Berkeley: University of California Press.

EastEnders [television series] (1985–present) Created by Julia Smith and Tony Holland: BBC 1 (UK).

EDCM (Every Disabled Child Matters) (2007) *Disabled Children and Child Poverty: Briefing Paper*. Online at: www.edcm.org.uk [accessed 2 December 2013].

Edwards, J. and Boxall, K. (2010) 'Adults with cystic fibrosis and barriers to employment', *Disability and Society*, 25, 4, pp. 441–453.

Edwards, M. L. (1997a) 'Constructions of physical disability in the ancient Greek world: The community concept', in Mitchell, D. T. and Snyder, S. L. (eds) *The Body and Physical Difference: Discourses of Disability*, Ann Arbor: University of Michigan Press, pp. 35–50.

Edwards, M. L. (1997b) 'Deaf and dumb in ancient Greece', in L. J. Davis (ed.) *The Disability Studies Reader*, New York: Routledge, pp. 29–51.

Edwards, S. D. (2008) Book review: *Disability Rights and Wrongs, Journal of Medical Ethics*, 34, p. 222.

Elephant Man, The [film] (1980) Directed by David Lynch.

Eleweke, C. J. (2013) 'A review of the challenges of achieving the goals in the African Plan of Action for people with disabilities in Nigeria', *Disability and Society*, 28, 3, pp. 313–323.

Enabling Education Network (EENET) (1998) 'Definition of inclusive education'. Online at: www.eenet.org.uk/EENET_def_of_IE.php [accessed 2 December 2013].

Erevelles, N. (2011) *Disability and Difference in Global Contexts: Enabling a Transformative Body Politic*, New York: Palgrave Macmillan.

Evans, S. (2004) *Forgotten Crimes: The Holocaust and People with Disabilities*, Chicago: Ivan R. Dee.

Ewing, D W. (2002) 'Disability and feminism: Goffman revisited', *Journal of Social Work in Disability and Rehabilitation*, 1, 2, pp. 73–82.

Fabrega, H. Jr (1991) 'The culture and history of psychiatric stigma in early modern and modern Western societies: A review of recent literature', *Comprehensive Psychiatry*, 32, 2, pp. 97–119.

Ferguson, P. M. (1994) *Abandoned to Their Fate: Social Policy and Practice toward Severely Retarded People in America, 1820–1920*, Philadelphia: Temple University Press.

Fiedler, L. A. (1978) *Freaks: Myths and Images of the Secret Self*, New York: Simon & Schuster.

Fiedler, L. A. (1996) [1991] Foreword, in Thomson, R. G. (ed.) *Freakery: Cultural Spectacles of the Extraordinary Body*, New York: New York University Press, pp. xiii–xvi.

Finger, A. (1999) *Past Due: A Story of Disability, Pregnancy and Birth*, Philadelphia: Women's Press.

Fink, M. (2013) 'People who look like things: Representations of disability in *The Simpsons*', *Journal of Literary and Cultural Disability Studies*, 7, 3, pp. 255–270.

Finkelstein, V. (1980) *Attitudes and Disabled People: Issues for Discussion*, New York: World Rehabilitation Fund.

Finkelstein, V. (1987) 'Disabled People and Our Culture Development', *DAIL Magazine*, no. 8 (June). Online at: www.independentliving.org/docs3/finkelstein87a.pdf [accessed 6 February 2010].

Fiske, J. (1987) *Television Culture*, London: Routledge.

Fitzgerald, M. (2004) *Autism and Creativity: Is There a Link between Autism in Men and Exceptional Ability?*, Hove: Brunner-Routledge.

Foucault, M. (1967) [1961] *Madness and Civilization: A History of Insanity in the Age of Reason*, trans. R. Howard, New York, Pantheon.

Foucault, M. (1970) [1966] *The Order of Things: An Archaeology of the Human Sciences*, London/ New York: Routledge.

Foucault, M. (1973) [1963] *The Birth of the Clinic: An Archaeology of Medical Perception*, trans. A. M. S. Smith, New York: Pantheon.

Foucault, M. (1977) [1975] *Discipline and Punish: The Birth of the Prison*, New York: Pantheon.

Foucault, M. (1980) *Power/Knowledge: Selected Interviews and Other Writings 1972–1977*, Brighton: Harvester.

Frankenberg, R. (1993) *White Women, Race Matters: The Social Construction of Whiteness*, Minneapolis: University of Minnesota Press.

French, S. (1993) 'Disability, impairment or something in between?', in Swain, J., Finkelstein, V., French S. and Oliver, M. (eds) *Disabling Barriers – Enabling Environments*, London: Sage/ Open University Press, pp. 17–25.

Frith, U. (2003) *Autism: Understanding the Enigma*, 2nd edn, Malden, MA: Blackwell.

Frohmader, C. and Meekosha, H. (2012) 'Recognition, respect and rights: Women with disabilities in a globalised world', in Goodley, D., Hughes, B. and Davis, L. J. (eds) *Disability and Social Theory: New Developments and Directions*, Basingstoke: Palgrave Macmillan, pp. 287–307.

Frost, L. (1996) 'The Circassian Beauty and the Circassian Slave: Gender, Imperialism, and American popular entertainment', in Thomson, R. G. (ed.) *Freakery: Cultural Spectacles of the Extraordinary Body*, New York: New York University Press, pp. 248–262.

Gallez, D. W. (1970) 'Theories of film music', *Cinema Journal*, 9, 2, pp. 40–47.

Game, A. and Metcalfe, A. (1996) *Passionate Sociology*, London: Sage.

Garber, Z. and Zuckerman, B. (1989) 'Why do we call the Holocaust "the Holocaust"? An inquiry into the psychology of labels', *Modern Judaism*, 9, 2, pp. 197–211.

Gartrell, A. (2010) '"A frog in a well": The exclusion of disabled people from work in Cambodia', *Disability AND Society*, 25, 3, pp. 289–301.

Gerber, D. A. (1992) 'Volition and valorization in the analysis of the "careers" of people exhibited in freak shows', *Disability, Handicap and Society*, 7, 1, pp. 53–69.

Ghai, A. (2001) 'Marginalisation and disability: Experiences from the Third World', in Priestley, M. (ed.) *Disability and the Life Course: Global Perspectives*, Cambridge: Cambridge University Press, pp. 26–37.

Ghai, A. (2002) 'Disability in the Indian context: Post-colonial perspectives', in Corker, M. and Shakespeare, T. (eds) *Disability/Postmodernity: Embodying Disability Theory*, London: Continuum, pp. 88–100.

Gleeson, B. (1999) *Geographies of Disability*, London: Routledge.

Goffman, I. (1963) *Stigma: Notes on the Management of a Spoiled Identity*, New York: Simon & Schuster.

Gold, N. and Auslander, G. (1999) 'Gender issues in newspaper coverage of people with disabilities: A Canada–Israel comparison', *Women and Health*, 29, 4, pp. 75–96.

Goleman, D. (2009) *Emotional Intelligence: Why It Can Matter More than IQ*, London: Bloomsbury.

Goodley, D. (2011) *Disability Studies: An Interdisciplinary Introduction*, London: Sage.

Goodley, D. (2013) 'Dis/entangling critical disability studies', *Disability and Society*, 28, 5, pp. 631–644.

Goodley, D. (2014) *Dis/ability Studies: Theorising Disablism and Ableism*, London: Routledge.

Goodley, D. and Lawthom, R. (2006) 'Disability studies and psychology: New allies?', in Goodley, D. A. and Lawthom, R. (eds) *Disability and Psychology: Critical Introductions and Reflections*, London: Palgrave Macmillan, pp. 1–16.

Goodley, D. and Runswick-Cole, K. (2010a) 'Emancipating play: Dis/abled children, development and deconstruction', *Disability and Society*, 25, 4, pp. 499–512.

Goodley, D. and Runswick-Cole, K. (2010b) 'Len Barton, inclusion and critical disability studies: Theorising disabled childhoods', *International Studies in Sociology of Education*, 20, 4, pp. 273–290.

Goodley, D. and Runswick-Cole, K. (2011a) 'Something in the air? Creativity, culture and community', *Research in Drama Education: The Journal of Applied Theatre and Performance*, 16, 1, pp. 75–91.

Goodley, D. and Runswick-Cole, K. (2011b) 'The violence of disablism', *Journal of Sociology of Health and Illness*, 33, 4, pp. 602–617.

Goodley, D. and Runswick-Cole, K. (2012a) 'Decolonizing methodologies: Disabled children as research managers and participant ethnographers', in Grech, S. and Azzopardi, A. (eds) *Communities: A Reader*, Rotterdam: Sense Publishers, pp. 215–230.

Goodley, D. and Runswick-Cole, K. (2012b) 'The body as disability and possability: Theorising the "leaking, lacking and excessive" bodies of disabled children', *Scandinavian Journal of Disability Research*, 15, 1, pp. 1–19.

Goodley, D. and Runswick-Cole, K. (2012c) 'Reading Rosie: The postmodern dis/abled child', *Educational and Child Psychology*, 29, 2, pp. 53–66.

Goodley, D. A., Lawthom, R., Clough, P. and Moore, M. (2004) *Researching Life Stories: Method, Theory and Analyses in a Biographical Age*, London: RoutledgeFalmer.

Goodley, D., Runswick-Cole, K. and Mahmoud, U. (2013) 'Disablism and diaspora: British Pakistani families and disabled children', *Review of Disability Studies*, 9, 2/3, pp. 63–78.

Grandin, T. (1996) *Thinking in Pictures: And Other Reports from My Life with Autism*, New York: Vintage Books.

Gray, P. (1999) 'Cursed by eugenics', *Time*, 153, 1, pp. 84–85.

Grech, S. (2008) 'Living with disability in rural Guatemala: Exploring connections and impacts on poverty', *International Journal of Disability, Community and Rehabilitation*, 7, 2. Online at: www.ijdcr.ca/VOL07_02_CAN/articles/grech.shtml [accessed 2 December 2013].

Grech, S. (2009) 'Disability, poverty and development: Critical reflections on the majority world debate', *Disability and Society*, 24, 6, pp. 771–784.

Grech, S. (2010) 'Recolonising debates or perpetuated coloniality? Decentring the spaces of disability, development and community in the global South', *International Journal of Inclusive Education*, 15, 1, pp. 87–100.

Green, S. E. (2001) '"Oh, those therapists will become your best friends": Maternal satisfaction with clinics providing physical, occupational and speech therapy services to children with disabilities', *Sociology of Health and Illness*, 23, 6, pp. 798–828.

Green, S. E. (2002) 'Mothering Amanda: Musings on the experience of raising a child with cerebral palsy', *Journal of Loss and Trauma*, 7, pp. 21–34.

Green, S. E. (2003) 'What do you mean "what's wrong with her?" Stigma and the lives of families of children with disabilities', *Social Science and Medicine*, 57, pp. 1361–1374.

Greenstein, A. (2013) 'Today's learning objective is to have a party: Playing research with students in a secondary school special needs unit', *Journal of Research in Special Educational Needs*. Online at: http://onlinelibrary.wiley.com/doi/10.1111/1471-3802.12009/abstract [accessed 16 December 2013].

Grue, L. and Lærum, K. T. (2002) '"Doing motherhood": Some experiences of mothers with physical disabilities', *Disability and Society*, 17, 6, pp. 671–683.

Guo, B., Bricout, J. C. and Huang, J. (2005) 'A common open space or a digital divide? A social model perspective on the online disability community in China', *Disability and Society*, 20, 1, pp. 49–66.

Hacking, I. (1999) *The Social Construction of What?* Cambridge, MA: Harvard University Press.

Haddon, M. (2003) *The Curious Incident of the Dog in the Night-Time*, London: Jonathan Cape.

Hahn, H. (1997) 'Advertising the acceptably employable image: Disability and capitalism', in Davis, L. J. (ed.) *The Disability Studies Reader*, New York: Routledge, pp. 172–186.

Hall, S. (1997) 'The spectacle of the "Other"', in Hall, S. (ed.) *Representations: Cultural Representations and Signifying Practices*, London: Sage, pp. 223–291.

Haller, B. A. (2010) *Representing Disability in an Ableist World: Essays on Mass Media*, Louisville, KY: Advocado Press.

Hammer, C. and Bosker, G. (1996) *Freak Show: Sideshow Banner Art*, San Francisco: Chronicle Books.

Haraldsdóttir, F. (2013) 'Simply children', in Curran, T. and Runswick-Cole, K. (ed.) *Disabled Children's Childhood Studies*, London: Palgrave Macmillan, pp. 13–21.

Harris, J. (2003) '"All doors are closed to us": A social model analysis of the experiences of disabled refugees and asylum seekers in Britain', *Disability and Society*, 18, 4, pp. 395–410.

Hasler, F. (1993) 'Developments in the disabled people's movement', in Swain, J., Finkelstein, V., French S. and Oliver, M. (eds) *Disabling Barriers – Enabling Environments*, London: Sage/ Open University Press, pp. 219–225.

Hawkins, J. (1996) '"One of us": Tod Browning's freaks' in R. G. Thomson (ed.) *Freakery: Cultural Spectacles of the Extraordinary Body*, New York: New York University Press, pp. 265–276.

Hepple, B. (2010) 'The new single Equality Act in Britain', *Equal Rights Review* 5, pp. 11–24.

Hevey, D. (1992) *The Creatures Time Forgot: Photography and Disability Imagery*, London: Routledge.

Hevey, D. (1997) 'The enfreakment of photography', in Davis, L. J. (ed.) *The Disability Studies Reader*, New York: Routledge, pp. 332–347.

Hodge, N. and Runswick-Cole, K. (2013) '"They never pass me the ball": Disabled children's experiences of leisure', *Children's Geographies*, 2, 3, pp. 311–325.

Hollyoaks [television series] (1995–present) Created by Phil Redmond: Channel 4 (UK).

Honkasalo, M.-L. (1998) 'Space and embodied experience: Rethinking the body in pain', *Body and Society*, 4, 2, pp. 35–57.

Hughes, B. (2009) 'Disability activisms: Social model stalwarts and biological citizens', *Disability and Society*, 24, 6, pp. 677–688.

Hughes, B. and Paterson, K. (1997) 'The social model of disability and the disappearing body: Towards a sociology of impairment', *Disability and Society*, 12, 3, pp. 25–40.

Humphrey, J. C. (1999) 'Disabled people and the politics of difference', *Disability and Society*, 14, 2, pp. 173–188.

Hunt, P. (ed.) (1966) *Stigma: The Experience of Disability*, London: Geoffrey Chapman.

Hunt, P. (1972) Letter to *The Guardian* (London). Online at: www.leeds.ac.uk/disability-studies/ archiveuk/Hunt/Hunt%201.pdf [accessed 3 December 2013].

Huson, S. M., Harper P. S. and Compston D. A. S. (1988) 'Von Recklinghausen neurofibromatosis: A clinical and population study in south-east Wales', *Brain*, 111, pp. 1355–1381.

Institute for the Study of the Neurotypical (ISNT) (1998) 'What is NT [neurotypical syndrome]? Online at: http://isnt.autistics.org [accessed 22 November 2012].

Islam, Z. (2008) 'Negotiating identities: The lives of Pakistani and Bangladeshi young disabled people', *Disability and Society*, 23, 1, pp. 41–52.

Jaarsma, P. and Welin, S. (2012) 'Autism as a natural human variation: Reflections on the claims of the neurodiversity movement', *Health Care Analysis*, 20, 1, pp. 20–30.

Jackson, P. (1989) *Maps of Meaning: An Introduction to Cultural Geography*, London: Routledge.

James, A. and Prout, J. (2001) *Constructing and Reconstructing Childhood: Contemporary Issues in the Sociological Study of Childhood*, London: Routledge.

Jarman, M. (2012) 'Disability on trial: Complex realities staged for courtroom drama: The case of Jodi Picoult', *Journal of Literary and Cultural Disability Studies*, 6, 2, pp. 209–225.

Jayasooria, D. (1999) 'Disabled people: Active or passive citizens: Reflections from the Malaysian experience', *Disability and Society*, 14, 3, pp. 341–352.

Johansen, R. E. B. (2002) 'Pain as a counterpoint to culture: Toward an analysis of pain associated with infibulation among Somali immigrants in Norway', *Medical Anthropology Quarterly*, 16, 3, pp. 312–340.

John, A. and Wheyway, R. (2004) *Can Play, Will Play: Disabled Children and Access to Outdoor Playgrounds*, London: National Playing Fields Association (NPFA).

Jones, A. H. (2013) 'Why teach literature and medicine? Answers from three decades', *Journal of Medical Humanities*, 34, 4, pp. 415–428.

Jönson, H. and Larsson, A. T. (2009) 'The exclusion of older people in disability activism and policies: A case of inadvertent ageism?', *Journal of Aging Studies*, 23, 1, pp. 69–77.

Kalyanpur, M. (1996) 'The influence of Western special education on community-based services in India', *Disability and Society*, 11, 2, pp. 249–270.

Kapp, S. K., Gillespie-Lynch, K., Sherman, L. E. and Hutman, T. (2012) 'Deficit, difference, or both? Autism and neurodiversity', *Developmental Psychology*, 49, 1, pp. 59–71.

Kassah, A. K., Kassah, B. L. L. and Agbota, T. K. (2012) 'Abuse of disabled children in Ghana', *Disability and Society*, 27, 5, pp. 689–701.

Keith, L. (2001) *Take Up Thy Bed and Walk: Death, Disability and Cure in Classic Fiction for Girls*, London: Women's Press.

Kidd, K. (2004) 'The mother and the angel: Disability studies, mothering and the "unreal" in children's fiction', *Disability Studies Quarterly*, 24, 1. Online at: http://dsq-sds.org/article/view/847/1022 [accessed 18 February 2014].

Kiani, S. (2009) 'Women with disabilities in the North West province of Cameroon: Resilient and deserving of greater attention', *Disability and Society*, 24, 4, pp. 517–531.

Kim, E. (2011) 'Asexuality in disability narratives', *Sexualities*, 14, 4, pp. 479–493.

Kim, K. M. (2010) 'The accomplishments of disabled women's advocacy organizations and their future in Korea', *Disability and Society*, 25, 2, pp. 219–230.

Kolářová, K. (2010) 'Performing the pain: Opening the (crip) body for (queer) pleasures', *Review of Disability Studies*, 6, pp. 44–52.

Kriegel, L. (1987) 'The cripple in literature', in Gartner, A. and Joe, T. (eds) *Images of the Disabled, Disabling Images*, New York: Praeger, pp. 31–46.

Kudlick, C. J. (2003) 'Disability history: Why we need another "Other"', *American Historical Review*, 108, 3, pp. 763–793.

Kuppers, P. (2003) *Disability and Contemporary Performance: Bodies on the Edge*, New York: Routledge.

Kuppers, P. (2007) *The Scar of Visibility: Medical Performances and Contemporary Art*, Minneapolis: University of Minnesota Press.

LaCom, C. (2002) 'Revising the subject: Disability as "third dimension" in *Clear Light of Day* and *You Have Come Back*', *Feminist Formations*, 14, 3, pp. 138–154.

Lamichhane, K. (2012) 'Employment situation and life changes for people with disabilities: Evidence from Nepal', *Disability and Society*, 27, 4, pp. 471–485.

Landsman, G. (1998) 'Reconstructing motherhood in the age of "perfect babies": Mothers of infants and toddlers with disabilities', *Signs: Journal of Women in Culture and Society*, 28, 1, pp. 69–101.

Landsman, G. (2003) 'Emplotting children's lives: Developmental delay vs. disability', *Social Science and Medicine*, 56, pp. 1947–1960.

Lawrence, D. H. (1993) [1928] *Lady Chatterley's Lover*, London: Penguin Books.

Lawson, W. (2000) *Life behind Glass: A Personal Account of Autism Spectrum Disorder*, London: Jessica Kingsley.

Lerner, N. W. (2010) 'Preface: Listening to fear/listening with fear', in Lerner, N. W. (ed.) *Music in the Horror Film: Listening to Fear*, New York: Routledge, pp. ix–xi.

Letham, J. (1999) *Motherless Brooklyn*, London: Vintage.

Lewis, A. (2002) 'Accessing, through research interviews, the views of children with difficulties in learning', *Support for Learning*, 17, 3, pp. 110–116.

Lewis, A. (2011) 'Silence in the context of "child voice"', *Children and Society*, 24, 1, pp. 14–23.

Lewis, A. and Porter, J. (2004) 'Interviewing children and young people with learning disabilities: Guidelines for researchers and multi-professional practice', *British Journal of Learning Disabilities*, 32, pp. 191–197.

Lindfors, B. (1996) 'Ethnological show business: Footlighting the Dark Continent', in R. G. Thomson (ed.) *Freakery: Cultural Spectacles of the Extraordinary Body*, New York: New York University Press, pp. 207–218.

Lloyd, M. (2001) 'The politics of disability and feminism: Discord or synthesis?', *Sociology*, 35, 3, pp. 715–728.

Loeb, M., Eide, A. H., Jelsma, J., Toni, M. K. and Maart, S. (2008) 'Poverty and disability in Eastern and Western Cape Provinces, South Africa', *Disability and Society*, 23, 4, pp. 311–321.

Longmore, P. K. (1987) 'Screening stereotypes: Images of disabled people in television and motion pictures', in Gartner, A. and Joe, T. (eds) *Images of the Disabled, Disabling Images*, New York: Praeger, pp. 65–78.

Lorber, J. and Farrell, S. A. (1990) *The Social Construction of Gender*, London: Sage.

Luna, C. (2009) '"But how can those students make it here?" Examining the institutional discourse about what it means to be "LD" at an Ivy League university', *International Journal of Inclusive Education*, 13, 2, pp. 157–178.

Maart, S., Eide, A. H., Jelsma, J., Loeb, M. E. and Ka Toni, M. (2007) 'Environmental barriers experienced by urban and rural disabled people in South Africa', *Disability and Society*, 22, 4, pp. 357–369.

McCall, L. (2005) 'The complexity of intersectionality', *Signs: Journal of Women in Culture and Society*, 30, 3, pp. 1771–1800.

McGuire, A. (2011) 'Representing autism: A critical examination of autism advocacy in the neo-liberal West', unpublished PhD thesis, University of Toronto.

McGuire, A. (2013) 'Buying time: The s/pace of advocacy and the cultural production of autism', *Canadian Journal of Disability Studies*, 2, 3, pp. 98–125.

McKay, G. (2009) '"Crippled with nerves": Popular music and polio, with particular reference to Ian Dury', *Popular Music*, 28, 3, pp. 341–365.

McKay, G. (2013) *Shakin' All Over: Popular Music and Disability*, Ann Arbor: University of Michigan Press.

McLaughlin, J., Goodley, D., Clavering, E., Tregaskis, C. and Fisher, P. (2008) *Families with Disabled Children: Values of Enabling Care and Social Justice*, Basingstoke: Palgrave Macmillan.

McLuhan, M. (1964) *Understanding Media: The Extensions of Man*, New York: Mentor.

McMillan, U. (2012) 'Mammy–memory: Staging Joice Heth, or the curious phenomenon of the "ancient negress"', *Women and Performance: A Journal of Feminist Theory*, 22, 1, pp. 29–46.

McNeil, D. Jr (2009) 'Outbreak of autism or statistical fluke?', *New York Times*, 16 March. Online at: www.nytimes.com/2009/03/17/health/17auti.html [accessed 21 November 2010].

McQuail, D. (1989) *Mass Communication Theory*, London: Sage.

McRuer, R. (2006) *Crip Theory: Cultural Signs of Queerness and Disability*, New York: New York University Press.

McRuer, R. (2007) 'Taking it to the bank: Independence and inclusion on the world market', *Journal of Literary and Cultural Disability Studies*, 1, 2, pp. 5–14.

Madriaga, M. and Mallett, R. (2010) 'Images of criminality, victimization, and disability', in Shoham, S. G., Knepper, P. and Kett, M. (eds) *International Handbook of Victimology*, Boca Raton, FL: Taylor & Francis, pp. 585–610.

Madriaga, M., Goodley, D., Hodge, N. and Martin, N. (2008) 'Enabling transitions into higher education for students with Asperger syndrome: Project report', London: Higher Education Academy.

Magubane, Z. (2001) 'Which bodies matter? Feminism, poststructuralism, race, and the curious theoretical odyssey of the "Hottentot Venus"', *Gender and Society*, 15, 6, pp. 816–834.

Mallett, R. (2007) 'Critical correctness: Exploring the capacities of contemporary disability criticism', unpublished PhD thesis, University of Sheffield.

Mallett, R. (2009) 'Choosing "stereotypes": Debating the efficacy of (British) disability-criticism', *Journal of Research in Special Educational Needs* (JORSEN), 9, 1, pp. 4–11.

Mallett, R. (2010) 'Claiming comedic immunity: Or, what do you get when you cross contemporary British comedy with disability?', *Review of Disability Studies*, 6, 3, pp. 5–14.

Mallett, R. and Runswick-Cole, K. (2010) 'Knowing me, knowing you, aha! Does the urge to know impairment reveal an urge to know normal?', paper presented at Theorizing Normalcy and the Mundane, Manchester Metropolitan University, 12–13 May.

Mallett, R. and Runswick-Cole, K. (2012) 'Commodifying autism: The cultural contexts of "disability" in the academy', in Goodley, D., Hughes, B. and Davis, L. J. (eds) *Disability and Social Theory: New Developments and Directions*, Basingstoke: Palgrave Macmillan, pp. 33–51.

Mallett, R. and Slater, J. (2014) 'Language', in Cameron, C. (ed.) *Disability Studies: A Student's Guide*, London: Sage, pp. 91–94.

Manchester City Council (no date) 'Acceptable language for use with disabled people'. Online at: www.manchester.gov.uk/info/200041/equality_and_diversity/106/disabled_people/4 [accessed 29 December 2011].

Masten, A. S. (2001) 'Ordinary magic: Resilience processes in development', *American Psychologist*, 56, 3, pp. 227–238.

Maya Dhungana, B. (2006) 'The lives of disabled women in Nepal: Vulnerability without support', *Disability and Society*, 21, 2, pp. 133–146.

Meekosha, H. (2004) 'Drifting down the Gulf Stream: Navigating the cultures of disability studies', *Disability and Society*, 19, 7, pp. 721–733.

Meekosha, H. (2008) 'Contextualizing disability: Developing southern/global theory', paper presented at the Fourth Biennial Disability Studies Conference, Lancaster University, UK, 2–4 September. Online at: http://wwda.org.au/meekosha2008.pdf [accessed 11 December 2013].

Meekosha, H. (2011) 'Decolonising disability: Thinking and acting globally', *Disability and Society*, 26, 6, pp. 667–682.

Meekosha, H. and Shuttleworth, R. (2009) 'What's so "critical" about critical disability studies?', *Australian Journal of Human Rights*, 15, 1, pp. 47–75.

Melendro-Oliver, S. (2004) 'Shifting concepts of genetic disease', *Science Studies*, 17, 1, pp. 20–33.

Merish, L. (1996) 'Cuteness and commodity aesthetics: Tom Thumb and Shirley Temple', in R. G. Thomson (ed.) *Freakery: Cultural Spectacles of the Extraordinary Body*, New York: New York University Press, pp. 185–203.

Meyer, S. (2005) *Twilight*, New York: Little, Brown.

Meyer, S. (2006) *New Moon*, New York: Little, Brown.

Meyer, S. (2007) *Eclipse*, New York: Little, Brown.

Meyer, S. (2008) *Breaking Dawn*, New York: Little, Brown.

Michalko, R. (2002) *The Difference Disability Makes*, Philadelphia: Temple University Press.

Miles, M. (1995) 'Disability in an eastern religious context: Historical perspectives', *Disability and Society*, 10, 1, pp. 49–70.

Miles, M. (2000) 'Signing in the Seraglio: Mutes, dwarfs and jesters at the Ottoman Court 1500–1700', *Disability and Society*, 15, 1, pp. 115–134.

Miles, S. (2013) 'Education in times of conflict and the invisibility of disability: A focus on Iraq?', *Disability and Society*, 28, 6, pp. 798–811.

Miller, K. A. (2012) 'The mysteries of the in-between', *Journal of Literary and Cultural Disability Studies*, 6, 2, pp. 143–157.

Mills, C. (2013) *Decolonizing Global Mental Health: The Psychiatrization of the Majority World*, London: Routledge.

Mitchell, D. T. and Snyder, S. L. (1997) 'Introduction: Disability studies and the double bind of representation', in Mitchell, D. T. and Snyder, S. L. (eds) *The Body and Physical Difference: Discourses of Disability*, Ann Arbor: University of Michigan Press, pp. 1–31.

Mitchell, D. T. and Snyder, S. L. (2001a) *Narrative Prosthesis: Disability and the Dependencies of Discourse*, Ann Arbor: University of Michigan Press.

Mitchell, D. T. and Snyder, S. L. (2001b) 'Representation and its discontents: The uneasy home of disability in literature and film', in Albrecht, G. L., Seelman, K. D. and Bury, M. (eds) *Handbook of Disability Studies*, Thousand Oaks, CA: Sage, pp. 195–218.

Mji, G., Gcaza, S., Swartz, L., MacLachlan, M. and Hutton, B. (2011) 'An African way of networking around disability', *Disability and Society*, 26, 3, pp. 365–368.

Molloy, H. and Vasil, L. (2002) 'The social construction of Asperger Syndrome: The pathologising of difference?', *Disability and Society*, 17, 6, pp. 659–669.

Monaco, J. (2000) *How to Read a Film: Movies, Media, Multimedia*, 3rd edn, New York: Oxford University Press.

Monk [television series] (2002–2009). Created by Andy Breckman. Burbank, CA: Mandeville Films.

Moraes, M. (2012) 'Can a blind person play dodge ball? Enacting body and cognition with a group of youths with visual disabilities', *Disability and Society*, 27, 5, pp. 663–673.

Morris, J. (1989) *Able Lives: Women's Experience of Paralysis*, London: Women's Press.

Morris, J. (1991) *Pride against Prejudice: Transforming Attitudes to Disability*, London: Women's Press.

Morris, J. (1992) 'Personal and political: A feminist perspective on researching physical disability', *Disability, Handicap and Society*, 7, 2, pp. 157–166.

Morris, J. (1993) 'Feminism and disability', *Feminist Review*, 43, pp. 57–70.

Morris, J. (1996) 'Introduction', in Morris, J. (ed.) *Encounters with Strangers: Feminism and Disability*, London: Women's Press, pp. 1–16.

Morris, J. (2003) 'Including all children: Finding out about the experiences of children with communication and/or cognitive impairments', *Children and Society*, 17, pp. 337–348.

Moswela, E. and Mukhopadhyay, S. (2011) 'Asking for too much? The voices of students with disabilities in Botswana', *Disability and Society*, 26, 3, pp. 307–319.

Munsaka, E. and Charnley, H. (2013) '"We do not have chiefs who are disabled": Disability, development and culture in a continuing complex emergency', *Disability and Society*, 28, 6, pp. 756–769.

Mulvey, L. (1975) 'Visual pleasure and narrative cinema', *Feminisms: An Anthology of Literary Theory and Criticism*, pp. 438–448.

Murray, S. (2008) *Representing Autism: Culture, Narrative, Fascination*, Liverpool: Liverpool University Press.

Murray, T. J. (1979) 'Dr Samuel Johnson's movement disorder', *British Medical Journal*, 1, pp. 1610–1614.

Murray, T. J. (2003) 'Samuel Johnson: His ills, his pills and his physician friends', *Clinical Medicine*, 3, 4, pp. 368–372.

Nadesan, M. H. (2005) *Constructing Autism: Unravelling the 'Truth' and Constructing the Social*, London: Routledge.

Naylor, C. (2005) 'Inclusion in British Columbia's public schools: Always a journey, never a destination?', paper presented at Canadian Teachers' Federation Conference, 'Building Inclusive Schools: A Search for Solutions', Ottawa, 17–19 November.

Norden, M. (1994) *The Cinema of Isolation: A History of Physical Disability in the Movies*, New Brunswick, NJ: Rutgers University Press.

Nunkoosing, K. and Haydon-Laurelut, M. (2011) 'Intellectual disabilities, referral texts and challenging behaviours: A critical discourse analysis', *Disability and Society*, 26, 4, pp. 405–417.

Nuwagaba, E. L., Nakabugo, M., Tumukunde, M., Ngirabakunzi, E., Hartley, S. and Wade, A. (2012) 'Accessibility to micro-finance services by people with disabilities in Bushenyi District, Uganda', *Disability and Society*, 27, 2, pp. 175–190.

Ogden, C. (2013) 'Surveillance of the leaky child: "Nobody's normal but that doesn't stop us trying"', in Ogden, C. and Wakeman, S. (eds) *Corporeality: The Body and Society*, Chester: University of Chester Press, pp. 80–98.

Oliver, M. (1990) *The Politics of Disablement*, Basingstoke: Macmillan.

Oliver, M. (1994) 'Politics and language: Understanding the disability discourse'. Online at:

http://disability-studies.leeds.ac.uk/files/library/Oliver-pol-and-lang-94.pdf   [accessed   13 December 2013].

Oliver, M. (1996) *Understanding Disability: From Theory to Practice*, Basingstoke: Macmillan.

Oliver, M. (2004) 'If I had a hammer: The social model in action', in Swain, J., French, S., Barnes, C. and Thomas, C. (eds) *Disabling Barriers – Enabling Environments*, 2nd edn, London: Sage, pp. 7–12.

Oliver, M. and Barton, L. (2000) 'The emerging field of disability studies: A view from Britain', paper presented at 'Disability Studies: A Global Perspective', Washington, DC, October. Online at: http://disability-studies.leeds.ac.uk/files/library/Oliver-Emerging-field.pdf   [accessed   3 December 2013].

Oliver, M., Zarb, G., Moore, M., Silver, J. and Salisbury, V. (1988) *Walking into Darkness: The Experience of Spinal Cord Injury*, Basingstoke: Macmillan.

Opini, B. M. (2010) 'A review of the participation of disabled persons in the labour force: The Kenyan context', *Disability and Society*, 25, 3, pp. 271–287.

Opini, B. M. (2012) 'Examining the motivations of women students with disabilities' participation in university education in Kenya', *Scandinavian Journal of Disability Research*, 14, 1, pp. 74–91.

Ortega, F. (2009) 'The cerebral subject and the challenge of neurodiversity', *BioSocieties*, 4, pp. 425–445.

Ott, K. (2005) 'Disability and the practice of public history: An introduction', *Public Historian*, 27, 2, pp. 9–24.

Overboe, J. (2007) 'Disability and genetics: affirming the bare life (the state of exception)', *Canadian Review of Sociology/Revue Canadienne de Sociologie*, 44, 2, pp. 219–235.

Overboe, J. (2012) 'Theory, impairment and impersonal singularities: Deleuze, Guattari and Agamben', in Goodley, D., Hughes, B. and Davis, L. J. (eds) *Disability and Social Theory: New Developments and Directions*, Basingstoke: Palgrave Macmillan, pp. 112–126.

Oxford English Dictionary (2007) Oxford: Oxford University Press.

Papatheodoru, T. (2005) 'Play and special needs', in Moyles, J. (ed.) *The Excellence of Play*, 2nd edn, Maidenhead: Open University Press/McGraw-Hill Education, pp. 39–58.

Papworth Trust (2012) *Disability in the United Kingdom: Facts and Figures*. Online at: www.papworth.org.uk/downloads/disabilityintheunitedkingdom2012_120910112857.pdf [accessed 11 March 2014].

Parashar, D. and Devanathan, N. (2006) 'Still not in vogue: The portrayal of disability in magazine advertising', *Journal of Applied Rehabilitation Counseling*, 37, 1. Online at: http://library.ncrtm.org/pdf/748.011A.pdf#page=15 [accessed 7 December 2013].

Parker, I. (2008) 'Emotional illiteracy: Margins of resistance', *Qualitative Research in Psychology*, 5, 1, pp. 19–32.

Parsons, J. G. (2012) 'The public struggle to erect the Franklin Delano Roosevelt Memorial', *Landscape Journal*, 31, 1–2, pp. 145–159.

Parsons, T. (1951) *The Social System*, London: Routledge.

Patrick, J. D. (1998) 'Representation of physical disability in colonial Zimbabwe: The Cyrene mission and *Pitaniko, the Film of Cyrene*', *Disability and Society*, 13, 5, pp. 709–724.

Patterson, S. (2011) 'Historical overview of disability and employment in the United States, 1600 to 1950', *Review of Disability Studies*, 7, 3–4, pp. 7–17.

Pfeiffer, D. (2005) 'Overview of the disability movement: History, legislative record, and political implications', *Policy Studies Journal*, 21, 4, pp. 724–734.

Pfeiffer, D. and Yoshida, K. (1995) 'Teaching disability studies in Canada and the USA', *Disability and Society*, 10, 4, pp. 475–500.

Pijl, S. J., Meijer, C. J. W. and Hegarty, S. (eds) (1997) *Inclusive Education: A Global Agenda*, London: Routledge.

Pingree, A. (1996) 'The "exceptions that prove the rule": Daisy and Violet Hilton, the "new woman," and the bonds of marriage' in Thomson, R. G. (ed.) *Freakery: Cultural Spectacles of the Extraordinary Body*, New York: New York University Press, pp. 173–184.

Pitts, V. (1998) ' "Reclaiming" the female body: Embodied identity work, resistance and the grotesque', *Body and Society*, 4, 3, pp. 67–84.

Play Safety Forum (2002) 'Managing risk in play provision: A position statement'. Online at: www.freeplaynetwork.org.uk/adventure/manage.htm [02.12.13].

Pink, J. (1996) ' "Do unto others" ' in Keith, L. (ed.) *'What Happened to You?' Writing by Disabled Women*, New York: New Press, pp. 179–180.

Pointon, A. (1997) 'Doors to performance and production', in Pointon, A. and Davies, C. (eds) *Framed: Interrogating Disability in the Media*, London: British Film Institute/Arts Council of England, pp. 110–116.

Priestley, M. (2001) *Disability and the Life Course: Global Perspectives*, Cambridge: Cambridge University Press.

Priestley, M. (2006) 'Disability and old age: Or why it isn't all in the mind', in Goodley, D. A. and Lawthom, R. (eds.) *Disability and Psychology: Critical Introductions and Reflections*, London: Palgrave Macmillan, pp. 84–93.

Proctor, R. N. (1988) *Racial Hygiene: Medicine under the Nazis*, Cambridge, MA: Harvard University Press.

Psycho (1960) Directed by Alfred Hitchcock.

Pyer, M. and Bush, M. (2009) *Disabled Families in Flux: Removing Barriers to Family Life*, London: Scope.

Quarmby, K. (2011) *Scapegoat: How We Are Failing Disabled People*, London: Portobello.

Radcliffe, L. (2013) 'Deconstructing the "normal" student: A discourse analysis of "prospective student" materials', unpublished undergraduate dissertation, Sheffield Hallam University.

Rain Man [film] (1988) Directed by Barry Levinson.

Ransome, P. (2010) *Social Theory for Beginners*, Bristol: Policy Press.

Rapley, M. (2004) *The Social Construction of Intellectual Disability*, Cambridge: Cambridge University Press.

Read, J. (2000) *Disability, Family and Society: Listening to Mothers*, Buckingham: Open University Press.

Read, J. and Walmsley, J. (2006) 'Historical perspectives on special education, 1890–1970', *Disability and Society*, 21, 5, 455–469.

Reeve, D. (2002) 'Negotiating psycho-emotional dimensions of disability and their influence on identity constructions', *Disability and Society*, 17, 5, pp. 493–508.

Reeve, D. (2006) 'Towards a psychology of disability: The emotional effects of living in a disabling society', in Goodley, D. A. and Lawthom, R. (eds) *Disability and Psychology: Critical Introductions and Reflections*, Basingstoke: Palgrave Macmillan, pp. 94–107.

Reeve, D. (2010) 'Ableism within disability studies: The myth of the reliable and contained body', paper presented at Theorizing Normalcy and the Mundane, Manchester Metropolitan University, 12–13 May.

Reiss, B. (1999) 'P. T. Barnum, Joice Heth and antebellum spectacles of race', *American Quarterly*, 51, 1, pp. 78–107.

Riach, K. and Loretto, W. (2009) 'Identity work and the "unemployed" worker: Age, disability and the lived experience of the older unemployed', *Work, Employment and Society*, 23, 1, pp. 102–119.

Richardson, D. (2005) 'Desiring sameness? The rise of a neoliberal politics of normalisation', *Antipode*, 37, 3, pp. 515–535.

Rieser, R. (2006) 'Disability equality: Confronting the oppression of the past', in Cole, M. (ed.) *Education, Equality and Human Rights: Issues of Gender, 'Race', Sexuality, Disability and Social Class*, London: Routledge, pp. 134–156.

Rose, G. (2001) *Visual Methodologies: An Introduction to the Interpretation of Visual Materials*, London: Sage.

Rothfels, N. (1996) 'Aztecs, aborigines, and ape-people: Science and freaks in Germany, 1850–1900', in Thomson, R. G. (ed.) *Freakery: Cultural Spectacles of the Extraordinary Body*, New York: New York University Press, pp. 158–172.

Runswick-Cole, K. (2007) 'The Tribunal was the most stressful thing: The experiences of families who go to the Special Educational Needs and Disability Tribunal (SENDisT)', *Disability and Society*, 22, 3, pp. 315–328.

Runswick-Cole, K. (2008) 'Between a rock and a hard place: Parents' attitudes to the inclusion of their children with special educational needs in mainstream schools', *British Journal of Special Education*, 35, 3, pp. 173–180.

Runswick-Cole, K. (2011a) 'Time to end the bias towards inclusive education?', *British Journal of Special Education*, 38, 3, pp. 112–120.

Runswick-Cole, K. (2011b) 'Parenting disabled children: Response paper', presented at Debates in Disability Studies Symposium II, Critical Disability Studies@Manchester Metropolitan University, Manchester Metropolitan University, 16 March.

Runswick-Cole, K. (2012a) 'Ethnography', in Banister, P., Bunn, G., Burman, E., Daniels, J., Duckett, P., Goodley, D., Lawthom, R., Parker, I., Runswick-Cole, K., Sixsmith, J., Smailes, S., Tindall, C. and Whelan, P. (2012) *Qualitative Methods in Psychology: A Research Guide*, 2nd edn, Maidenhead: Open University Press/McGraw-Hill Education, pp. 75–88.

Runswick-Cole, K. (2012b) '(Neuro)diversity: Pros and cons in a social policy context', paper presented at Disability Research Forum, Sheffield Hallam University, 18 December.

Runswick-Cole, K. and Goodley, D. (2011) 'Celebrating cyborgs: Photovoice and disabled children', paper presented at 'Researching the Lives of Disabled Children and Young People, with a Focus on their Perspectives', ESRC Research Seminar Series, Norah Fry Research Unit, Bristol University, 21 January.

Runswick-Cole, K. and Goodley, D. (2012) 'Resilience in the lives of disabled people across the life course: The literature review'. Online at: http://disabilityresilience.wordpress.com/2013/06/23/disability-resilience/ [accessed 29 July 2012].

Rush, B. (2004) 'Mental health service user involvement in England: Lessons from history', *Journal of Psychiatric and Mental Health Nursing*, 11, 3, pp. 313–318.

Rushton, P. (1982) 'Women, witchcraft, and slander in early modern England: Cases from the church courts of Durham, 1560–1675', *Northern History*, 18, 1, pp. 116–132.

Ryan, D. F. (2005) 'Deaf people in Hitler's Europe: Conducting oral history interviews with deaf Holocaust survivors', *Public Historian*, 27, 2, pp. 43–52.

Ryan, M.-L. (2003) 'On defining narrative media', *Image and Narrative*, 6. Online at: www.imageandnarrative.be/inarchive/mediumtheory/marielaureryan.htm [accessed 7 December 2013].

Ryan, S. and Runswick-Cole, K. (2008) 'Repositioning mothers: Mothers, disabled children and disability studies', *Disability and Society*, 23, 3, pp. 199–210.

Sandahl, C. and Auslander, P. (2009) *Bodies in Commotion: Disability and Performance*, Ann Arbor: University of Michigan Press.

Segal, L. (1997) 'Sexualities', in Woodward, K. (ed.) *Identity and Difference*, London: Sage/Open University Press, pp. 183–238.

Semonin, P. (1996) 'Monsters in the marketplace: The exhibition of human oddities in early modern England', in Thomson, R. G. (ed.) *Freakery: Cultural Spectacles of the Extraordinary Body*, New York: New York University Press, pp. 69–81.

Shakespeare, T. (2000) 'Disabled sexuality: Towards rights and recognition', *Disability and Society*, 18, 3, pp. 159–166.

Shakespeare, T. (2006) *Disability Rights and Wrongs*, London: Routledge.

Shakespeare, T. and Watson, N. (2001) 'The social model of disability: An outdated ideology?', *Research in Social Science and Disability*, 2, pp. 9–28.

Shakespeare, T., Gillespie-Sells, K. and Davies, D. (1996) *The Sexual Politics of Disability*, London: Cassell.

Shakespeare, T., Barnes, C., Priestley, M., Cunningham-Burley, S., Davis, J. and Watson, N. (1999) *Life as a Disabled Child: A Qualitative Study of Young People's Experiences and Perspectives*, Leeds: Disability Research Unit: University of Leeds.

Sharp, K. and Earle, S. (2002) 'Feminism, abortion and disability: Irreconcilable differences?', *Disability and Society*, 17, 2, pp. 137–145.

Sheldon, A., Traustadóttir, R., Beresford, P., Boxall, K. and Oliver, M. (2007) 'Disability rights and wrongs?' (review article), *Disability and Society*, 22, 2, pp. 209–234.

Sherry, M. (2004) 'Overlaps and contradictions between queer theory and disability studies', *Disability and Society*, 19, 7, pp. 769–783.

Sherry, M. (2007) '(Post)colonising disability', *Wagadu*, 4, pp. 10–22.

Siebers, T. (ed.) (2000) *The Body Aesthetic: From Fine Art to Body Modification*, Ann Arbor: University of Michigan Press.

Siebers, T. (2005) 'Disability aesthetics', *PMLA*, 120, 2, pp. 542–546.

Sinclair, J. (1993) 'Don't mourn for us'. Online at: www.autreat.com/dont_mourn.html [accessed 8 January 2013].

Slater, J. (2012) 'Youth for sale: Using critical disability perspectives to examine the embodiment of "youth"', *Societies*, 2, 3, pp. 195–209.

Slater, J. (2013) 'Research with dis/abled youth: Taking a critical disability, "critically young" positionality', in Curran, T. and Runswick-Cole, K. (eds) *Disabled Children's Childhood Studies*, Basingstoke: Palgrave Macmillan, pp. 180–194.

Slee, R. (1997) 'Imported or important theory? Sociological interrogations of disablement and special education', *British Journal of Sociology of Education*, 18, pp. 407–419.

Slingblade [film] (1996) Directed by Billy Bob Thornton.

Sloper, T. and Beresford, B. (2006) 'Families with disabled children', *British Medical Journal*, 333, 4, pp. 928–929.

Snow Cake [film] (2006) Directed by Marc Evans.

Snyder, S. L. and Mitchell, D. T. (2006) *Cultural Locations of Disability*, Chicago: University of Chicago Press.

Snyder, S. L., Brueggemann, B. J. and Thomson, R. G. (2002) 'Introduction: Integrating disability into teaching and scholarship', in Snyder, S. L., Brueggemann, B. J. and Thomson, R. G. (eds) *Disability Studies: Enabling the Humanities*, New York: Modern Language Association of America, pp. 1–12.

Souza, M. A., Sampaio, R. F., Aguiar, N. and Augusto, V. G. (2013) 'Exploring the organization of daily life among women with disabilities in Belo Horizonte, Brazil: Perspectives of functionality and temporality', *Disability and Society*, 28, 2, pp. 161–175.

Stalker, K. and Connors, C. (2007) 'Children's experiences of disability: Pointers to a social model of childhood disability', *Disability and Society*, 22, 1, pp. 19–33.

Stalker, K. and McArthur, K. (2012) 'Child abuse, child protection and disabled children: A review of recent research', *Child Abuse Review*, 21, 1, pp. 24–40.

Staples, J. (2011) 'At the intersection of disability and masculinity: Exploring gender and bodily difference in India', *Journal of the Royal Anthropological Institute*, 17, 3, pp. 545–562.

Stemp, J. (2004) 'Devices and desires: Science fiction, fantasy and disability in literature for young people', *Disability Studies Quarterly*, 24, 1. Online at: http://dsq-sds.org/article/view/850 [accessed 2 December 2013].

Stephens, E. (2005) 'Twenty-first century freak show: Recent transformations in the exhibition of non-normative bodies', *Disability Studies Quarterly*, 25, 3. Online at: http://dsq-sds.org/article/view/580/757 [accessed 2 December 2013].

Stiker, H. J. (1999) *The History of Disability*, trans. W. Sayers, Ann Arbor: University of Michigan Press.

Stuart, O. (1992) 'Race and disability: Just a double oppression?', *Disability, Handicap and Society*, 7, 2, pp. 177–188.

Stuart, O. (1993) 'Double oppression: An appropriate starting point', in Swain, J., Finkelstein, V., French S. and Oliver, M. (eds) *Disabling Barriers – Enabling Environments*, London: Sage/Open University Press, pp. 93–100.

Stubblefield, A. (2007) '"Beyond the pale": Tainted whiteness, cognitive disability, and eugenic sterilization', *Hypatia*, 22, 2, pp. 162–181.

Susman, J. (1994) 'Disability, stigma and deviance', *Social Science and Medicine*, 38, 1, pp. 15–22.

Swain, J., French, S. and Cameron, C. (2003) *Controversial Issues in a Disabling Society*, Buckingham: Open University Press.

Taylor, S. J., Bogdan, R. and Lutfiyya, Z. M. (eds) (1995) *The Variety of Community Experience: Qualitative Studies of Family and Community Life*, Baltimore: Paul H. Brookes.

Theorizing Normalcy and the Mundane (2013) *Book of Abstracts*, Sheffield: Sheffield Hallam University.

Thomas, C. (1997) 'The baby and the bath water: Disabled women and motherhood in social context', *Sociology of Health and Illness*, 19, 5, pp. 622–643.

Thomas, C. (1999) *Female Forms: Experiencing and Understanding Disability*, Buckingham: Open University Press.

Thomas, C. (2007) *Sociologies of Illness and Disability: Contested Ideas in Disability Studies and Medical Sociology*, Basingstoke: Palgrave Macmillan.

Thomas, M. (2000) 'Albert Einstein and LD: An evaluation of the evidence', *Journal of Learning Disabilities*, 33, 2, pp. 149–157.

Thomson, R. G. (1996a) 'Benevolent maternalism and physically disabled figures: Dilemmas of female embodiment in Stowe, Davis, and Phelps', *American Literature*, 68, 3, pp. 555–586.

Thomson, R. G. (ed.) (1996b) *Freakery: Cultural Spectacles of the Extraordinary Body*, New York: New York University Press.

Thomson, R. G. (1997) *Extraordinary Bodies: Figuring Physical Disability in American Culture and Literature*, New York: Columbia University Press.

Thomson, R. G. (2001) 'Seeing the disabled: Visual rhetorics of disability in popular photography', in Longmore, P. K. and Umansky, L. (eds) *The New Disability History: American Perspectives*, New York: New York University Press, pp. 335–374.

Thoreau, E. (2006) 'Ouch! An examination of the self-representation of disabled people on the internet', *Journal of Computer-Mediated Communication*, 11, 2, pp. 442–468.

Timimi, S., Gardner, N. and McCabe, N. (2011) *The Myth of Autism*, Basingstoke: Palgrave Macmillan.

Tincknell, E. and Raghuram, P. (2002) 'Big Brother: Reconfiguring the "active" audience of cultural studies?', *European Journal of Cultural Studies*, 5, 2, pp. 199–215.

Titchkosky, T. (2001) 'Disability: A rose by any other name? People-first language in Canadian society', *Canadian Review of Sociology*, 28, 2, pp. 125–140.

Titchkosky, T. (2008) *Reading and Writing Disability Differently: The Textured Life of Embodiment*, Toronto: University of Toronto Press.

Tolkien, J. R. R. (1937) *The Hobbit: or There and Back Again*, London: George Allen & Unwin.

Tolkien, J. R. R. (1954a) *The Fellowship of the Ring: being the first part of The Lord of the Rings*, London: George Allen & Unwin.

Tolkien, J. R. R. (1954b) *The Two Towers: being the second part of The Lord of the Rings*, London: George Allen & Unwin.

Tolkien, J. R. R. (1955) *The Return of the King: being the third part of The Lord of the Rings*, London: George Allen & Unwin.

Tomlinson, A. (2004) 'The Disneyfication of the Olympics: Theme parks and freak-shows of the body', in Bale, J. and Christensen, M. K. (eds) *Post-Olympism? Questioning Sport in the Twenty-First Century*, Oxford: Berg Publishers, pp. 147–163.

Tøssebro, J. (2004) 'Understanding disability': Introduction to the special issue 'Understanding Disability', *Scandinavian Journal of Disability Studies*, 6, 1, pp. 3–7.

Traustadóttir, R. (1995) 'A mother's work is never done: Constructing a "normal" family life', in Taylor, S. J., Bogdan, R. and Lutfiyya, Z. M. (eds) *The Variety of Community Experience: Qualitative Studies of Family and Community Life*, Baltimore: Paul H. Brookes.

Traustadóttir, R. (2004) 'Disability studies: A Nordic perspective', keynote paper presented at British Disability Studies Association Conference, Lancaster, UK, 26–28 July.

Tregaskis, C. (2002) 'Social model theory: The story so far', *Disability and Society*, 17, 4, pp. 457–470.

Treloar, L. L. (2002) 'Disability, spiritual beliefs and the church: The experiences of adults with disabilities and family members', *Journal of Advanced Nursing*, 40, 5, pp. 594–603.

Trnka, S. (2006) 'Languages of labor: Negotiating the "real" and the relational in Indo-Fijian women's expressions of physical pain', *Medical Anthropology Quarterly*, 21, 4, pp. 388–408.

UNESCO (1994) *The Salamanca Statement and Framework for Action on Special Educational Needs*. Online at: www.unesco.org/education/pdf/SALAMA_E.PDF [accessed at 2 December 2013].

UNICEF (1989) *UN Convention on the Rights of the Child*, Geneva: Office of the High Commissioner for Human Rights.

United Nations (2007) *Convention on the Rights of Persons with Disabilities*. Online at: www.un.org/disabilities/default.asp?id=150 [accessed 2 December 2013].

UPIAS (1974/1975) *Policy Statement*, London: Union of Physically Impaired Against Segregation.

UPIAS (1976) *Fundamental Principles of Disability*, London: Union of Physically Impaired Against Segregation.

Uprety, S. K. (1997) 'Disability and postcoloniality in Salman Rushdie's *Midnight's Children* and Third-World novels', in Davis, L. J. (ed.) *The Disability Studies Reader*, New York: Routledge, pp. 366–381.

Valentine, J. (2001) 'Disabled discourse: Hearing accounts of deafness constructed through Japanese television and film', *Disability and Society* 16, 5, pp. 707–721.

Van Dijck, J. (2002) 'Medical documentary: Conjoined twins as a medical spectacle', *Media, Culture and Society*, 24, pp. 537–556.

Vaughan, C. A. (1996) 'Ogling Igorots: The politics and commerce of exhibiting cultural Otherness, 1898–1913', in Thomson, R. G. (ed.) *Freakery: Cultural Spectacles of the Extraordinary Body*, New York: New York University Press, pp. 219–233.

Walker, S. (2004) 'Disability equality training: Constructing a collaborative model', *Disability and Society*, 19, 7, pp. 703–719.

Walkerdine, V. (1993) 'Beyond developmentalism?', *Theory and Psychology*, 3, 4, pp. 451–469.

Walmsley, J. (2001) 'Women and the Mental Deficiency Act of 1913: Citizenship, sexuality and regulation', *British Journal of Learning Disabilities* 28, 2, pp. 65–70.

Walz, M. and James, M. (2009) 'The (re)making of disability in pop: Ian Curtis and Joy Division', *Popular Music*, 28, 3, pp. 367–380.

Wardi, A. J. (2005) 'Freak shows, spectacles, and carnivals: Reading Jonathan Demme's *Beloved*', *African American Review*, 39, 4, pp. 513–526.

Watermeyer, B. and Swartz, L. (2008) 'Conceptualising the psycho-emotional aspects of disability and impairment: The distortion of personal and psychic boundaries', *Disability and Society*, 23, 6, pp. 599–610.

Watson, N. (2002) 'Well, I know this is going to sound very strange to you, but I don't see myself as a disabled person: Identity and disability', *Disability and Society*, 17, 5, pp. 509–527.

Weinstock, J. A. (1996) 'Freaks in space: "extraterrestrialism" and "deep-space multiculturalism"', in Thomson, R. G. (ed.) *Freakery: Cultural Spectacles of the Extraordinary Body*, New York: New York University Press, pp. 327–337.

Welcome to Our World . . . Living with Autism (2011) Exhibition at V&A Museum of Childhood, London, March.

West, D. (2007) *The Death of the Grown-Up*, New York: St Martins Press.

White, J. (2005) '"Krazy kripples": Using *South Park* to talk about disability', in Ben-Moshe, L., Cory, R. C., Feldbaum, M. and Sagendorf, K. (eds) *Building Pedagogical Curb Cuts: Incorporating Disability into the University Classroom and Curriculum*, Syracuse, NY: Graduate School, Syracuse University, pp. 83–91.

Whyte, S. R. and Ingstad, B. (2007) 'Introduction: Disability connections', in Ingstad, B. and Whyte, S. R. (eds) *Disability in Local and Global Worlds*, Berkeley: University of California Press, pp. 1–29.

Wilde, A. (2004a) 'Performing disability: Impairment, disability and soap opera viewing', in M. King and K. Watson (eds) *Representing Health: Discourses of Health and Illness in the Media*, Basingstoke: Palgrave Macmillan, pp. 66–88.

Wilde, A. (2004b) 'Disabling masculinity: The isolation of a captive audience', *Disability and Society*, 19, 4, pp. 355–370.

Wilde, A. (2010) 'Spectacle, performance and the re-presentation of disability and impairment', *Review of Disability Studies*, 6, 3, pp. 34–44.

Williams, R. (1981) *Culture*, London: Fontana.

Wilton, R. D. (2003) 'Locating physical disability in Freudian and Lacanian psychoanalysis: Problems and prospects', *Social and Cultural Geography*, 4, 3, pp. 369–389.

Wolfensberger, W. (1980) 'The definition of normalization: Update, problems, disagreements, and misunderstandings', in Flynn, R. J. and Nitch, K. E. (eds) *Normalization, Social Integration, and Community Services*, Baltimore: University Park Press.

Woodward, K. (1997a) 'Introduction', in Woodward, K. (ed.) *Identity and Difference*, London: Sage/Open University Press, pp. 1–6.

Woodward, K. (1997b) 'Concepts of identity and difference', in Woodward, K. (ed.) *Identity and Difference*, London: Sage/Open University Press, pp. 7–62.

Woodward, K. (ed.) (1997c) *Identity and Difference*, London: Sage/Open University Press.

World Health Organization (2011) *World Report on Disability*. Online at: www.who.int/disabilities/world_report/2011/report/en [accessed 7 December 2013].

Wright, D. (2000) 'Learning disability and the new Poor Law in England, 1834–1867', *Disability and Society*, 15, 5, pp. 731–745.

X-2 [film] (2003) Directed by Bryan Singer.

Yenika-Agbaw, V. (2011) 'Reading disability in children's literature: Hans Christian Andersen's tales', *Journal of Literary and Cultural Disability Studies*, 5, 1, pp. 91–108.

Young, R. and Nettlebeck, T. (1995) 'The abilities of a musical savant and his family', *Journal of Autism and Developmental Disorders*, 25, pp. 231–248.

Yuan, D. D. (1996) 'The celebrity freak: Michael Jackson's "grotesque glory"', in R. G. Thomson (ed.) *Freakery: Cultural Spectacles of the Extraordinary Body*, New York: New York University Press, pp. 368–384.

Zames Fleischer, D. and Zames, F. (2001) *The Disability Rights Movement: From Charity to Confrontation*, Philadelphia: Temple University Press.

Zola, I. (1987) 'Any distinguishing features? The portrayal of disability in the crime-mystery genre', *Policy Studies Journal*, 15, 13, pp. 487–513.

Index

Page numbers in **bold** denote figures.

global South: disability in 27–33; impairment
as key issue 28; mapping **18**; suggested
academic sources for Disability Studies on
30; Western or Eurocentric assumptions
about development in 28
Goffman, E. 88
Gold, N. 63
Goodley, D. 8, 16, 40, 43, 100, 113, 120
Graber, D. 48
Grech, S. 15, 19, 27–8, 30–2
Greenstein, A. 114

Haller, B. A. 48, 53, 56, 63–4
Hammer, C. 81
The Hardest Hit 93
Hartmann v. *Loudoun County Board of Education*
64
hate crime 70
Haydon-Laurelut, M. 41
health and safety, and children's play 113
Hepple, B. 70, 102
heteronormativity 101, 103
historical perspectives: advocacy potential 75;
availability of sources 72–3; benefits for
Disability Studies 75; benefits for disabled
people 74; benefits of research 74–6;
conceptualisations of disability 72;
contextualising 'disability' in history 76, 78;
the 'disability' Holocaust 81–4 (*see also*
Holocaust); evaluating sources 73–4;
Finkelstein's phases of history 69; and
Foucault 74, 76–8; infanticide 67;
interpretation issues 74; lack of interest in
histories of disability 71; legislation 69;
medical treatment of 'crippled' children
77–8; medicalisation of impairment 77, 81;
mental illness 67, 68; usefulness of Disability
Studies to the discipline of history 76
historical roots of stigma 75–6
Hitler, Adolf 82
The Hobbit (Tolkien) 124
Hodge, N. 113
Hollyoaks (Channel 4) 56
the Holocaust: barriers to and solutions for
telling the 'disability' Holocaust story **85**;
connotations and meanings 81–2; eugenic
justifications 82–3; killing of children with
impairment 83–4; sterilisation law 83; T4
adult programme 84
homosexuality 83, 88, 100–1, 103, 129
Honkasalo, M 130
Hoskins, Steven 70
Hughes, B. 95, 122–3
Hugo, V. 52
human rights 4, 20, 28, 38, 123
The Hunchback of Notre-Dame (various) 52
hysteria 129

Iceland 19, 43, 110
identity politics: beyond 104–5; use of the
term 86; what it involves 89–90
identity politics perspectives: compatibility of
differing identity positions 86–7; disability
activism in the UK 90–3 (*see also* disability
activism); and disability culture 61;
'equality'/'diversity' paradox 103;
essentialism vs non-essentialism 88–9;
feminist vs disability identity politics 103;
gender identity 98; impairment as a political
identity 95–7; intersecting identities 97–102
(*see also* intersectionality); neurodiversity
95–6; 'new' social movements 89–90; non-
identification 94; problems with 'groups'
102–5; sexual identity 97–8 (*see also* sexual
identity); symbolic interactionism 88; 'us'
and 'them' 87, 103, 104
Idiots Act (UK, 1886) 69
impairment: experiencing pain 130–2 (*see also*
pain); hierarchy of 126; implications of
impairment-specific research 125–7;
invalidation of childhood by 40; as key issue
in the global South 28; negative
characterisation 45; and persecution 68;
place of in disability activism 122–3; place
of in the social model 13; 'real' vs 'socially
constructed' 120–2; relevance of in
Disability Studies 123–5; relevance of to
Disability Studies 123–5; as sign of
supernatural or demonic activity 67; social
and cultural contexts 127–9
impairment effects, Thomas's explanation of
the concept 14
impairment-specific research, implications of
125–7
In My Language (Baggs) 96
inclusive education: and autism in the news
media 64; barriers to 112; Barton on 111;
debates in the global North 111; discussions
in England 112; enshrinement in
international law 111; impact of the social
model 15
India: postcolonial perspective 30–1; religious
perspectives on disability 31
indigenous communities 26
individual rights, notion of as global North
idea 39
infanticide: historical perspective 67; Indian
perspective 31
institutionalisation, Nordic criticisms 20
intersectionality: and anti-discrimination
legislation 102; and assumptions of white
male heterosexual identity 97–8; between the
experiences of queer and disabled individuals
101; 'double disadvantage' 99; living multiple
'minority' identity positions 98–102;